# COUTURE
# SEWING
## Techniques

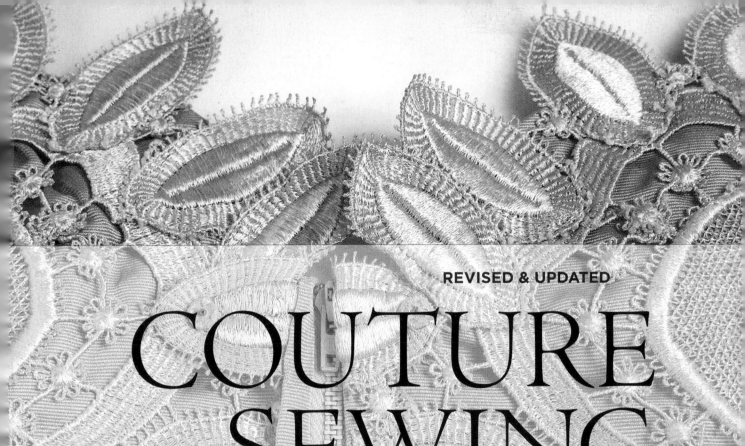

REVISED & UPDATED

# COUTURE SEWING
## Techniques

CLAIRE B. SHAEFFER

The Taunton Press, Inc., 63 South Main Street, PO Box 5506,
Newtown, CT 06470-5506
e-mail: tp@taunton.com

Editor: Erica Sanders-Foege
Copy editor: W. Anne Jones
Technical editor: Linda Conner Griepentrog
Indexer: Lynne Lipkind
Cover design: Kimberly Adis
Interior design/Layout: Kimberly Adis
Illustrators: Steve Buchanan and Christine Erikson
Cover photography: (front) Ken Howie, author's Collection; (back, clockwise
from top) Ken Howie, author's collection; Steven H. Bluttal, courtesy of the
Museum of the City of New York, Costume Collection. Costume worn by
Katharine Cornell in "No Time for Comedy" [1939] by S. N. Behrman; Photo
by Brian Sanderson, Courtesy of the FIDM Museum at the Fashion Institute
of Design & Merchandising, Los Angeles, CA. Gift of Mrs. Herbert Lawrence,
1956; Claire B. Shaeffer.

The following names/manufacturers appearing in *Couture Sewing
Techniques* are trademarks: Harper's Bazaar[SM], Mylar®, PlastDip®, Rigilene®,
Teflon®, Vogue Patterns®.

**Library of Congress Cataloging-in-Publication Data**

Shaeffer, Claire B.
  Couture sewing techniques / Claire Shaeffer. -- Rev. and updated.
    p. cm.
  Summary: "Best-selling couture sewing reference that presents in clear
photos and illustrations and concise prose the basics and applications of
couture sewing, as well as its cultural importance"-- Provided by publisher.
  ISBN 978-1-60085-335-7 (pbk.)
  1.  Dressmaking. 2.  Tailoring (Women's)  I. Title.
  TT515.S483 2011
  646.4--dc22

                          2011007172

Printed in the United States of America
10 9 8 7 6 5 4 3 2 1

# Acknowledgments

A BOOK OF THIS KIND cannot be written without much help and cooperation. I am greatly indebted to the couture industry, which helped me enormously with the research for the original edition of *Couture Sewing Techniques*. My thanks in particular go to the *Chambre syndicale de la couture parisienne*, the governing body in Paris of the couture industry, and to the

couture houses, bespoke tailors, embroiderers, and custom shirtmakers in Paris, Rome, London, Florence, and New York.

Special thanks to the late Mme Marguérite Carré for her personal memories of the techniques used at Christian Dior, when she was the "première de premières," and to the late Charles Kleibacker for sharing his knowledge of couture techniques.

For the 2nd Edition of *Couture Sewing Techniques*, I thank Ralph Rucci and James Galanos for allowing me to visit their workrooms, observe the techniques which they used, and interview their employees. I am grateful to the Fondation Pierre Bergé and Yves Saint Laurent for arranging an interview with Jean-Pierre Derbord, the premier of the atelier du tailler, who shared his expertise and described the techniques used at Yves Saint Laurent.

I am very grateful to Phyllis Magidson, the curator at the Museum of the City of New York, with whom I worked on a research project that focused on Mainbocher and Charles Frederick Worth. This project expanded my knowledge while reminding me that many couture techniques which I had written about earlier had changed little, if at all.

A special thanks to Ken Howie and Sherill Taylor, who photographed the designs in my vintage collection, and to their staffs and the stylists who assisted them as well as the Phoenix Art Museum and Neil's of Palm Desert, who loaned mannequins.

I also want to thank the museums that loaned photographs and sketches, their curators, and photographers: Dennita Sewell at Phoenix Art Museum, Phyllis Magidson at the Museum of the City of New York, Gayle Strege at The Ohio State University Historic Costume Collection, Valerie Steele at the Fashion Institute of Technology, the Metropolitan Museum of Art, Kevin Jones at the Fashion Institute of Design and Merchandising in Los Angeles, Söjic Phaff at Christian Dior, John Wirchanski and the estate of Charles Kleibacker, and Lynn Cook at Australian Stitches.

I want to thank Sarah Benson who helped with so many things from typing and editing, making samples and photos, organizing, repairing, and pressing the garments to dressing mannequins.

I'm particularly grateful to The Taunton Press for undertaking such a challenging project and to its staff, especially my editor Erica Sanders-Foege, whose skills and enthusiasm helped to transform my dreams into reality.

And last, but not least, my thanks to my mother, the late Juanita Sumner Brightwell, who taught me that only my best was good enough, and to my husband, Charlie Shaeffer, MD, whose support and encouragement make it all possible.

# Contents

# Introduction

IF YOU CAN SEW, YOU CAN SEW COUTURE. Very few techniques are difficult, but they require time and patience. This edition, like the original, describes couture techniques as practiced in the ateliers of the haute couture. They are not adapted for home-sewers because I feel strongly that grasping the principles used in the haute couture will help you better understand garment construction and fitting, and in turn, help you to solve many problems you encounter.

My focus is on the craftsmanship, even though elements like draping and design, proportion and balance, fit and fabric are equally important. I've concentrated on classic couture techniques that can be applied to a variety of designs and fabrics and also offer the most value to the greatest number of readers.

The book itself is divided into two sections. The first five chapters introduce you to the world of haute couture, how it differs from expensive ready-to-wear, basic couture skills, and essential techniques. My instincts as a teacher compel me to suggest that you read these chapters first.

The last seven chapters focus on the application of these techniques to garments. The new chapter —Chapter 11: Designing with Fabric—describes particular details I've seen on specific fabrics.

Many of the photographs in the first edition were no longer available so I've selected new ones from various museums; and I've included photographs of some garments in my vintage collection.

The measurements used throughout the book are only guidelines; I suggest that you always purchase extra fabric so you can make samples before sewing the actual garment. This allows you to fine-tune the dimensions and practice your skills.

No matter what your sewing expertise, this book will expand your horizons. Most importantly, it is a practical guide for learning the craft of haute couture, and it will also provide new ideas for applying the techniques that you already know.

While some techniques are less suitable for beginners, most will be of value to the average home-sewer; they are easy to duplicate and can be applied to many designs and fabrics.

I find sewing by hand extremely rewarding. The pleasure of both making and wearing beautifully constructed garments far exceeds the time and effort required to complete them. I hope this book will help you develop these same skills and perfect old ones, and, in turn, reward you with years of pleasure—and a closet full of beautifully made garments.

# PART ONE

# The Basics
## *of* Couture Sewing

This stunning two-piece dress was made in the I. Magnin Custom Salon in 1948 for Mrs. Moon, the manager. Apparently influenced by Christian Dior's New Look collection in 1947, this dress is a very subtly designed border print on silk muslin.

(Photo by Ken Howie. Author's collection.)

# Inside the World of Haute Couture

WHEN I LEFT FOR PARIS in January 1991 for a week of press previews of the haute couture collections, the Gulf War had just begun and the weather was brutally cold. Although I had visited the workrooms of many couture houses over the years, this would be the first time I would have the opportunity to attend the runway shows debuting their collections,

Inspired by a Guy Laroche dress, the author designed this evening gown for Vogue Patterns. Fabricated in an unusual satin/ wool brocade, the dress is cut on the bias. It has a single seam at center back with darts positioned vertically and horizontally to enhance the figure. The muslin toile, or working pattern, at the right was used to refine the fit and determine the best construction techniques.

(Photo by Ken Howie. Author's collection.)

and I did not know what to expect. I soon found that each show was as different from the next as the designs it presented. All were extravagant and exhilarating to watch. The designs themselves were magnificent, although some were so flamboyant that it seemed they were not really intended to be worn off the runway. Many, however, would set the next season's fashion trends. Literally translated, the French phrase *haute couture* means "sewing at a high level," but a better translation might be the "finest high-fashion sewing." Although the haute couture designs shown on runways in Paris and Rome are too expensive for most pocketbooks, their influence on styles, colors, and accessories echoes throughout the women's clothing industry worldwide. For the home-sewer, haute couture designs have a special relevance.

Custom-sewn for a select group of women who can afford them, couture garments are simply the most beautifully made in the world. It may surprise some to learn that most of the techniques used in couture workrooms can be duplicated at home.

Originating in mid-19th-century Paris with the designs of an Englishman named Charles Frederick Worth (see "A Brief History of Couture" on p. 12), haute couture represents an archaic tradition of creating garments by hand with painstaking care and precision. In an elaborate process that's very much the same today as it was in the 1850s, each couture garment is custom cut, fitted, and even frequently redesigned for a particular individual. The process involves numerous steps and people with specialized skills, from the couturier, or designer, who creates the design to the team of assistants, fitters, and needleworkers who bring it to life.

Today, even though there are excellent couturiers in Rome, the center of haute couture remains in Paris, where there is still an enormous support structure of skilled workshops and needleworkers who specialize in hand embroidery, beading, feather work, braiding, fabric flowers, and custom-made accessories. In France, the term haute couture is strictly controlled by the *Chambre syndicale de la couture parisienne* (Parisian High Fashion Syndicate), the governing body of French fashion houses. The use of this term is reserved exclusively for the group's eleven members, who meet the strict qualifying rules outlined below. The official list for haute couture spring/summer 2010 for members included Adeline André, Anne Valérie Hash, Chanel, Christian Dior, Christian Lacroix, Dominique Sirop, Franck Sorbier, Givenchy, Jean Paul Gaultier, Maurizio Galante, and Stéphane Rolland. There are also five Correspondent (foreign) Members including Elie Saab, Giorgio Armani, Maison Martin, Margiela, and Valentino as well as 14 Guest Members. Two Americans—Mainbocher and Ralph Rucci—are former members; Oscar de la Renta was the couturier for Pierre Balmain. To be named to the list remains the highest recognition that a designer can achieve.

To earn the right to call itself a couture house and use the term "haute couture" in its advertising or in any other way, a member of the *Chambre syndicale* must design fashions that are made to order for private clients and involve one or more fittings, have a workroom in Paris with at least 15 full-time workers, present a collection of at least 35 designs, including day and evening garments, to the press in Paris in January for spring/summer season and in July for the autumn/winter season, and show the collection to potential clients in the respective couture houses.

The *Chambre syndicale's* definition of a couture house is so limiting that it excludes such notables as the houses of Renato Balestra, Gattinoni Couture, Romeo Gigli, and Sarli Couture, who both work and show their collections in Italy. Even

Deceptively simple, this timeless design features pin-tucking on the cashmere knit.

(Photo by Ken Howie, courtesy of Chado Ralph Rucci and the Phoenix Art Museum.)

The only American designer to have an eponymous couture house in Paris, Main Bocher changed his name to Mainbocher and gave it a French pronunciation. This boned-strapless gown was considered old-fashioned in 1934 when Mainbocher created it.

(Photo by David Arky, courtesy of the Museum of the City of New York, gift of the Estate of Tilly Losch, Lady Carnarvon, ca. 1956.)

the many old, established French couture houses do not qualify because, although their workrooms are in Paris, they do not present a collection.

## What makes couture "haute"?

What's so special about haute couture designs that simple day dresses range in price from $8,000 to $20,000, suits from $10,000 to $50,000, and evening gowns from $15,000 to as much as $500,000? There are many factors, notably the fabulous, exclusive fabrics used, the flawless design, cut and fit of each garment, the exquisite craftsmanship, and the time required.

Haute couture begins with strong, innovative design—the couturier's ability to interpret the mood of the time for the mode of the world. Whether classically styled or exaggerated, couture designs rely on such basic design principles as proportion, balance, color, and texture, and they conform to the image of the couture house.

Maintaining the integrity of a design while making adjustments to suit a client's figure and personal preferences is a delicate balancing act. Most couture houses will go to great lengths to do both. Several years ago, for example, when I visited the workrooms of English designer Hardy Amies, the staff had just fitted a client's dress, which she felt was about 1 in. too short. The black velvet, asymmetrical design featured a 4-in. pleated taffeta ruffle inserted in a seamline that began at the left shoulder, curved gently downward and ended at the right side seam about 4 in.—a ruffle's width— above the hemline. Since the garment had a wide hem allowance, it could have been lengthened by simply lowering the hem, but then the proportion of the ruffle's width and distance to the hemline would have been spoiled. Rather than demean the design, the house decided to lower the seamline, even though it meant cutting a new right front that positioned the ruffle precisely 4 in. above the hem.

Couture designs are enhanced by the extraordinary fabrics from which they are sewn. Only the finest luxury fabrics are used in couture, and they frequently cost hundreds of dollars a yd.— some cost more than a thousand dollars a yd. Most fabrics are made of natural fibers, but they can be made of silver threads; and a few couturiers use metallic, plastic, and man-made fibers for special effects. In the 1960s, designers experimented with new materials like Mylar®. See Chapter 12, p. 214, for a Mylar dress designed by Chanel.

Designs by Balenciaga, Yves Saint Laurent, and Givenchy have what initially appears to be an unnecessary use of an expensive fashion fabric for the lining or backing. When examined closely,

The "Swan" ball gown from 1954, like many others by Charles James, is heavily boned with a lowered back waist. As is typical for a couture design, the dress was made to fit its owner and cannot be altered successfully for another individual.

(Photo courtesy of Chicago History Museum, gift of Mrs. Corson Ellis.)

it is apparent that there was a reason for the extravagance. The two most common reasons are to eliminate a hem at the lower edge and to provide an inconspicuous lining fabric that might show when the garment is worn. My favorite is a short, special occasion dress by YSL. On the outside, the skirt has pleats at the waist; on the inside, the same fabric is tucked under the pleats to provide support. There is only a fold at the hemline.

Many printed fabrics are made with exclusive patterns or colorways, meaning the same design in different colors, designed by either the couturier or a fabric designer. A few couturiers work closely with a fabric house to develop new fabrics. Some fabrics, such as the extra-wide silks manufactured for Vionnet, the silk gazar designed in 1958 for Balenciaga by the noted fabric-design firm of Abraham (see below) and the printed silk muslin designed in 1947 for Dior by the firm of Bianchini-Ferier (see the photo in Chapter 12 on p. 220), are still widely used. Many other original fabrics are, of course, no longer available.

The long-standing liaison between the House of Chanel and the fabric firm of Linton Tweeds began with Chanel's first collection in 1919 and continues today. Frequently used for Chanel suits, Linton fabrics are often a combination of wool and mohair, but many incorporate acrylic, metallics, novelty yarns, and even cellophane. The House of Chanel chooses from 15 to 40 exclusive patterns for the firm of Linton to weave in lengths of small amounts of 6 to 8 meters so they can make prototype designs for the runway. Linton will also weave fancy selvages, which might include the more expensive yarns in the fabric and supply matching yarns and narrow trims when requested.

Designed by Cristobal Balenciaga in the 1950s, the simple lines of this coat showcase the unusual fabric, which appears to be gazar woven like a matelassé. The coat is completely lined with self-fabric even though it most certainly added to the cost.

(Photo by Taylor Sherrill. Author's collection.)

## The Atelier

In the atelier, or workroom, of a couture house, fabric patterns are sometimes cut apart, rearranged, and sewn back together to create special effects for a particular design (for example, see the blouse by Chanel on p. 208). This procedure is most often used to rearrange the color bars on striped fabrics or to appliqué motifs where there is a void on the garment, but I've seen fabrics that were literally created in the atelier. Some are relatively simple creations—such as the red-and-blue-striped Chanel blouse I saw that was made by cutting red and blue fabrics into narrow strips and seaming them together. Others, such as the fabric customized in Valentino's atelier for a wedding gown, are extremely labor intensive. That particular fabric had pink-and-white-ruffled diamond patterns completely covering the gown's tulle skirt, which took four workers four weeks to make.

Buttons and trims are often custom-made as well. Braids run the gamut from silver crocheted trims to re-embroidered braids to thread-wrapped embroidered topstitching. Buttons range from Worth's fabric covered buttons with an embroidered flower on top to Schiaparelli's avant-garde, whimsical designs with plastic cicadas or ceramic trapeze artists to Chanel's simpler double-C gilt designs or ornate camellia buttons.

In addition to the array of high-quality trims employed on a couture garment, the fit is also a highly conceived element of any couture piece. A couture garment fits flawlessly as a result of multiple fittings on the client's dress form, which has been customized to duplicate her figure, but more impressive than the fit are the subtle ways in which a couture garment is proportioned for the individual client. For an asymmetrical figure, for example, the collar, pockets, and shoulder seam may be slightly narrower on one side. For a full figure, vertical seamlines are moved in or out as needed to create the most flattering line, while for a short figure, all horizontal seamlines are adjusted, not just the waistline and hem.

The size of the client's garment also affects the way it is embellished. On a garment with embroidery or beading, the embellished design is scaled to the dimensions of the client's garment, so that it does not overwhelm a smaller figure or float against the sizable background on a larger one.

## Craftsmanship

Impeccable craftsmanship is the essence of haute couture, and it begins long before the fabric is cut. With the help of a muslin pattern, or toile, every design is planned so the motifs, stripes, or plaids are not only matched, but also positioned most attractively for the client's figure. At garment openings, floral motifs match so perfectly you have

*continued on p. 17*

The legendary designer Christian Dior drapes silk taffeta on a model to begin a design for his 1948 collection. According to Mme. Marguerite, who worked closely with him, he would then make quick sketches from which the atelier premiers would cut and sew the first toile.

(Photo by Bellini, courtesy of Christian Dior.)

# A Brief History of Haute Couture

**IN THE BEGINNING, FRANCE** was recognized as the world's foremost fashion leader when Louis Napoleon Bonaparte established the Second Empire in 1852. About the same time, an Englishman named Charles Frederick Worth, a sales assistant at the famous Parisian fabric store, Gagelin-Opigez et Cie., persuaded his employers to allow him to open a new department with a few dressmakers. By combining his extensive knowledge of fabrics and garment construction with a talent for promotion, Worth soon established himself as the

Designed by Jeanne Pacquin, this silk velvet and satin gown illustrates the designer's talent for creating an afternoon dress that could be worn to dinner.

(Courtesy of Chicago History Museum.)

only male dressmaker in Paris. Worth executed each of his original designs in several Gagelin fabrics, distinguishing himself from conventional dressmakers, well-trained technicians who combined the customer's design and fabric. In so doing, he became the father of *haute couture,* a phrase coined in 1863 by an American client, a Mrs. Moulton.

## THE HOUSE OF WORTH

In 1858, Worth created his own couture house with his partner Gustof Bobergh. Within two years, he secured the patronage of the French Empress Eugénie, one of the most important fashion leaders of all time. Worth was the first to establish a house style and create a collection of seasonal designs shown on live models. In 1868, Worth established the *Chambre syndicale de la couture parisienne,* the governing body of French fashion.

Worth was also the first to understand the relationship of the fabric to the design. He began cutting garment sections with the grain and used one of the concepts of mass production—interchangeable, modular parts—to create a variety of different designs. But the fashion change he made that pleased him most

was abolishing the "cage," or hoop skirt, in favor of a more relaxed silhouette.

When the Franco-Prussian War toppled the Second Empire in 1870, the fairy tale ended, and Worth lost his most important client when Empress Eugénie went into exile. Paris, nonetheless, continued as the international center of high fashion—albeit more restrained fashion—and Worth continued to design for women of wealth and note.

At the same time, aesthetic dress, which was initially inspired by designs from late medieval and early renaissance periods, was introduced. These soft, loose dresses were simply embellished and worn without a corset. The aesthetic movement reached its height in the 1880s.

## THE BELLE EPOQUE

As La Belle Epoque dawned, the first important woman designer, Madame Pacquin, founded her couture house in 1891. Although she became known for glamorous evening gowns, exquisite workmanship and innovative mix of materials, Pacquin was also a practical designer. She introduced a dress style tailored enough for daywear but elegant enough for informal evening occasions. She was the first French designer to

Known for superb workmanship, intricate cuts, lace, and embroidered embellishments, the atelier Callot Sœurs specialized in formal eveningwear.

(Photo by Steven H. Bluttal, courtesy of the Museum of the City of New York, gift of Mrs. Robert L. Stevens & Mrs. Cornelius Vanderbilt.)

publicize her designs by sending several models to the races at Longchamps wearing the same outfit, and she was the first to open international branches of her couture house.

## CHANGING TIMES

When the new century dawned, women were still confined in tightly laced corsets and elaborately ornamented clothing, but the fashion world was ready for a change. Credited with modernizing dress design, Paul Poiret introduced the straight silhouette in 1907, which has dominated fashion for most of the century. Worn with a less confining corset, the forerunner of the brassiere, his new design—the shift—was a simple narrow tube with a high waist.

The first couturier to collaborate with artists such as Raoul Dufy, Poiret produced new fashions that were bold, brilliantly colored and exotic, and were often distinguished more by their decoration than by their cut.

Madeleine Vionnet, another innovative designer, showed her radical new designs in 1907 while working for French couturier Jacques Doucet, one of the major competitors of the House of Worth at the turn of the century. Cut entirely on the bias and worn over uncorseted figures, Vionnet's dresses appeared simple in design, but their construction was quite complex.

Mass production of various goods began during the war, and many women entered the work force. Even though clients from the Austrian, German, Balkan, and Russian courts had vanished, the couture houses thrived after the war. They created simpler, less individualized designs intended for wealthy, fashionable women in France and abroad, but most sales were now made to retailers, who purchased hundreds of models or to manufacturers who planned to copy them. As a result, many couture houses became specialists in handmade designs.

During the 1920s, the "garçonne," or boyish look, became popular, introducing a new informality to the haute couture fashion scene, which was dominated by Jean Patou

This avant-garde Poiret ensemble is from about 1919. The coat is fabricated in a single layer of wool double cloth. Wool inserts conceal seaming on the face of the coat.

(Photo by Steven H. Bluttal, courtesy of the Museum of the City of New York, gift of Mrs. Henry Clews.)

Cut on the bias, this asymmetrical Vionnet design from 1922 is fabricated in multiple layers of silk crepe georgette and trimmed with lamé.

(Photo by Ken Howie, courtesy of the Phoenix Art Museum, gift of the Arizona Costume Institute in honor of the Museum's 50th anniversary, 2009.)

and Coco Chanel. Inspired by sportswear, Patou invented the V-neck sweater and the short pleated skirt, and was the first to use his monogram as a design element. Chanel put her rich clients, who had been wearing satin and lace day dresses, into casual, unstructured jersey dresses and woolen cardigan jackets.

The 1929 Wall Street crash abruptly ended the prosperous Roaring Twenties. When the United States raised import taxes on couture designs, many houses began selling designs and toiles to retailers and manufacturers, which could be imported to America duty free.

In the 1930s, fashions changed dramatically once more. Italian-born designer Elsa Schiaparelli created outlandish fashions in unique color combinations. Known for her hard-edge chic and fantasy, "la Schiap" created styles that often featured prints and embellishments designed by such artists as Dali and Cocteau. She is credited with inventing the long dinner suit and voluminous evening trousers. Inspired by masculine uniforms, she introduced the broad-shouldered, boxy silhouette that

dominated fashion from 1933 to the late 1940s.

After Germany invaded France in 1940, many couture houses closed, while others moved—Molyneux to London and Mainbocher to America—but most continued to present small collections.

During the war years, American designers like Gilbert Adrian, Irene, Jean Louis, Charles James, Valentina, Claire McCardell, Mainbocher, Norman Norell, Hattie Carnegie, and Sophie Gimbel developed an American style. Intended for a more active lifestyle, this style was straightforward and more youthful than the European tradition on which it was built.

### THE NEW LOOK

Women's fashions remained virtually unchanged after the war until Christian Dior showed his first collection in 1947. Dubbed a "New Look" by Carmel Snow, editor of *Harper's Bazaar*[SM] magazine, Dior's designs featured long, full skirts, wasp waists, and narrow sloping shoulders. Influenced by La Belle Epoque, Dior restored femininity to a world tired of uniforms and uniformity and made fashion exciting once more. The couture industry was revitalized.

During the postwar boom and into the 1950s, haute couture continued to flourish. Pierre Balmain created magnificent ball gowns, Jacques Fath introduced pastels to bridal wear, and Hubert de Givenchy introduced separates to high fashion. In the early 1950s, an unfitted silhouette was ushered in with Cristobal Balenciaga's introduction of the sack dress in 1951. By the mid-1950s, many designers were showing designs that bypassed the waist. Notable was Yves Saint Laurent's trapeze dress, created for his first collection at Dior in 1958. The new relaxed silhouette was off and running but, unfortunately, its success,

later combined with fashion and fabric developments in the 1960s, would have a devastating effect on haute couture.

By the mid-1960s, couture fashions were less structured and even more casual, inspired by the loose-fitting fashions of the hippie movement. With the demise of the bra and fitted silhouettes, the fashions coming out of Paris were easily copied in all price ranges. For the first time in history, couture had lost its leading edge, and many couture

houses launched *prêt-a-porter*, or luxury ready-to-wear, collections. Pierre Cardin, the first to do so in 1959, was promptly, though temporarily, expelled from the *Chambre syndicale*.

By 1975, luxury ready-to-wear was an important industry. Unfortunately, the success of the new luxury ready-to-wear clothing came at the expense of haute couture fashions. The easy availability of luxury ready-to-wear meant that retailers and manufacturers no longer had to purchase toiles and designs for copying.

### The "Me" Decade

Dubbed the "Me Decade" by writer Tom Wolfe, the 1970s offered many choices. Fashions were romantic, individualistic, and unstructured, with extravagant interpretations of Russian, Chinese, African, Indian, and gypsy themes, as well as "retro" looks from the 1920s, '30s, and '40s. The decade, too, was dominated by pants—from very short hot pants, stovepipes, and bell-bottoms to Yves Saint Laurent's trouser suit for women.

### The Big '80s

With the 1980s came an English royal wedding, an infusion of Middle Eastern petrol dollars, the ostentatious Reagan Era, and new clients from Japan. There was lots of new money, younger customers, and a renewed

The "Petal" ballgown was constructed like many Charles James designs with a boned bodice and elaborate skirt. Fabricated in black velvet and silk taffeta, the skirt has numerous underskirts, all cut in different shapes, to support the approximately 25 yd. of fabric in the overskirt.

(Photo by Ken Howie, courtesy of Phoenix Art Museum, gift of Mrs. Eleanor Searle Whitney McCollum, 1975.)

interest in haute couture. Karl Lagerfeld was hired to modernize the Chanel style and resuscitate the couture house. The innovative Christian Lacroix revived the House of Patou and promptly left to establish his own label, putting us all in pouf dresses. Yves Saint Laurent perfected his classic styles for day and rich fantasies for evening, Pierre Cardin continued to develop his geometric-inspired futurist shapes, and Givenchy and Valentino created the elegant luxuries their clients adore.

## COUTURE TODAY

The finest jewel in fashion's crown, haute couture is an anachronism today. Having peaked in the 1940s and 1950s, when its sales were the major

source of income for the great design houses, couture clothing has largely been replaced by luxury ready-to-wear, which is generally called couture in America. Couture sales have dropped to a fraction of their all-time high. The couture customer base has dwindled to an estimated 2,000 with perhaps only a few hundred women purchasing regularly, and the number of couture houses has dropped from a high of 53 after World War II to 21 at the beginning of 1993. By 2010, there were just 11. Given the shrinking clientele and rising prices of haute couture, it's not surprising that its future is frequently a subject for speculation. Many couture houses such as Givenchy, Ungaro, and Balmain have discontinued their haute couture collections.

Today, couture is considered the engine that pulls the train as the most successful houses spin off lucrative licenses for ready-to-wear clothing, fragrances, cosmetics, fashion and home accessories, chocolates and even automobile interiors. The House of Cardin, for example, had

840 licenses in 94 countries, including one for car tires. Although supported by bigger and more profitable business operations, haute couture is still an art form practiced by a few creative men and women and a small group of skilled artisans. Whether classic in style or playfully outrageous, the designs that emerge from couture workrooms influence women's fashions throughout the industrialized world.

In 1959, Pierre Cardin was banished from the *Chambre Syndicale* because he introduced a ready-to-wear collection. After his reinstatement, his sculptured space-age designs set the fashion trends for several years. This dress from 1965 is fabricated in a thick wool double knit.

(Photo by Ken Howie, courtesy of the Phoenix Art Museum, Donor Mrs. Peter Lipton.)

Ralph Rucci is the master of simple, modern silhouettes that belie their complexity. This design, from his 2010 collection, features a bias-cut satin slip and sweater with bugle beads.

(Photo courtesy of Chado Ralph Rucci.)

to look twice to see the fasteners, and on suits and two-piece designs, the fabric pattern continues uninterrupted from neck to hem.

During the construction process, most of the sewing is done by hand. Thousands of perfectly spaced basting stitches mark or hold the garment layers together temporarily so a design can be fitted on the client or dress form, stitched or hand-sewn permanently or precisely pressed. Then these stitches are taken out so the construction can continue. Again and again, the fabric is painstakingly shaped and manipulated in the hands or on a form until the garment is completed. Even the seams may be permanently sewn by hand. The construction of the dress, gown or suit that emerges may look effortless, but it takes many hours to produce that effortless look.

All of the hand sewing that goes into making a couture garment distinguishes it from a comparable design in luxury ready-to-wear, which is known in France as *prêt-à-porter*. Priced from $200 for a cotton shirt, for example, to $30,000 for an evening gown, luxury ready-to-wear is sewn from high-quality fabrics and sold in better stores and boutiques all over the world. Hundreds of copies of each design are sewn, primarily by machine operators, who are part of a piecework system— each one performs the same operation over and over. As a result, there's considerably less hand work on many luxury ready-to-wear garments by such designers as Armani, Ralph Lauren, Oscar de la Renta, or Versace. The garments are nonetheless lovely, and most are clean-finished, or lined with rayon or silk to conceal serged, pinked, or unfinished seams.

## Creating a Couture Collection

Twice a year, in January and July, each couture house spends millions of dollars to present its collections. Although the couture shows were once sedate affairs held in couture salons, they have become theatrical extravaganzas produced with lights and loud music. Designed to lure almost

1,500 members of the media to Paris, the shows generate important publicity for the designers. The most successful designs that make headlines in January and July are eventually copied or translated into mass-produced clothing in all price ranges. As a laboratory for women's fashions, the couture industry has a major impact on what women wear.

A couture collection is frequently developed around a theme such as a major art exhibit, an exotic vacation spot, or a period in fashion history. The collection will have some day dresses, some suits (and occasionally trouser suits), a few short evening designs, and a number of long gowns. Some designs will be comfortable and may flatter older or less-than-perfect figures. Others may include a few glitzy showstoppers to promote the house's image and excite the press.

## Designing the Couture Collection

The first phase of assembling a collection begins in the couturier's design studio many months before the press show. The couturier will begin with either the fabric or the silhouette. They must be compatible because the combined qualities of the fabric, that is, its weight, drape, texture, and hand (the fabric's crispness or softness), will make it appropriate for some types of silhouettes and not for others. If the designer is contemplating an exaggerated, sculpted look, a crisp, tightly woven fabric will probably be chosen. If, on the other

Designed by Christian Dior, this sketch of "Mexico" for Summer 1953 is called a croquis. A photograph of the design is shown on p. 220.

(Photo courtesy of Christian Dior.)

hand, the designer begins with a bolt of soft fabric, the design will probably fall more gently and follow the lines of the body. One designer known for his ability to use a fabric to its fullest potential was the Spaniard Cristobal Balenciaga (see one of his designs on p. 10).

When the fabrics arrive, the couturier drapes unfolded lengths of each one over a dress form or a model to see how it hangs on the lengthwise grain, crossgrain, and bias. Then, using this information as a guide, he makes hundreds of *croquis*, or design sketches, for his collection. Since it is impossible to develop toiles for every sketch, the editing process to select the best designs and fine-tune the focus of the collection begins at once. This is usually done by the couturier with the help of design assistants and the premières, the heads of the ateliers, whose technical expertise is highly regarded. The design sketches are then distributed to the workrooms.

## Tailoring Workrooms

Depending on the type of garment the couturier has designed, his sketch will go to the *atelier du tailleur* (tailoring workroom) or to the *atelier du flou* (dressmaking workroom). The garments made in the tailoring workroom are more structured than those created in the dressmaking workroom, and the tailoring fabrics, usually woolens, tend to be heavier than dressmaker fabrics. In the tailoring workroom, the fabric is often shaped by stretching and shrinking it (see p. 64) and is supported by the garment's entoilage, or inner structure of interfacings and pad stitching.

A few houses have two tailoring workrooms: one that concentrates on tailored, menswear-influenced designs made of fabrics similar in texture, weave, and weight to those used for menswear; and a second that concentrates on softer dressmaker styles made of soft wools, mohairs, bouclés, or chenilles.

In the dressmaking atelier, where many gowns, dresses, blouses, and other garments are sewn, silk is the predominant fabric. Many of the garments made in this workroom are softly draped designs

that have to be sewn on a dress form from the right side of the garment in order for the draped folds of the design to be accurately pinned and stitched in place. Some designs have no inner structure and rely completely on the body to give them shape (see the bias-cut dress designed by Madeleine Vionnet, shown on p. 14). Others, like the Charles James gown (see p. 15), may be backed or rely on an elaborate inner structure.

After discussing the design with the couturier, the première decides who will make the toiles and sew the prototypes, called *modèles*. The toiles and prototypes are usually sewn by the *premières mains* or "first hands," who are the most experienced workers in the atelier, and a small group of workers, or *mains* ("hands"), with a variety of skills and training. Then a muslin fabric in the appropriate weight for the design is selected, and the toile is draped on a dress form to duplicate the couturier's sketch and provide the basic pattern from which the garment will be sewn. Depending on the complexity of the design, this process usually takes four to eight hours.

Even though the toile is just a working pattern, it is made carefully with the necessary underpinnings and sometimes even with buttonholes. During its development, the toile is basted and rebasted for fittings on one of the house models and is examined and modified again and again until the couturier is satisfied.

In the New York workroom at Scaasi, this dressmaker is basting the hem. Notice that the bulk of the garment is supported on the table and she is holding a small section of the hem in her hand.

(Photo by Author.)

This timeless evening gown is fabricated in silk velvet. A very successful New York designer, Valentina made many designs that were cut off grain but not on the true bias.

(Photo by Steven H. Bluttal, courtesy of the Museum of the City of New York, Costume Collection. Costume worn by Katharine Cornell in "No Time for Comedy" [1939] by S. N. Behrman.)

Once the toile is approved by the couturier, he reviews the fabric selection for the prototype to make certain it is still appropriate for the design. The toile is then carefully ripped apart and pressed so it can serve as a pattern for cutting the fashion fabric. After the fashion fabric is cut and marked with thread tracing (see Chapter 3, "Marking the Garment" on p. 48), the prototype is completely basted for a first fitting on a house model. Then it is modified and corrected as needed; this usually involves two or three fittings, until the couturier is satisfied with the results. To save time finishing the prototypes, the edges are sometimes serged, pinked, or zigzagged, and it is not uncommon for tailored garments to be left unlined. Finally, jewelry, hats, and shoes are selected by the couturier or his assistants for the press show and the design is entered in the *livre de fabrications*, or production book.

## Ordering a Couture Design

Let me take you on an imaginary shopping spree to purchase your first couture design. The best times to visit are in February or September shortly after the *grand défilé* (press preview) so you can see the private fashion show, called the *défilé*, which is held several days each week immediately after the collection is shown to the press. If this is not convenient, you can visit another time and watch a videotape of the fashion show.

To make an appointment, you should write the *directrice*, who manages the salon, or wait until you arrive in Paris and ask the concierge at your hotel to contact her for you. If you have a friend who shops at a particular house, she may recommend that you ask for her *vendeuse* (salesperson); otherwise, one will be assigned to you. This assignment is permanent unless you request a change. You will get to know each other well, and she will provide expert fashion advice on selecting the clothes that are appropriate for your lifestyle and figure and how to accessorize your wardrobe. In fact, a *vendeuse* is sometimes trusted so implicitly that some clients allow her to select their garments and do not bother to come in until they are ready for the first fitting. Do not worry if you do not speak French; most of the salespeople speak excellent English.

If you arrive a little early on the day of the fashion show, you can browse in the boutique, where you will find the luxury ready-to-wear collection, lingerie, accessories, and often some decorative items for the home. Present yourself at the reception desk so you can meet your vendeuse, who will show you to your seat. During the show, note the numbers of the designs you want to see.

# HAUTE COUTURE vs. READY-TO-WEAR

| HAUTE COUTURE | HIGH-END READY-TO-WEAR |
|---|---|
| ➤ Not available in stores | ➤ Sold in boutiques/fine stores |
| ➤ Limited availability; garments must be ordered | ➤ Garments are ready to be purchased and worn |
| ➤ Little hanger appeal | ➤ Designs have hanger appeal |
| ➤ Designed for individual client | ➤ Designed for target customer |
| ➤ Designs limited availability<br>➤ One of a kind or few duplicates | ➤ Multiple identical garments |
| ➤ Design may appeal to only one client<br>➤ Design must fit only one client<br>➤ Design can be complex with little or no opportunity for alterations | ➤ Design must appeal to many customers, fit a variety of figure types and sizes, be suitable for alterations, fit into a specific price range, reflect the manufacturer's image |
| ➤ Client can sometimes choose a different fabric or color or request design changes | ➤ Customer has no input in fabric selection or design |
| ➤ Fine-quality fabrics<br>➤ Limited quantities<br>➤ Limited availability<br>➤ Fabrics sometimes custom made (red/blue stripes—seamed to make striped fabric<br>➤ Couturier may work with textile manufacturer to create exclusive fabrics | ➤ Fine-quality fabrics<br>➤ Designer selects colors and fabric patterns<br>➤ Fabrics used as designed by textile mill |
| ➤ Embroideries designed and proportioned for individual | ➤ Embroidery designs may not change with the garment's size |
| ➤ Design is proportioned for individual client | ➤ Design proportioned for target customer<br>➤ Patterns graded up and down specific amounts for larger/smaller figures |
| ➤ Design proportion sometimes adjusted for asymmetrical figure | ➤ Design proportion is symmetrical |
| ➤ Not cut until client orders | ➤ Cut when retailer orders |
| ➤ Pattern made by draping muslin on client's dress form | ➤ Pattern made by flat-pattern method |
| ➤ Fitted on client and/or client's dress form | ➤ Fitted on fit model or fit model's dress form |

**CONSTRUCTION**

| | |
|---|---|
| ➤ Made by "hand," preponderance of hand sewing | ➤ Mass-produced with little or no hand sewing |
| ➤ Stitching lines—seams, darts, pleats—thread-traced | ➤ Relies on precision cutting so edges can be matched when assembled |
| ➤ Seam allowances generally wider, not precise widths, can be different widths—one wide, one narrow | ➤ Seam allowances are precise widths<br>➤ Some seams very narrow (¼") so they can be stitched quickly and accurately |

| HAUTE COUTURE | HIGH-END READY-TO-WEAR |
|---|---|
| ➤ Matchpoints located on seamlines | ➤ Notches (matchpoints) located on cut edge with short clips |
| ➤ Seams, darts, tucks, pleats hand basted before stitching<br>➤ Basting sometimes from face side and/or on dress form | ➤ Little or no basting |
| ➤ Layers frequently sewn together by hand with wrong sides together | ➤ Layers stitched by machine with face sides together |
| ➤ At edges, extended facing folds to wrong side to avoid bulk of seam | ➤ At edges, separate facing joined to garment |
| ➤ Understitching is by hand with a backstitch | ➤ Understitching by machine |
| ➤ Darts slashed open or balanced | ➤ Darts pressed to one side |
| ➤ Garment front marked with cross-stitches or "F" | ➤ Garment front generally not marked |
| ➤ Dresses frequently backed, not lined<br>➤ Untrained eye considers inside "rough" or unfinished | ➤ Dresses lined |
| ➤ Most common seam/hem finish today is hand overcasting, because it is soft and inconspicuous | ➤ Most common seam/hem finish is overlocking (serging) |
| ➤ Hand-rolled hems, sometimes picot edges | ➤ Narrow, machine-stitched hems |
| ➤ Buttonholes—hand bound, or in-seam | ➤ Buttonholes—machine stitched, bound, or in-seam |
| ➤ Snaps frequently fabric covered | ➤ Snaps not covered |
| ➤ Patch pockets—made by hand, handsewn to garment | ➤ Patch pockets made and applied by machine |
| ➤ Waistbands often faced with silk or ribbon<br>➤ Finished by hand | ➤ Waistband faced with self-fabric, finished by machine |
| ➤ Jacket sleeve vents finished with hand-folded miter or no miter | ➤ Jacket sleeve vents mitered at corner |
| ➤ Sewn-in interfacings for support | ➤ Fusible interfacings |
| ➤ Underpinnings frequently sewn into garment | ➤ Underpinnings generally not sewn in and may require separate purchase |
| ➤ Stays used to hold garment in place on body, to hold design in desired position, or to reduce bulk. | ➤ Stays rarely used |
| ➤ Shoulder pads handmade, sometimes unusual shapes | ➤ Mass-produced shoulder pads |

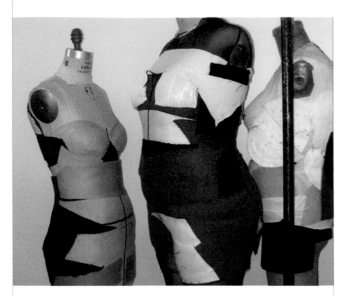

In couture, a dress form is padded to the individual customer's measurements so the design can be draped and fitted on the dress form before it is fitted on the client. (Courtesy of *Threads* magazine.)

If you want to try some on, you can stay afterward or make an appointment to come back another day.

You will probably want to "try the house" with a small order—a day dress or a suit. During the 1940s and 1950s, many clients had their entire wardrobes from a single couturier. Although some clients will order an entire wardrobe from the same designer, many prefer nowadays to patronize several houses.

To look at the designs you have selected, you will be escorted to a dressing room. The designs will be brought from the *cabine,* or models' dressing room, where the prototypes are stored. Since they are custom-made for tall, extremely thin models, they may not fit, but do not worry.

Depending on your size, you can get an idea of what you will look like in a given design by slipping into the prototype without zipping it, or by having it pinned to your slip. If you prefer, one of the house models will model it so you can see it on the figure at close range. Since you probably are not accustomed to shopping this way, you might be alarmed at the idea of ordering a costly garment that you have not tried on in your size. But your

vendeuse has had years of experience, and since the business of haute couture depends on loyal customers, she is not going to let you purchase an unflattering design.

Once you have made your selection, discuss any changes you want with the *vendeuse*—for example, a different neckline or sleeve, another color or fabric, a longer or shorter skirt or possibly two skirts. How much you can change a design depends on the couturier and the available fabrics. Most designers do not mind as long as the integrity of the design is not compromised.

At most houses, a new client will be asked to pay 50 percent of the entire order when it is placed and before your measurements are taken. If you are a high profile client, you may not be asked for a deposit and the price may be less because you will be a walking advertisement for the house.

## GETTING MEASURED

The première of the workroom that will make your garment will take your measurements. You will be measured from head to toe—about 30 measurements altogether; these will be turned over to the première main, who will be responsible for your design. She will pad a dress form with cotton batting or lambswool to duplicate your figure, including any quirks or irregularities noted by the première, and cover the form with a *toile de corps,* which is a muslin body suit that zips up the back.

Using the design's original prototype or its muslin toile as a guide, the première main will make a toile of the design on your dress form. She will drape, mold, and pin pieces of muslin to the form until she is pleased with its design and fit.

If you were to lay your toile on top of the original toile for the prototype, you would probably find that they are quite different in cut even though they look exactly the same on dress forms. This is one of the most fascinating aspects of the construction of a couture garment. Your toile will reflect the changes made to accommodate, flatter, and fit your individual figure. It takes an atelier worker many years to learn which adjustments will be most

This label from the House of Worth is on the waist stay or Petersham. The garment's number, which is sometimes called the "passage," is written in ink on the underside.

(Photo by Author, courtesy of the Museum of the City of New York, gift of Mrs. Calvin Brice.)

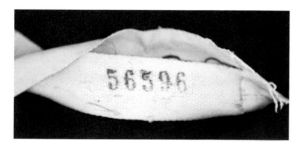

When the Chanel couture label is turned wrong side up, you can see the "bolduc" or tape with the garment's number on it. (Photo by Author.)

flattering to the client and then execute them on a toile without visibly altering the design.

After the fabric for your garment has been cut, the garment sections are marked with thread tracing. Then, almost every detail of the design, including the hem, zipper, and sometimes even the lining, is hand basted for the first fitting.

About a week after you have ordered your garment, you will have your first fitting. Even though the garment will have thread tracings to mark the garment centers and balance lines so the fit can be evaluated easily, it may look finished because the basting stitches are so fine and regular. For your fitting, your vendeuse and the directrice or couturier, and the première or première main, who is making the garment will evaluate the fit and design of your garment.

Back in the workroom, all the basted seams are ripped apart and the sections are laid flat on the table. Called *mis à plat*, or "laying out flat," this

procedure is one of the distinguishing techniques of couture construction. The corrections marked during the fitting are made on the garment sections and also on the toile for future reference, should you want a similar design. When necessary, a new garment section is cut to replace one that can not be corrected.

If the garment has embroidery, beading or another type of embellishment, it is done at this point. Often the garment sections to be embellished are sent out to one of the small firms in Paris that specializes in ornamentation. Then the corrected and embellished garment sections are rebasted, pockets are added, and the permanent stitching is completed on seams and details that do not require further fitting.

At your second fitting, the garment is checked to be sure it fits and hangs correctly, and any minor adjustments are indicated so the design can be completed. If the design is very complex or your figure is difficult to fit, there may be additional fittings.

Although heavily embellished designs may require several months to complete, most designs are finished in two to three weeks, for special clients they are sometimes made in less time.

When your own garment is complete, you will have your final fitting, and assuming all is well, the *griffe* (label) will then be sewn in. It is considered bad luck to sew it in before the final fitting. At Dior, the date of the collection is woven on the label, and the fabrication number (the cumulative number of garments produced by the house) is stamped on it. At many houses, the number is handwritten on the *bolduc* or plain cotton tape. Finally, the design is logged into the *livre de compte*, or sales book, carefully packed and delivered to your hotel or shipped to your home.

At most houses, your new outfit comes with an unspoken, unconditional guarantee of satisfaction. If the color is wrong, you may return it even though the error was yours. If you lose or gain weight, the garment will be altered, frequently at no extra charge; but, if you want it restyled, there is often a fee.

# 2

# The Art of Hand Sewing

THERE ARE THOUSANDS OF temporary stitches sewn by hand into a couture garment during its construction, and hundreds of permanent hand stitches on the finished piece. The first thing you notice when visiting a couture atelier is that the workers (referred to in French as *mains* ["hands"] or *petites mains* "little hands" are seated at tables where they sew by hand, rather than at sewing machines. In fact, there are only a few sewing machines in the atelier.

Hand stitching has many virtues. The most important is the control you have to shape the garment when handling the fabric. You can sew inconspicuously from the right side and work in sections that are too narrow to be stitched on a sewing machine; and you can sew very precisely. If the hand stitches must be removed, they are less likely to mar the fabric than machine stitches.

In this country, home sewers tend to be much more familiar with machine stitching than with sewing by hand, so it's worth reviewing some hand sewing basics and choosing tools and supplies.

Designed by Chanel in the 1930s, this extraordinary silk chiffon blouse features alternating strips of handsewn pintucks and lace insertions. The body of the blouse is backed with flesh-colored silk chiffon. On the front, the shaping for the bust is hidden in the seams joining the lace and chiffon. Narrow overcast seams at the armscye are cleverly hidden by the lace at the top of the sleeves. The French seams at the underarm and shoulder seams are sewn with short running stitches.

(Photo by Ken Howie. Author's collection.)

# Needles and Thread

Needles come in various types and sizes. The needle type is determined by its length, the size and shape of its eye, and whether it's point is sharp or blunt. Dressmaking and tailoring needles are sized from 1 to 18, and tapestry needles and yarn darners are sized from 14 to 26. The higher the number, the finer and shorter the needle.

Use long needles to pick up multiple short stitches and for long stitches used for thread tracing, uneven basting and stab stitches; use shorter needles for general sewing, short basting stitches, hemming, and other finishing techniques. Fine needles are appropriate for lightweight and medium-weight fabrics, and sturdier needles for heavier materials. Use needles with oval or long eyes for coarse threads and easy threading. To prevent rusting, store your extra needles in their original packages or on a piece of fabric.

Use an emery bag, usually shaped like a strawberry, to sharpen and polish needles—simply push the needle back and forth through the bag several times. If you leave needles in the emery bag for long periods, they may rust.

A thimble is indispensable in couture sewing. It not only protects your finger but helps you make neater stitches with greater speed. There are two types of thimbles: the frequently used closed-end dressmaker's thimble, and the open-end tailor's thimble. Each type of thimble is used for similar tasks, but as their names suggest, they are worn by workers in different workrooms of a couture house.

Threads come in a variety of fibers and sizes (see "Thread Types and Their Uses" on the facing page). It has a twist. When you're hand sewing, the thread will knot and kink less if you work *with* the twist. The twist usually runs in the direction from the loose end of the spooled thread toward the spool.

## BASIC SEWING TOOLS AND SUPPLIES

Horsehair braid (1), wigan (2), stay tape (3), Petersham (4), seam binding (5), weights (6), spiral boning (7), magnifier (8), boning stays (9), tracing wheel (10), reducing glass (11), measuring and drafting equipment (12), homemade pouncer triangle (13), basting cotton (14), scissors (15), beeswax (16), thread (17), chalk (18), pins (19), machine needles (20), thimbles (21), tambour hooks (22), needles (23), silk pin bag (24). (Photo by Taylor Sherrill. Author's collection.)

# THREAD TYPES AND THEIR USES

| TYPE | FEATURES | USES |
| --- | --- | --- |
| **All-purpose cotton** (size 50/3, 50/2, or 3-cord cotton, sometimes called Silk Finish) | All-purpose thread for hand and machine sewing; usually mercerized; may fade or crock (rub off) | Basting, hemming, padstitching, zippers, button stems, buttonholes on cotton fabric, machine stitching |
| **Basting thread, skeined cotton, embroidery floss** | Loose twist, soft finish, breaks easily; does not fall out of fabric; rarely leaves impression on fabric when pressed | Thread-tracing, tailor's tacks, hand basting |
| **Cotton-wrapped polyester core** | All-purpose thread, stronger than mercerized cotton | General hand and machine sewing |
| **Extra-fine cotton-wrapped polyester** | Strong, all-purpose thread | Hand and machine stitching on lightweight fabrics |
| **Fine machine embroidery thread** (size 60, cotton) | All-purpose thread for lightweight fabrics; more sheen than mercerized cotton | General hand and machine stitching, buttonholes on lightweight fabrics |
| **Glazed cotton** (sizes 40, 50, or 60) | Strong, starched thread; easy to pull up; usually leaves an impression when pressed | Basting, thread-tracing, gathering |
| **Mercerized cotton** (size 50/3 or 3-cord cotton, sometimes called Silk Finish) | All-purpose thread for hand and machine sewing, may fade or crock | Basting, thread-tracing, gathering |
| **Polyester** | All-purpose thread for all types of fabrics | Machine stitching on synthetic fabrics |
| **Serger thread** | Lightweight thread | Finishing raw edges, seaming lightweight synthetic fabrics |
| **Silk basting** (100 weight) | Very fine; rarely leaves impression on fabric when pressed | Top basting, rolled hems, machine-stitching chiffon |
| **Silk buttonhole twist** (sizes D, E, F, 9 weight) | Heavy silk thread | Buttonholes on medium- to heavy-weight fabrics, button stems |
| **Silk line stitch or silk embroidery** (30 weight) | Medium-weight silk thread; similar to silk machine twist, but stronger | Buttonholes on light- to medium-weight fabrics, machine topstitching, thread chains and loops, button stems |
| **Silk machine twist** (50 weight) | Versatile, medium-weight silk thread | Hand and machine stitching |
| **Topstitching** | Heavy polyester thread, stiffer than silk buttonhole twist | Topstitching, buttonholes, buttons; rarely used in couture |

Thread the needle with the end that first comes off the spool just as you would thread a sewing machine needle. Thread the end that's pointed like a flower bud and knot the end that flares open.

When used for permanent hand stitches, all thread types should be pulled once or twice through a small cake of beeswax, and then pressed to strengthen. Pressing with a warm iron also prevents knotting and fraying and keeps the wax from rubbing off on the fabric. Do not use beeswax on basting threads; it will leave a permanent stain if pressed over.

In couture workrooms, the type of thread selected depends on whether it is to be used for hand or machine sewing, the kind of stitch—temporary or permanent, decorative or utilitarian—the garment section to be sewn, the fabric fiber content, the degree of strength required, and the sewer's preference.

## Beginnings and Endings

For most hand sewing, sit at a table and let the bulk of the garment rest on the tabletop. If you are right-handed, rest your left forearm at the edge of the table with your palm curled toward you; pick up the edge of the garment. Rest your right forearm on the edge of the table and sew from right to left with the bulk of the garment on the table

In couture, hand sewing is done at long tables, which support the garments and allow the workers to sew easily. (Photo by Author.)

below the needle—unless, of course, the stitch you are sewing requires reversing sewing direction or holding the garment vertically. (If you are left-handed, reverse these directions.)

Once you are ready to begin stitching, fasten the thread with a simple knot, waste knot, or backstitches at the beginning of your work. Keep the knots small and inconspicuous to prevent an impression from showing through when the fabric is pressed. To make a simple knot, wrap the thread end around your forefinger. Use your thumb and forefinger to roll the thread off the finger; pull the knot taut. The waste knot is used to anchor the thread temporarily for sewing buttons, buttonholes, and bastings; it is a simple knot trimmed away once the thread is fastened permanently or the seam is stitched. The thread is frequently anchored with backstitches, then the knot trimmed away.

An alternative to a knot, backstitches are used at the beginning and end of temporary and permanent hand stitches. Make two or three stitches on top of each other.

The figure-8 knot is used to secure permanent hand stitches. Pick up a very small backstitch; wrap the thread around the point of the needle in a figure 8. Pull the needle through.

To hide the thread end, I insert the needle next to the knot; pull it out about ½ in. away. Then I hold it taut and cut close to the fabric so the thread end will disappear between the layers.

The tailor's knot is used to secure machine stitching at the beginning and the end of a seam. Make a loose loop; use your thumb and forefinger to work the knot down to the fabric, and pull it taut. When learning this knot, it sometimes helps to insert a pin into the loop; then pull the thread taut.

## Temporary Stitches

Hand-sewn stitches fall into two basic categories according to their use: temporary and permanent. Generally referred to as basting stitches, temporary stitches are used to mark the garment, prepare

## KNOTS

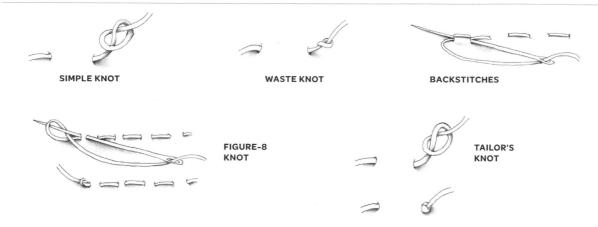

**SIMPLE KNOT**

**WASTE KNOT**

**BACKSTITCHES**

**FIGURE-8 KNOT**

**TAILOR'S KNOT**

it for fittings, and hold the various fabric layers in position during construction. Temporary or basting stitches are sewn into a garment again and again throughout its construction, only to be removed a short time later after serving their purpose. By contrast, permanent stitches are sewn once and removed only if an error has been made or if the garment is altered.

In fact, most of the actual stitches used for basting—even, uneven, diagonal, and slip basting—are the same as those used for permanent functions. Four basic basting stitches are described in this section; two additional stitches—thread tracing and tailor's tacks—are described in Chapter 3 (see p. 48). Gathering and ease-basting stitches, also described in Chapter 3, are used as temporary and permanent stitches (see pp. 53–54). Slip-basting and fell stitches are used to baste from the right side.

For most applications, a soft basting thread is best; it will break easily when stitched over and will not disturb the permanent stitches when it is removed.

All directions are given for right-handed sewers. Left-handed sewers should reverse these directions; and unless noted otherwise, stitches are sewn from right to left.

**Even Basting.** Even basting stitches are similar to permanent running stitches (see "Running Stitch,"

p. 32). They are used to join two edges under some stress; for example, the seams of a closely fitted garment or curved seams. They are also used for easing one layer, or a gathered section, to another shorter layer or section.

1. Use a long needle such as a cotton darner so you can pick up several stitches on the needle before pulling the thread through.

### EVEN BASTING

*CLAIRE'S HINT I use cotton basting thread so I can machine stitch on the basted line. When it's removed, the thread will break; but it will not disturb the machine stitching.*

2. Anchor the thread with a backstitch or waste knot.
3. Right sides together, pick up several stitches about ¼ in. long and equal in length on both sides. When basting tight curves, use shorter stitches.
4. Anchor the thread with a backstitch.

**Uneven Basting.** Uneven basting stitches are used for marking, basting hems, and straight seams that don't need to be particularly strong and for top basting. Longer on one side than the other, the stitches—the spaces—are usually ⅛ in. to ¼ in. with the threads measuring between ¼ in. to 1 in., but they can be longer.

CLAIRE'S HINT *When basting long seams, I pin one end of the work to a weight, such as a tailor's ham, so I can hold the fabric taut while sewing.*

### UNEVEN BASTING

1. Use a long needle and cotton basting thread.
2. Anchor the thread with a backstitch or waste knot.
3. Right sides together, pick up several short stitches (⅛ in. to ¼ in.), spacing them about ¼ in. to 1 in. apart.
4. Continue, so the stitches on one side of the garment are two to three times the length of the stitches on the other side.
5. Anchor the thread at the end with a backstitch.

**Double Basting.** Double basting is two rows of basting stitches with the second row on top of the first to fill the "spaces" in the first row. It is used to hold two or more fabric layers securely and prevent shifting when stitched. The first row is often even basting, but it can be slip basting (see the facing page).

**Top-Basting.** Top-basting is used on the right side of the fabric to hold the layers in place for fitting or pressing. Top-basting can be made with even or uneven basting stitches.

1. Use a long needle and cotton or silk basting thread.
2. Anchor the thread with a backstitch or waste knot.

### TOP BASTING

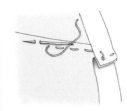

3. To top baste seamlines for fittings, fold the seam allowances in one direction; top baste through all layers a scant ¼ in. from the seamline.
4. To top baste seamlines for matching plaids or fabric patterns, turn under the seam allowance on the upper layer at the seamline. Align the folded edge with the seamline on the underlayer, and top baste a scant ¼ in. from the seamline.

5. To top baste edges for pressing, or for fitting, even-baste through all layers, basting about ¼ in. from the edge when possible.

CLAIRE'S HINT *When you sew right at the edge, it often distorts the edge.*

6. Anchor the thread at the end with a backstitch.

### LAP BASTING

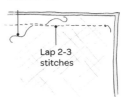

Leave 2" tail

Lap 2-3 stitches

**Lap-Basting.** Use lap-basting when basting bias seams that are stretched when stitched.

1. Use a long needle and cotton basting thread.
2. Anchor the thread with a backstitch or waste knot at the beginning.
3. Baste 6 in. to 8 in. Cut the thread, leaving a 2-in. tail.
4. Begin again, using a 2 in. tail instead of a knot. Overlap the last few stitches about ½ in.
5. Continue to the end, basting short segments so the threads overlap at the beginnings and ends.
6. Anchor the thread at the end with a backstitch.

**Diagonal Stitches.** Diagonal stitches can be temporary basting stitches or permanent stitches. The stitch can be worked vertically or horizontally, depending on how you hold the fabric, and from top to bottom, or vice versa. When used for basting, diagonal stitches hold two or more layers together such as pleats, backings, and interfacings to prevent shifting, as well as to baste pile fabric layers together.

1. Use a between or crewel needle and cotton basting thread.
2. Anchor the thread with a backstitch.
3. Hold the fabric vertically and insert the needle horizontally from right to left. Pull the thread through; make the next stitch ¼ in. to 2 in. directly below or above the first stitch. On one side of

the fabric, the stitches will form a vertical column of diagonal stitches; on the other, short horizontal "dashes."

## DIAGONAL STITCHES

**Cross-stitches.** A variation of diagonal stitches, cross-stitches look like catchstitches, but they're made by working a pair of diagonal basting stitches in opposite directions. They can be temporary or permanent stitches.

## CROSS-STITCHES

3. Work the first row from top to bottom and the second row from bottom to top.
4. Fasten the thread at the end with a backstitch.

**Slipbasting.** Use slipbasting to baste seams from the right side of the fabric when matching stripes and plaids, or for sewing intricately shaped seamlines and easing one edge to another. Generally, one slip-basted edge overlaps the other. Occasionally, the two edges can abut, or the two garment sections and their edges can be sewn one on top of the other as, for example, at the end of a

CLAIRE'S HINT *I use two rows of diagonal stitches to baste velvet seams. When I baste the second row, I place the stitches in between the stitches of the first row.*

4. Fasten the thread at the end with a backstitch.

permanent stitches. In addition to their use as temporary marking stitches, cross-stitches are also used permanently to mark the garment front so you can identify how it is to be worn.
1. Use a between or crewel needle.
2. Anchor the thread with a backstitch.

## SLIPBASTING

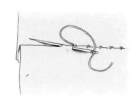

belt or waistband. Slipbasting is sewn with the same slipstitch used for permanent seams joined from the right side (see "Slipstitch," p. 33). Since slipbasting alone does not always keep layers from shifting when stitched, it's frequently reinforced with an additional row of even basting.

Fellstitching is often substituted for slipbasting when you need to match patterns or edges precisely, since fellstitches are less likely to shift than slip-basted stitches. Fellstitching is also sometimes reinforced with a row of even basting (see "Fellstitch," p. 33).
1. With the garment right-side-up, turn under the overlap seam allowance; align the seamlines and match the design.
2. Use a between or crewel needle and cotton basting thread.
3. Anchor the thread with a backstitch or waste knot, and work right to left. Take a short stitch in the folded edge and pull the needle through.
CLAIRE'S HINT *Generally, I find it easier to work with the overlap edge toward me.*

4. Directly opposite this point, pick up a small stitch $\frac{1}{16}$ in. to $\frac{1}{4}$ in. long in the lower layer.
5. Begin the next stitch in the folded edge directly opposite this small stitch. Make several stitches alternating between the two layers so they form a perfect ladder.
6. Pull up the thread.

# Permanent Stitches

Permanent stitches are used to shape the garment, finish edges and details, and manipulate the fabric with pleats, tucks, or gathers. These stitches can be simple and utilitarian, such as catchstitches, pad-stitches, running, and hemming stitches, or they can be both functional and decorative, such as blanket stitches, buttonhole stitches, and cross-stitches.

Permanent stitches such as blanket and buttonhole stitches have limited applications while others such as backstitches, catchstitches, hemming, and running stitches can be adapted for a variety of tasks. The stitches here are listed in order of frequency of their use.

**Running Stitch.** Running stitches are short, even stitches used mainly for staystitches, setting stays, securing the folds on a draped design, and seams that require little strength. By lengthening the stitch or sewing it unevenly, it can be adapted for other uses such as setting zippers, joining two layers permanently, or securing the folds of a draped design.

1. Use a long needle such as a cotton darner in a small size.

2. Anchor the thread with a knot or backstitch and take several small, even stitches about ⅛ in. long on the needle. Pull the needle through and repeat the process to the end of the work.

CLAIRE'S HINT *When sewing a seam that needs more strength, I add a backstitch after every third or fourth stitch. Combining running stitches and backstitches produces a combination stitch. This stitch is softer and weaker than the backstitch alone but can be sewn much more quickly.*

3. Anchor the thread at the end. Running stitches are also used for staystitching. Use staystitching to prevent a curved or bias edge, such as an armscye or neckline, from stretching out of shape during the garment's construction.

RUNNING STITCH

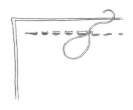

To staystitch by hand, sew a row of short running stitches on the seamline, either before or after a backing has been applied to the garment section. Then tighten the thread as needed to prevent the edge from losing its shape.

**Backstitch.** The backstitch is one of the strongest and most adaptable permanent stitches. Its primary function is to join seams that need strength and elasticity, such as those used for setting sleeves. At Gieves and Hawkes, a well-known men's bespoke tailor in London, the backstitch is the preferred stitch for joining the crotch seam on trousers.

BACKSTITCH

This stitch can be sewn two ways: as either a full backstitch or a partial backstitch. On the front side, the full backstitch looks like machine stitching, which makes it very useful for repairing seams. The partial backstitch looks like a simple running stitch on the front side. Sewn either way, these stitches can be varied in length and tension for a great deal of control.

1. Use a short needle such as a between or crewel needle.

2. Anchor the thread, and work right to left. Pick up a ⅛-in. stitch. Pull the thread through and insert the needle 1/16 in. to ⅛ in. behind the thread.

3. Complete the stitch by passing the needle under the fabric and out again ⅛ in. ahead of the thread.

CLAIRE'S HINT *On the mid-19th century Worth designs, the stitches are 1/16 in.*

4. When you make the next stitch, insert the needle either at the end of the previous stitch for a full backstitch or with a short space separating the two stitches for a partial backstitch.

5. Anchor the thread.

CLAIRE'S HINT *In this book, whenever the term backstitch appears, it refers to either a full or partial backstitch.*

The prickstitch and pickstitch are variations of the backstitch. Both are only about 1/16 in. long and spaced about 3/16 in. apart. The pickstitch is used as a decorative stitch on the edges of collars and lapels; it does not show on the underside. It can also be used for understitching. The prickstitch is used for setting zippers; it looks like the pickstitch on the top side, but it goes through all layers.

To understitch a finished edge with a facing or lining, begin with the garment wrong side up. Sew through the facing or lining and both seam allowances 1/16 in. to 1/4 in. from the seamline using a pickstitch. If you are understitching where there's no seam allowance (on an extended facing, for example), sew the understitches to the garment backing, interfacing or stay.

**Slipstitch.** A slipstitch is used to permanently join two layers from the right side such as a waist or appliqué seam, intricately shaped seam or two folded edges on the end of a band or belt. It can also be used for hemming and for basting (see "Slipbasting," p. 31).

### SLIPSTITCH

To prevent slipstitches from showing on the right side when hemming, be careful to pick up only a single thread on the garment.

Couture skirts rarely have a label so cross-stitches are used to mark the center front to facilitate dressing.

(Photo by Taylor Sherrill. Author's collection.)

**Drawstitch.** A variation of the slipstitch, the drawstitch is used in tailoring to join two folded edges such as the collar and lapel.

1. Use a short needle.
2. Right side up, anchor the thread. Take a short stitch 1/16 in. to 1/8 in. long in one folded edge, and then take a stitch in the other. Continue, alternating between the two edges.

### DRAWSTITCH

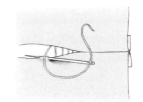

3. Draw the thread taut so the two folded edges are close together. The drawstitch can be worked like a slipstitch or a fellstitch. However, each stitch must be taken separately, the stitches must be close together, and evenly spaced and parallel to each other, so the finished seam looks as if it's been machine stitched.

4. Anchor the thread.

**Fellstitch.** A fellstitch is used to sew a raw or folded edge flat against the fabric beneath it, such as setting an undercollar, sewing seams permanently from the right side, sewing flat-felled seams, and finishing narrow and rolled hems. These directions are for fell stitching, or felling, a lining to a facing; however, they apply to other uses of fell stitching, except for hemming and felling a French seam flat, which are described on p. 51.

1. Use a short needle.
2. Begin with the facing and lining right side up, fold under the lining and match the seamlines.

### FELLSTITCH

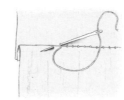

3. Work from right to left with the bulk of the garment below the needle.

4. Anchor the thread and bring the needle out through the lining fold. Insert it into the facing directly opposite the point it just exited.

5. Take a stitch in the facing, and bring the needle out through the lining fold ⅛ in. to ¼ in. away.

6. Pull the thread taut. Continue to finish the seam. The finished stitches should be perpendicular to the edge of the lining and invisible on the right side. On the wrong side, there will be a row of diagonal stitches, unless the layers are so thick that your needle does not pass through all of them.

7. Anchor the thread.

CLAIRE'S HINT *When using the fell stitch for hemming such as on a rolled hem or when felling a French seam flat against the background fabric, take very small stitches, picking up only a single thread of the background fabric.*

**Whipstitch.** A whipstitch is similar to an overcasting stitch (see the facing page), but it's used for seaming and hemming rather than finishing raw edges. It can be sewn with either right or wrong sides of the garment together.

### WHIPSTITCH

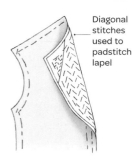

1. Use a short needle.

2. Anchor the thread. The best method for anchoring the thread for a whipstitch is to leave a long tail and lay it over the seamline so the first few stitches are sewn over the thread tail.

3. Insert the needle from the back of the fabric through all layers, bring it out just below the edge and pointing toward you.

4. Repeat, inserting the needle 1/16 in. to the left of the previous stitch. Pull the thread taut after each stitch.

CLAIRE'S HINT *If you are careful to insert the needle just a few threads below the edge, the finished seam will be smooth and flat.*

5. To join a new thread, cut the previous thread end to ½ in. and sew over it when you begin with the new thread.

6. To finish a whipstitched seam or hem, sew six whipstitches in the opposite direction, and hide the thread end between the edges.

**Stabstitch.** The stabstitch is used for sewing bound buttonholes and pockets, setting shoulder pads and zippers, and joining thick fabric layers.

### STABSTITCH

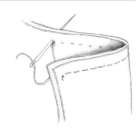

1. Use a long needle.

2. Right side up, anchor the thread and stab the needle vertically into the fabric layers pulling it through to the underside.

3. Reverse the procedure and stab the needle vertically into the fabric to bring the needle back to the top side, placing the stitches from ⅛ in. to ¼ in. apart for a zipper to ⅜ in. to ½ in. apart for setting a shoulder pad.

CLAIRE'S HINT *When setting a shoulder pad, keep the stitches loose to prevent dimples. When possible, locate the stitches in the well of the shoulder seam and don't pull too tightly so they will be inconspicuous on the right side of the garment.*

### DIAGONAL STITCH

Diagonal stitches used to padstitch lapel

**Diagonal Stitch.** Diagonal stitches are used to join two or more fabric layers together permanently and to shape collars and lapels. When used in tailoring, this stitch is called padstitching. For information on how to sew diagonal stitches (see "Diagonal Stitches," p. 30) and padstitches (see "Finish the Undercollar," p. 188).

**Catchstitch.** Catchstitches look like a row of Xs on the right side of the fabric with two parallel rows of dashes on the wrong side. They are often used when hemming to hold one edge flat against another. A very elastic stitch, the catchstitch can be used to form casings for elastic and tapes, and to tack pleats and attach labels.

## CATCHSTITCH

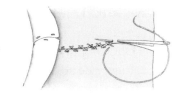

1. Use a short needle.
2. Working from left to right, anchor the thread.
3. Insert the needle horizontally in one row so it points to the left and take a small stitch.
4. Move to the second row, position the needle a little to the right and slightly below the first stitch, insert the needle horizontally and take a second stitch.
5. Move back to the first row, to the right and slightly above the last stitch position the needle as before and take the next stitch. Repeat this process, alternating between the two rows, keeping the stitches in each row aligned with one another. Pull the thread taut after each stitch.
6. Anchor the thread at the end.

**Hemming Stitches.** The blindstitch and blind catchstitch are the two hemming stitches used most often by both couturiers and home sewers. For hems on sheers, ruffles, and scarves, use the slipstitch (see p. 33) and/or the fell stitch (see p. 33).

## BLINDSTITCH

**Blindstitch.** Sometimes called the blind-hemming stitch, the blindstitch is worked inconspicuously between the hem and garment.
1. Use a short needle and anchor the thread in the hem allowance.
2. Take a tiny stitch in the garment skimming the backs of several threads.
3. Pull the sewing thread through, then pick up a small stitch on the hem allowance 1/4 in. to 1/2 in. to the left of the previous stitch. Alternate the stitches between the garment and hem to create a series of small Vs, keeping the stitches loose and pulling the thread through on every stitch.
4. Fasten the thread on the hem allowance.

**Blind Catchstitch.** The blind catchstitch is stronger, more durable, and more elastic than the blindstitch. It is used for hemming heavy fabrics. This stitch is actually a catchstitch worked between two layers of fabric, like a blindstitch.

## BLIND CATCHSTITCH

1. Use a short needle. Work left to right, anchor the thread on the hem allowance.
2. Pick up a small stitch on the garment to the right; then pick up a stitch on the hem.
3. Alternate the stitches between the garment and hem.
4. Anchor the work at the end.

**Overcasting Stitch.** Used to prevent raveling, overcasting stitches are small, slanted stitches sewn over a raw edge. Generally made on a single layer, they can also be sewn on a double layer and worked in either direction. They should be about 1/16 in. deep and evenly spaced 1/16 in. to 1/8 in. apart. (See Chapter 3, p. 44, for an example of overcasting stitches.)
1. Use a short needle and work from left to right.
2. Hold the raw edge horizontally so it's parallel to your index finger. Anchor the thread on the underside with a simple knot and insert the point of the needle under the edge about 1/16 in. from it. Bring the needle out at a 45° slant.

3. Pull the thread through and the needle up, while holding the thread against the fabric with your left thumb.

4. Insert the needle for the next stitch ⅛ in. from the first. Continue, making each stitch separately rather than trying to take several stitches on the needle at once then pulling the thread through.

5. Anchor the work at the end.

**Cross Your Hand.** For fabrics that ravel, overcast a row in one direction; then overcast a second row in the opposite direction. In haute couture, this is called "cross your hand." When done well, the finished stitches look like a machine zigzag.

BLANKET
STITCH

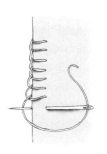

**Blanket Stitch.** Use the blanket stitch to cover hooks and eyes, finish thread bars and thread chains, and as a decorative edging. Blanket stitches can be worked from top to bottom, or vice versa.

1. Use a short needle and hold the work right side up with the raw edge positioned vertically in your hand.

2. Anchor the thread; insert the needle horizontally into the fabric about ¼ in. from the edge. Loop the thread under the needle point; pull the thread taut, but not tight. Once you get the knack of this stitch, you'll be able to position the thread loop at the edge before inserting the needle.

3. Continue to the end and anchor the thread.

**Buttonhole Stitch.** The buttonhole stitch is used to control fraying on hand-worked buttonholes as well as to make button shanks, decorative button loops, and decorative edges. It is important to wax and press the thread used for buttonhole stitches, because waxing will strengthen it and keep it from twisting while you sew. Buttonhole stitches can be worked in any direction—top to bottom, left to right, or vice versa.

1. Wax and press the thread.

2. Use a short needle and hold the work right side up with the raw edge positioned vertically in your hand.

BUTTONHOLE
STITCH

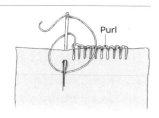

Purl

Insert needle into
wrong side of fabric

3. Anchor the thread with a waste knot.

4. Pass the needle point under the fabric edge and bring it out about 1/16 in. away. Loop the thread under the needle point in the direction in which you are working—right to left. Pull the needle through so it is perpendicular to the fabric edge. Tighten the thread and use your thumbnails to position the purl portion of the stitch on top of the fabric.

5. Anchor the thread at the end.

**Thread Bar.** Made by sewing buttonhole or blanket stitches over several strands of thread anchored at two points in the fabric, thread bars serve various purposes and are referred to by different names, depending on their function and location on the garment. Used at the top of pleats and slits, at the bottom of zippers, on lining pleats, at V-shaped openings, and at any other

THREAD BAR

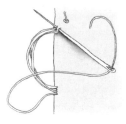

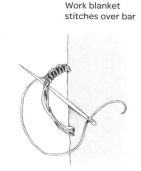

Work blanket
stitches over bar

Make a bar with
several strands

point of stress on a garment, a thread bar becomes a reinforcing bar tack. Used at a garment edge instead of a fabric button loop or metal eye, the thread bar is called a thread loop.

1. Wax and press the thread.
2. Anchor the thread with a waste knot.
3. Sew two to four stitches, one on top of the other, the length you need for the thread bar or loop.
4. Work blanket or buttonhole stitches over the length of the strands. Work the stitches tightly, but do not crowd them.
5. At the end, push the needle to the wrong side of the fabric and fasten the thread securely.

**Thread Chain.** A thread chain is made with a hand-crocheted chain stitch. When used to hold two or more layers or garment sections loosely together, the thread chain is called a French tack, or swing tack.

Thread chains are softer and less durable than thread bars and can range in length from ¼ in. to several inches. Scaasi used long French tacks to hold together the various layers of hems on his famous ball gowns. Chanel used short ones to attach ties to necklines, and to keep the ends of collars and flaps from lifting up.

1. Wax and press the thread.
2. Anchor the thread with a waste knot.
3. Take a small backstitch to make a loop.
4. Hold the loop open over the thumb and index finger of one hand; hold the thread in the needle taut with the other thumb and index finger.
5. Then, using the middle finger on the hand holding open the loop as a crochet hook, pull a new thread loop through the first one and allow the first loop to slip off the fingers.
6. Open the new loop as you pull the last loop taut on the chain.
7. Continue making loops in this fashion until the chain is the desired length.
8. To finish, pick up a small stitch on the corresponding garment section before slipping the needle through the last loop of the chain.
9. Fasten the thread securely.

## THREAD CHAIN

Pick up stitch in fabric, then last loop

# Shaping the Garment

3

SEAMS, DARTS, AND PRESSING TECHNIQUES are crucial elements of garment construction. Combined with support fabrics, they shape a two-dimensional fabric to fit the three-dimensional contours of a body. Essential to home sewing and ready-to-wear, these elements are practiced with the greatest skill in haute couture workrooms, where both the fit and construction of a garment are intended to be flawless. Seams and darts shape a garment visibly, while support fabrics and expert pressing shape it invisibly. For this reason, perfectly sewn seams and darts are perhaps appreciated more than the selection of appropriate support fabrics and skillful pressing, but the latter are equally significant in the garment's construction. In fact, in the case of pressing, a couture pattern may appear to have little relationship to the final garment because many sections have been stretched and/or shrunk extensively during construction.

One of the best examples I've seen on a finished garment was a jacket with princess seams from the shoulders. At first glance, the jacket front appeared to be a single piece of fabric. When I examined it carefully,

An important costume designer before he opened his couture salon in 1942, Gilbert Adrian Greenburgh was known for his architectural designs and padded shoulders. He liked working with the fabric grain, intricate seams, insets, and free-floating tabs. This jacket, like many others, fastens with hooks and eyes and ties at the neck and waist instead of buttons and buttonholes.

(Photo by Ken Howie. Author's collection.)

# Machine-stitching Basics

**BEFORE LOOKING AT SEAMS,** let's quickly review the fundamentals of machine stitching. In haute couture, most machine stitching is done on only a straight-stitch machine. When sewing on a zigzag machine, I use a straight-stitch foot and a round-hole throatplate. When sewing lightweight fabrics on a machine with a very wide (9mm) zigzag stitch, the foot does not hold the fabric firmly because the feed dogs are set too far apart.

Before you begin machine stitching, clean the seams by removing all but essential bastings. Check the machine's stitch length, tension, and needle size on a fabric scrap. Since the seams are basted before machine stitching, you'll have fewer stitching problems than usual and can disregard many of the commonly held rules, such as stitching with the fabric grain or with the ease or gathers on top.

To fasten the thread ends when machine stitching, use a tailor's knot (also called an overhand knot; see p. 28) or thread the ends into a needle and sew a few backstitches by hand. Machine backstitching is never used in couture because it adds stiffness and bulk to the seamline; and it is almost impossible to remove without marring the fabric. I use a calyx-eyed or easy-threading needle to secure the thread ends. To make a tailor's knot, pull the bottom thread through to the upper layer. Give the threads a sharp tug to be sure they are firmly locked; knot the ends. To remove the bastings after you have machine stitched, clip the basting threads every 3 in. to 4 in. and pull them out, using tweezers if necessary.

I found that the front and side front sections had been shaped instead of cut, to create the shape of the princess seams. When I visited the workroom of London bespoke tailor Gieves and Hawkes, the presser was shaping the trouser legs on a uniform for one of the Queen's guards. Using heat and moisture he shrank and stretched the straight, narrow-legged pants again and again until they duplicated the shape of the guard's legs (see "Pressing Techniques," p. 61).

Only a few seam types—plain, lapped, abutted, and French seams—are used extensively in haute couture. Except for novelty seams, all other seams are variations of these four basic seams. The plain seam is by far the most frequently used and the most versatile. The lapped seam epitomizes the attention lavished on a couture garment (one of its variations, the appliqué seam, is painstakingly hand-stitched around the motifs of luxurious, costly lace and special-occasion fabrics). The French seam is very narrow and frequently used for sheer fabrics so it will be inconspicuous on the finished design. Novelty seams, such as piped, slot, tucked, and welt seams, are not used as frequently in haute couture as in luxury ready-to-wear, and since basic directions for these seams are included in many sewing books, they are not included in this chapter.

Many seams in couture are sewn by hand, with machine stitching reserved for structural seams and darts. The shoulder and armscye seams on linings are always sewn by hand, as are those that join the lining to the garment. Seams joining a tailored collar to a neckline and lapels are generally sewn by hand, and those attaching a skirt or sleeve to a bodice are sometimes hand-sewn.

The seams discussed here can be sewn by hand or by machine depending on their location, whether they need to be sewn from the right or wrong side, the fabric bulk, and the strength and elasticity needed. One type of lapped seam, the appliqué seam for woven fabrics, is sewn by alternating between machine and hand stitches.

This chapter focuses on permanent seams. In couture construction, all seamlines are marked at the outset with thread tracing and matchpoints or notches (see "Marking the Garment," p. 48), and basted for the first fitting. After the fitting, the bastings, but not the thread tracing, are removed and adjustments are made to correct the fit. Finally the seams are stitched permanently (see "Assembling the Garment," p. 42).

## Plain Seams

The plain seam serves as the foundation for many other seams. Although this seam is used on luxury ready-to-wear and home-sewn designs as well as on couture garments, there are important differences in how each sector constructs it. In ready-to-wear and home sewing, the cut edges of the seam allowances are used as guides for stitching the seams. In haute couture, the seam allowances are frequently too wide, uneven or varied in width to be used as accurate guides. So, in couture, seamlines are marked with thread-tracing, tailor's tacks, and matchpoints. These markings become the guidelines for assembling and fitting the garment.

Although the traditional plain seam is very inconspicuous when pressed open, it is not appropriate for all fabrics. For lightweight and transparent fabrics, the five variations on the plain seam described in this chapter—narrow plain seam, false French seam, drapery French seam, self-bound seam, and whipped seam—are more suitable. However, unlike the traditional plain seam, these seams cannot be altered.

## BASTING SEAMS

In couture, most plain seams are basted together at least once before they are machine stitched, and many are basted, ripped, and rebasted several times.

1. Right sides together, align the thread-traced seamlines and matchpoints; pin. Use a long needle and short, even basting stitches to baste intricately shaped seams and those that join close-fitting sections of the garment. Use long, uneven stitches for seams that will receive little stress. Check carefully as you sew to be sure you are basting precisely on both seamlines.

2. When basting seams that cross darts or other seamlines, work carefully to avoid catching the seam allowances or dart fold. When basting seams and darts, begin basting at the intersecting seamline, rather than at the raw edge, to make it easier to fit the garment accurately. Press the closed seam lightly. Do not press the seam open firmly until you are certain the seam will not be changed after the fitting.

3. To prepare for a fitting, fold the basted seam to one side and top baste through all layers $1/8$ in. to $1/4$ in. from the seamline.

CLAIRE'S HINT *Used instead of pressing to hold the seam flat, top basting lets you evaluate the garment's fit and visual effect easily.*

4. If there are no corrections to be made after the fitting, remove the top-basting, press the seam flat once more, and machine stitch on the basted lines. Remove the bastings and thread tracings before pressing.

5. Press the seam flat to "marry" the seam so the stitches will sink into the fabric layers. If the fabric is thick or heavy, turn the seam over and press the other side (see "Pressing Techniques," p. 61).

6. Wrong side up, open the seam with your fingers. Using just the iron point, not the entire soleplate, press the stitched line firmly with a sharp up-and-down movement.

CLAIRE'S HINT *Do not press the edges of the seam flat against the garment. This is easier if you place the seam on a seam stick, point presser, or seam roll.*

# Assembling the Garment

**THE PROCESS OF ASSEMBLING** a garment in haute couture is less straightforward than in home sewing and luxury ready-to-wear.

## DRAPING THE PATTERN

The garment usually begins with draping several rectangles of muslin on the right side of a dress form padded to duplicate the customer's figure. Since only half a pattern is usually needed for a symmetrical design, the design is draped on the right side, then it's duplicated for the other half. The left side of the garment is draped in muslin only for bias-cut, asymmetrical, or complex designs; fabrics with patterns to be matched, asymmetrical figures that are difficult to fit, and embellished designs that need to be scaled to the garment's proportions.

The draper pins and shapes the muslin to create a toile, or muslin pattern, for the customer's design. As the design takes shape, the excess muslin is trimmed away, and changes are made in proportion and scale to fit and flatter the client's figure. Once the draping is completed, the toile is carefully marked with grainlines and matchpoints, unpinned and pressed. The toile is doubled and basted together to check the fit on the client's dress form. After any corrections are made, the toile is ready for use as the garment pattern. If it will be used for several garments, a clean copy is made on muslin rectangles.

## CUTTING THE GARMENT

The toile's bodice and skirt sections are laid on the garment fabric with the lengthwise grains aligned and with ample space between for seam allowances at least 1 in. wide. Any backing is cut, but the sleeves, collar facings, pockets, and lining are often left uncut until needed, particularly when there are fabric patterns to match.

All the cut sections are marked with thread tracings at stitching lines, hemlines, matchpoints, garment centers, and horizontal balance lines. Since the garment fabric and muslin drape differently, the garment is hand-basted together and fitted on the dress form so corrections can be made. The bastings are then removed, the sections laid flat again, and the fitting corrections made.

## PREPARING FOR THE FIRST FITTING

For the client's first fitting, the garment is rebasted with short basting stitches to make the

7. When using steam, a damp cloth, or sponge, press the entire section until it is almost dry. Let it cool before moving the work so the fabric will "remember" the pressed position.

8. Finish the raw edges of the seams appropriately (see "Seam Finishes," p. 44).

**Basting from the Right Side.** When matching fabric patterns or assembling intricately shaped or lapped seams, it's more practical to baste the seams from the right side instead of the wrong side. This is much easier to do in couture because the seamlines are thread-traced and can be aligned easily from the right side.

1. Turn under and pin; baste as needed to control the seam allowance on a shaped edge.

2. Right sides up, match the seamlines, aligning matchpoints; pin.

3. Slip baste the two sections together.

garment appear machine stitched.

Instead of pressing and permanently creasing the seams, they are folded to one side and top basted about ¼ in. from the seamline for the fitting. The edges are basted under at plackets, hems, and seam allowances, and clipped only as needed to turn under smoothly. Shoulder pads and stays are basted in place. Some premières even baste the zipper, pockets, and lining in, while others fit with few facings and may even fit a toile sleeve instead of a fabric sleeve.

## PREPARING FOR THE SECOND FITTING

Corrections are carefully marked and matchpoints added as needed. Again the bastings are removed and the garment laid flat to make corrections. Any sections requiring shaping are eased, shrunk, or stretched to mold the fabric permanently, and the pockets and stays are set. At this point, the garment is rebasted and checked on the dress form.

If the garment has set-in sleeves, they're pinned into the armscye while the garment is still on the dress form. The sleeves are basted in place with sleeve heads and shoulder pads so the garment appears finished for the second fitting. The fit is then examined to be sure earlier alterations are correct and to see if additional fine-tuning is needed.

## PREPARING FOR THE FINAL FITTING

After the second fitting, the sleeves are carefully marked and removed so underarm seams can be stitched and pressed, and cuffs, vents, and any linings can be finished. Before permanently stitching the garment, each seamline is carefully checked to be sure intersecting seams match precisely and bastings are taut enough to keep the layers from shifting. Except for bastings that hold seams together, all other bastings, including thread-tracings, are removed, and the seams are stitched precisely on the basted seamlines.

The sleeves are then basted and permanently stitched into the armscyes. Any remaining unfinished seams are basted, stitched permanently, and pressed. The garment is hemmed, lingerie guards added, zipper set, and all raw edges finished.

After a final check to make sure all bastings have been removed, the garment is pressed lightly and ready for the final fitting on the client. After the fit and drape are examined a last time and the client accepts the design, the label is sewn in place.

One vendeuse told me that it's considered bad luck to sew the label in before the final fitting; and if the garment already has a label, she will rip it out before the fitting. It's sent back to the workroom to be resewn after the fitting.

## NARROW PLAIN SEAM

This plain seam variation is trimmed and finished with the raw edges overcast together. Used frequently on the armholes of unlined blouses and dresses, this seam is especially appropriate for curved seams that are not pressed open and for firmly woven, sheer fabrics.

1. Right sides together, stitch a plain seam.
2. Remove the bastings and press the closed seam flat.

### NARROW PLAIN SEAM

3. Baste the seam allowances together ⅛ in. from the seamline.

CLAIRE'S HINT
*When the fabric ravels badly, I stitch again next to the basting.*

4. Trim the seam so it is no wider than ¼ in.

# Seam Finishes

**SEAM FINISHES ARE USED TO** prevent the edges of seams, facings, and hems from fraying. Overcasting seams by hand is the preferred finish in couture because it is the flattest, softest, and least likely to show on the right side of the garment. Although it's the most popular finishing method, it's also the most time consuming and therefore the most expensive.

**CLAIRE'S HINT** *To reduce expense, a few couture workrooms now use a narrow, machine-sewn zigzag finish or a serged edge. A bound edge, called a Hong Kong finish by home sewers, is also selectively used.*

You can see the overcasting on this inside view of the red Dior dress, shown on p. 131.

(Photo by Greg Rothschild, courtesy of *Threads* magazine.)

## HAND OVERCASTING

Hand overcasting is used to finish individual seam allowances. It can also be used on the raw edges of hems and facings to reduce bulk, on a narrow plain seam that finishes two seam allowances together (see p. 43), and to finish narrow seams on transparent fabrics. When two layers are overcast together, extra care must be taken to be sure there's no strain or pull that shows on the face of the garment.

**1.** Use a short needle and fine cotton or silk thread. Anchor the thread and work from left to right.

**2.** Use overcasting stitches no more than ⅛ in. deep and ⅛ in. apart at the edges (see left). For fabrics that ravel badly, work a second row of stitches in the opposite direction.

## BINDING

A seam, hem, or facing can also be finished with a binding to encase the raw edges. On seams, the allowances can be bound together or separately. Binding them together produces the bulkiest and stiffest edge; and when the fabric is lightweight to medium-weight, it may show as a ridge on the right side of the garment. Binding the two edges separately is suitable for fabrics that ravel or irritate the skin and for unlined or backed garments.

This type of binding is also often used to finish a hem or facing on heavy or bulky fabrics. When working with lightweight and many medium-weight fabrics, this finish may show on the right side, in which case the edge should be overcast rather than bound.

To make a seam binding, choose a lightweight fabric like chiffon, plain-weave silk, or organza.

**1.** Cut 1-in.-wide bias strips (see p. 82).

**2.** Trim the seam or hem allowances so they are even in width and ¾ in. to 1¼ in. wide.

**3.** Right sides together, pin the strip to the seam allowance, matching the raw edges. Stitch a ¼-in. seam by hand or machine and trim to ⅛ in. or less.

**CLAIRE'S HINT** *For a softer finish and more control, I sometimes sew the binding with short running stitches.*

### BIAS BINDING

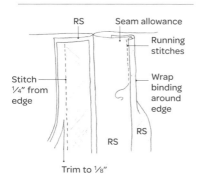

RS
Seam allowance
Running stitches
Stitch ¼" from edge
Wrap binding around edge
RS
RS
Trim to ⅛"

A favorite finish of designer James Galanos, a narrow silk binding is used to finish the raw edges of the pocket. Here you can see the finished side as well as the raw edge on the underside.

(Photo by Author.)

**4.** Wrap the binding around the raw edge and pin it in place. Use short running stitches close to the first seamline to secure the binding.

**5.** Press and trim the excess binding width to ¼ in.

**6.** When finishing armholes or seams on transparent fabrics, baste the seam allowances together. Trim the seam to ¼ in. to ½ in., and apply the binding to the both edges together.

**7.** To finish the binding, turn under its raw edge and sew it to the seamline joining the bias and seam allowances.

Bound with flesh-colored silk chiffon, this seam will be almost invisible when the dress is worn.

(Photo by Greg Rothschild, courtesy of *Threads* magazine.)

(although armscye seams can be as wide as ½ in.); overcast the edges together.

5. Remove the basting and press again. The location of the seam will determine the direction of its final pressing. On an armscye, press it flat; then fold it toward the sleeve. On the shoulder, press it toward the garment front.

CLAIRE'S HINT *Many sewing references, suggest pressing the shoulder seam toward the back. When this is done, the seam is more noticeable from the front of the garment.*

## FALSE FRENCH SEAM

Unlike the traditional French seam it resembles (see p. 51), the false French seam is stitched with right sides together and can be used on lightweight fabrics to finish shaped and closely fitted seams.

1. Right sides together, stitch a plain seam; remove the bastings and press the seam flat.

2. Trim the seam allowances to between ¼ in. and ½ in.

3. Fold one seam allowance in toward the other and pin along the fold. Fold and pin the remaining seam allowance.

4. Align the folded edges; baste them together.

5. Sew the edges together with slipstitches or whipstitches; press again.

---

FALSE FRENCH SEAM

---

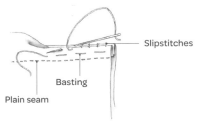

## SELF-BOUND SEAM

Called a standing fell seam in factory production, the self-bound seam is so named because one seam allowance wraps around and binds the other. The finished seam is generally less than ⅜ in.

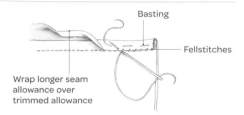

Basting

Fellstitches

Wrap longer seam allowance over trimmed allowance

wide and is frequently used on the armholes of unlined blouses and dresses. This seam is only suitable for lightweight fabrics.

1. Right sides together, stitch a plain seam; remove the bastings, and press the seam flat.

2. Trim one seam allowance so it's ¼ in. narrower than the other.

CLAIRE'S HINT *At the armscye, trim the sleeve seam allowance to ⅛ in. to ¼ in. wide; trim the bodice seam allowance to ⅜ in. to ½ in. wide.*

3. Wrap the wider seam allowance around the narrower one, and fold under the raw edge. Baste the folded edge at the seamline.

4. Use fell stitches or slipstitches to sew it permanently. Press lightly.

## WHIPPED SEAM

Another variation of the plain seam, the whipped seam looks more like a heavy cord than a seam. It is used on transparent fabrics like chiffon, silk mousseline, and organza.

1. Right sides together, stitch a plain seam.

### WHIPPED SEAM

2. Fold both seam allowances over ¹⁄₁₆ in. from the stitched line.

3. Overcast the fold and trim the seam allowances close to the overcasting.

# Lapped Seams

The lapped seam is made by lapping one garment section over another. The overlap is folded under and permanently sewn to the underlap from the right side with fell stitches or slipstitches and sometimes blindstitches or machine stitching.

Compared with a plain seam, the lapped seam is more visually defined on the surface of the garment. Many couture houses use this seam to join a gathered skirt to the bodice. A few designers use it for setting sleeves, even though the stitches nearly always show. The lapped seam is sometimes used as an alternative to an abutted seam (see p. 51) when joining seams and darts on interfacings and backings.

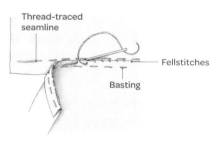

Thread-traced seamline

Fellstitches

Basting

1. Using the thread tracing as a guide, turn under the overlap seam allowance. Baste ⅛ in. from the edge with soft cotton basting thread or silk thread.

CLAIRE'S HINT *When sewing a lapped seam on a curve, stretch or shrink the seam allowance as needed so it will lie flat when turned under. If necessary, clip or trim the seam allowance to remove excess bulk. If the overlap is shaped with an outward corner, miter the seam allowances. If it has an inward corner, face the corner (see p. 56).*

2. Wrong side up, press the folded edge lightly. Remove the thread tracing on the seamline and press.

3. Right sides up, align and pin the seamlines and matchpoints on the two sections; top baste next to the earlier basting.

4. Sew the seam permanently with slipstitches or fell stitches.

CLAIRE'S HINT *I use blindstitches about 1/16 in. from the edge so the stitches are not noticeable or I sew from the wrong side with running stitches, using the basting as a guide.*

5. Remove all bastings and press lightly.
6. When joining seams and darts on interfacings and backings, trim away the seam allowance on the overlap, and leave a small seam allowance on the underlap. Lap and pin the sections. Sew permanently with catchstitches or running stitches.

## APPLIQUÉ SEAMS

Appliqué seams are among the most intricate seams sewn in couture workrooms. Used to seam lace and patterned fabrics, they are variations of the lapped seam and often used on couture bridal gowns and special-occasion designs. There are many ways to sew appliqué seams, most of them labor intensive, difficult to alter, and rarely used except in haute couture.

Lace appliqué seams can join intricately shaped lace designs without visible seamlines. When an appliqué seam joins patterned fabrics, the seamline is often adjusted to avoid disrupting the motifs of the fabric design. The resulting seam zigzags or meanders around motifs that cross the seamline and returns to a regular straight seam between motifs. The sections outlining a motif are sewn by hand; the straight sections between the motifs are sewn by machine. This seam is inconspicuous but rarely invisible.

1. Use the fitted toile to plan the layout before cutting the fabric.
2. Cut off the seam allowances or make a paper pattern without seam allowances so you can see the motifs at the seamlines when you place the pattern on the fabric.
3. Spread the fabric right side up; place the toile or pattern on top of it, positioning the motifs attractively on the garment sections. Wherever the major motifs cross the seamline, you will cut

This blouse is beautifully constructed with appliqué seams and motifs. Notice that the sleeves are cut crosswise and the bodice lengthwise
(Photo by Ken Howie. Author's collection.)

around the motif and appliqué it to the seam. Leave plenty of room between the garment sections for cutting around appliqué motifs.

4. Before cutting out the sections, thread-trace all seamlines and darts. Leave at least 1/4-in. seam allowances around the motifs and 1 in. to 1 1/2 in. on straight seams.

**Lace Appliqué Seams.** A lace-on-lace appliqué seam is the simplest appliqué seam. It's made by whipstitching a finished or cut lace edge to another piece of lace. Only a small seam allowance is needed if you are working with a cut lace edge since this edge will not be turned under. Instead,

# Marking the Garment

MARKING A GARMENT, AN important element of couture sewing, is essential for its assembly since, unlike in ready-to-wear construction and home sewing, raw edges are rarely used as a guide for seaming. In addition to indicating seamlines, hemlines, darts, and matchpoints, markings are also used to note fabric grainlines and design details such as pocket positions and buttonholes.

A garment can be marked with thread, chalk, or a tracing wheel. In couture, marking with thread is generally preferred because it's visible on both sides of the fabric and durable enough to stay in position as long as needed during construction without damaging the fabric. Since information on chalking and tracing-wheel markings is readily available in other sewing books (see Bibliography on p. 244), the focus here is on thread tracing.

If you've never marked with thread, the process may seem tedious at first, but you'll soon discover how invaluable it is for assembling and fitting garments. There are two basic marking stitches: thread tracings, most often used in dressmaking workrooms to mark dresses, blouses, and gowns; and tailor's tacks, used in tailoring workrooms on suits, pants, and tailored dresses. Both types of markings are made before the pattern is removed from the fabric and sometimes even before the fabric is cut.

## THREAD-TRACING

Thread-tracings are usually made with soft basting cotton; but you may want to use silk basting thread to mark the garment centers and balance lines since silk is less likely to leave an impression on the fabric when pressed. When thread-tracing seamlines and darts, first mark the stitching lines on the garment with chalk or dressmaker's carbon or transfer them directly from the toile.

**1.** To use a toile on a single layer of fabric, begin with the fabric face up and the toile on top.

**2.** Fold the toile back on the seamline, and mark the garment at the folded edge.

**3.** To use a toile on a double layer, thread-trace only the upper layer.

CLAIRE'S HINT *To avoid catching the lower layer, many workers place the scissor points between the two layers.*

**4.** Pin the layers together on the thread-tracing, turn the sections over, and thread-trace between the pins.

**5.** Use a long needle and soft basting cotton. Anchor the thread with a backstitch. Use alternating long and short basting stitches to mark the seamlines. Continue basting about 1 in. past the intersection; do not pivot at the corner.

CLAIRE'S HINT *At the end of each seamline, I mark the intersection clearly by inserting the needle at the intersecting seamline.*

**6.** To thread-trace the adjacent seamlines, begin again in the seam allowance about 1 in. from the intersecting seam; continue to thread-trace the seamline (see the drawing, on the facing page).

## TAILOR'S TACKS

Tailor's tacks are generally used only on wool fabrics since they tend to fall out of slippery and open-weave materials and are cumbersome to use on a muslin toile.

**1.** Use a pattern without seam allowances—or with the seam allowances folded back—as a marking guide. Usually sewn through two layers of fabric with a double strand of soft, unglazed thread such as basting cotton or hand embroidery floss, tailor's

Couture construction begins with marking. Most pieces are marked with thread-tracing or tailor's tacks, which can be seen on both sides of the fabric.

(Photo by Susan Kahn.)

tacks are a series of connected thread loops (see the photo above) that are then cut apart, leaving tufts of thread in each layer of the fabric.

**2.** Cut out the garment sections first. With the pattern still on the fabric, mark all seamlines, garment centers, darts, placket openings, button and buttonhole locations.

**3.** To mark straight lines, take a short stitch, then pick up another short stitch about 1 in. away.

**4.** To mark a curved line, make the stitches about ¼ in. apart and leave a loop when you pull up the thread.

**5.** Gently pull the fabric layers apart about ¼ in. and clip the center of the loops, leaving short thread tufts on each layer.

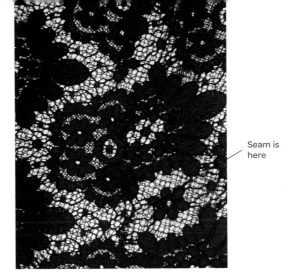

Seam is here

Designed by Castillo, this evening gown from the 1980s (shown on p. 203) was assembled with lace appliqué seams and darts to camouflage the seamlines and avoid interrupting the motifs of the lace pattern.

(Photo by Author.)

to stop any raveling that may occur, the cut edge is whipstitched to the corresponding section and the excess seam allowance is trimmed away.

1. Right sides up, lap the sections, aligning the thread-traced seamlines and matchpoints; pin.

CLAIRE HINT *If it will be more attractive, lap part of the seam in one direction and part in the other. Clip to the seamline between the motifs each time you change the direction of the lap.*

2. Pin all seams together and examine your work, making sure the motifs are attractively positioned.

## LACE-ON-LACE APPLIQUÉ SEAM

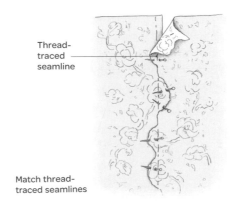

Thread-traced seamline

Match thread-traced seamlines

To be worn over a long black dress, this cropped top was assembled with appliqué seams and darts. Look closely at the large red flower; it laps the armscye seam, making the seam almost invisible. The fabric is silk taffeta with silk embroidery and chenille.

(Photo by Author.)

CLAIRE'S HINT *If you find a "bald spot" or two, cut out extra motifs and apply them as needed. Equally important, do not try to save every motif or the seamline will be more noticeable.*

3. Baste using diagonal stitches; then sew the new seamline with small whipstitches. Trim away the excess lace at the overlap edges; generally, the underlap is not trimmed.

4. Remove the thread tracings and bastings, and press the garment wrong side up on a softly padded surface.

**Fabric Appliqué Seams.** Suitable for fabrics with large, widely spaced motifs, the appliqué seam for patterned fabrics has been used on designs by Schiaparelli, Lanvin, Dior, Balmain, Balenciaga,

and other couturiers. This seam is usually machine stitched between the motifs and hand-sewn around them, and it must be planned before the fabric is cut. The motifs on the two sections don't have to match, but they should merge attractively. One section can consistently overlap the other; or they can alternate overlap directions.

1. Thread trace all seamlines and matchpoints.

2. To sew a simple appliqué seam with one section overlapping the other, clip the seam allowance on the overlap to the seamline above and below each motif to be lapped.

CLAIRE'S HINT *When the motifs alternate from side to side, establish one side as the primary overlapping side, clip above and below any motifs that are to overlap.*

3. Using the thread tracing as a guide, fold under the seam allowance between the motifs. Press lightly from the wrong side.

CLAIRE'S HINT *Sometimes I alternate the overlaps, but it is more difficult when working with woven fabrics than when working with lace.*

4. Right sides up, align the seamlines and matchpoints; top baste the sections together about ⅛ in. from the thread-traced seamline. Baste the edges of the motifs flat.

5. Slip baste the part of the seam to be machine stitched.

6. Remove the top-basting; and reposition the sections with right sides together. Stitch the basted sections between the motifs.

## APPLIQUÉ SEAM FOR PATTERNED FABRIC

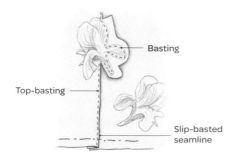

Top-basting

Basting

Slip-basted seamline

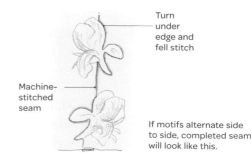

Turn under edge and fell stitch

Machine-stitched seam

If motifs alternate side to side, completed seam will look like this.

7. Remove the bastings, secure the thread ends and press open the machine-stitched sections, clipping as needed to make them lie flat.

8. Right side up, trim the seam allowance around the motif so it can be folded under smoothly; clip as needed at the curves and corners. Pin and baste the motifs in place.

CLAIRE'S HINT *I use a fine needle to work the raw edges of the motifs under, and finger-press the edges.*

9. Use fell stitches or slipstitches to sew the edges of the motifs permanently.

10. Remove the bastings and trim away the excess fabric under the appliqué. Press lightly from the wrong side.

## ABUTTED SEAM

The abutted, or butted, seam has no seam allowances and is used for joining seams and darts on interfacings where you want to minimize bulk. Occasionally it is used for piecing fabrics. This seam is usually sewn with an underlay, which adds strength; but it can be sewn without one.

1. Use plain-weave linen or cotton tape, rayon seam binding, lightweight selvage cut from silk organza or georgette, or muslin selvage for the underlay.

2. Cut away the seam allowances or the dart take-upfold.

3. Center one raw edge on the underlay and baste. Butt the second edge to the first and baste.

4. Stitch the edges permanently by hand with catchstitches or by machine with straight or zigzag stitches. Press.

Eliminating the underlay produces a softer, more flexible seam. To finish the seam without an underlay, sew the edges together with a catchstitch and press.

### ABUTTED SEAM

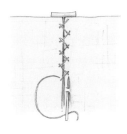

Butt edges together and catchstitch to underlay

## FRENCH SEAM

Called an English seam in France and a French seam in the English-speaking world, the French seam looks like a tuck on the wrong side of the garment. Its neat appearance on both sides of the garment makes it appropriate for handmade silk lingerie and fine blouses, and for some garments made of transparent fabrics. Because of its strength, this seam is also suitable for fine infant's wear and other lightweight, washable garments. French seams, however, are unsuitable for intricately shaped seamlines and for garments that are closely fitted or might require alterations.

A French seam is actually two seams: the first is sewn in the seam allowance, and the second on the seamline. Either seam can be sewn by hand or machine, but if you sew them both by hand, they will be softer and interfere less with the drape of the fabric.

1. To prepare the garment for a fitting, baste right sides together as you would for a plain seam.

2. After the fitting, and after all corrections are made, remove the seam bastings—but not the thread tracings—so you can lay the garment flat.

3. Wrong sides together, match and pin the thread-traced seamlines together. Baste.

CLAIRE'S HINT *On very lightweight fabrics like chiffon, georgette, or organza, I baste the first stitching line ⅛ in. from the thread-traced seamline. On heavier fabrics, I baste a scant ¼ in. away.*

### FRENCH SEAM

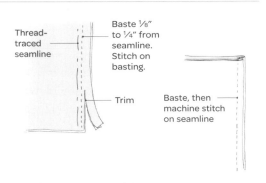

Thread-traced seamline

Baste ⅛" to ¼" from seamline. Stitch on basting.

Trim

Baste, then machine stitch on seamline

4. Shorten the stitch length, machine stitch over the basting; or if you are sewing by hand, use short running stitches.

5. Remove the seam bastings, but not the thread tracings.

6. Press the seam flat; then open.

7. Reposition the sections with right sides together with the seam at the edge. Press the fold with the iron point.

8. Open the sections and trim so the seam is slightly less than the finished width.

9. Right sides together, baste on the thread-traced seamline and stitch.

10. Remove the basting; press the seam flat; then to one side. Press shoulder and side seams toward the front of the garment so they will be inconspicuous when the garment is worn.

CLAIRE'S HINT *For a stronger seam, fell stitch the free edge of the French seam to the wrong side of the garment.*

## Stitching Intricate Seams

Couture garments often feature intricate seamlines that require special attention. The seamlines on Adrian's stunning jacket (see p. 38), for example, join reverse corners, which need to be handled differently from the standard plain seam. Most of these seams require additional reinforcement since the inward corner is clipped to the seamline. More common than either seams with reverse corners or reverse curves are intersecting seams. When encountering any of these seams, you will find these guidelines helpful.

### INTERSECTING SEAMS

Most designs have at least one or two seams that either meet or cross one another. In home sewing and ready-to-wear, the second seam is stitched across the seam allowances of the first seam. However, this can interfere with the drape of the garment—and cause a pull when the body moves. Many seams in haute couture are sewn without stitching across the seam allowances at the intersecting seamlines. Instead, the seam is stitched up to the intersecting seamline. Then it begins again just on the other side of the seamline, with the seam allowances held out of the way. Shoulder seams are often stitched in this way when they intersect the armscye seam. When considering whether to cross one seam with another, base your decision on whether the stitching will create an unwanted tension in the seam. If so, interrupt the seamline when it meets an intersecting seam.

**Matching Seamlines, Method One.** To perfect your skill at matching seamlines, make a patchwork sampler with twenty 3-in. squares just as the students at the school of the Chambre syndicale do.

On this sampler the strips are stitched across the intersecting seams.

1. Cut twenty 3-in. squares; make four long strips of five squares joined together with ½-in. seams; press all the seams open.

2. Right sides together, baste the long edges of the strips with ½-in. seams.

CLAIRE'S HINT *I double-baste at the intersections to keep the layers from slipping.*

3. Machine stitch across the intersecting seam allowances. Check to be sure the intersections match exactly. Remove the bastings and press.

**Matching Seamlines, Method Two.** On this sampler the strips are stitched together without stitching across the intersecting seams.

1. Cut twenty 3-in. squares and make four long strips.

2. Right sides together, baste the long edges of the strips with ½-in. seams keeping the seam allowances free.

3. When stitching the seam, push the seam allowances away from the presser foot as you approach each intersection and sew precisely up to it. Cut the thread, leaving long thread tails.

4. Rearrange the seam allowances to avoid stitching across them. Start again precisely on the other side of the seam; stitch to the next seam. Repeat to the end of the strip.

## INTERSECTING SEAMS

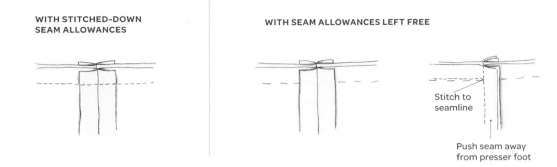

**WITH STITCHED-DOWN SEAM ALLOWANCES**

**WITH SEAM ALLOWANCES LEFT FREE**

Stitch to seamline

Push seam away from presser foot

5. Secure the thread ends with tailor's knots or backstitches. Remove the bastings and press.
CLAIRE'S HINT *I use the calyx-eye needle (easy-threading) to pull the threads through to one side.*

**Stitching Over Darts.** The garment will drape better if you do not stitch over the folded dart. This situation is handled in the same way as the intersecting seams whose seam allowances are left free.

1. Stitch the dart stopping at the seamline.
2. Cut and press the dart open.
3. Baste the seam. With the dart on top, stitch to the dart, stop and cut the threads, leaving long thread tails.
4. Fold the dart over the stitched section and begin again on the other side of the dart.
5. At the end of the seamline, pull all thread ends toward the undarted layer; fasten with tailor's knots or backstitches before pressing.

## ENCLOSED SEAMS

These seams are enclosed between the garment and its facing or lining; they can be located at any faced edge. Since these edges can be bulky, enclosed seams require some special handling to make them smooth, flat, and inconspicuous.

1. Right sides together, baste and stitch the seam; press.
CLAIRE'S HINT *I press the seam open first so it will lie flatter.*

2. Grade the seam to reduce the bulk, trimming the individual seam allowances to different widths. To ensure a smooth finish on the right side, trim the garment seam allowance to ¼ in.; trim the facing seam allowance slightly more.
CLAIRE'S HINT *To avoid making an unwanted cut on the garment when trimming, I hold the edge I'm trimming above the table with my left hand immediately under the scissor points.*

3. At curved edges, clip or notch the seam allowances as needed so they will lie flat and smooth. Make the clips on the bias, rather than on grain, to avoid weakening the seam. At corners, trim away only a small triangle. After grading the seam, I catchstitch one seam allowance to the interfacing or backing; then I sew the remaining seam allowance to the first one.
4. Turn the edge right side out so it's covered by the facing or lining; press lightly from the wrong side.

## EASED SEAMS

Eased seams join a longer section to fit a shorter one smoothly, such as a back shoulder joined to a front shoulder. Ease basted with tiny running stitches to hold in the excess fabric, these stitches smoothly ease rather than gather or pleat the fabric.

1. Wrong side up, begin with a simple knot and stitch a row of short, even basting stitches on the seamline with approximately 20 stitches to the in. leaving the thread slack with a long tail.

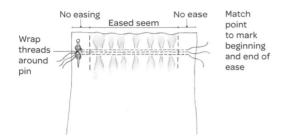

No easing | Eased seem | No ease | Match point to mark beginning and end of ease

Wrap threads around pin

2. Add two more rows of identical basting ⅛ in. one above and one below the first line of stitches.

3. Pull up the threads and evenly distribute the fullness until the section is the desired length. I set the pin at the end of the basting by picking up a very tiny bight. Then I pull up the threads and wrap them around the pins in a figure-8.

4. Shrink out the excess fullness with your iron until the eased area is smooth (see p. 64). If there is a lot of ease or the fabric is difficult to ease, I pull up the ease-basting some to shrink a little, then I pull it more and shrink until it is the appropriate length.

5. Baste and complete the seam like a plain seam.

## GATHERED SEAMS

Use small running stitches to gather a large, full section into a smaller one. This technique is similar to ease basting, but the extra fabric length is much fuller, not shrunk out with the iron, and has a softly gathered decorative effect. Use this seam to join gathered edges to waistbands, cuffs, and yokes.

1. Use a long needle and a strong thread like glazed cotton. Anchor the thread and begin the first row of gathering stitches on or just inside the seamline of the longest layer. Pick up five or six small stitches on the needle before pulling it through the fabric; continue until the entire section is gathered.

2. At the end of the gathering, leave a long thread tail.

3. Sew two more gathering rows ⅛ in. above and below the first.

4. Pin the beginning end of each row to a weight (such as a tailor's ham) and pull up all rows as

# Stays

**MADE FROM STRIPS OF SEAM** binding, plain-weave tape, or selvage, stays are used to stabilize seamlines or garment edges so they hug the body and prevent stretching. A seam stabilized in this manner is called a stayed or taped seam. Stays are also used on eased or gathered seams to control the fullness, make the garment section easier to handle during construction, and prevent the finished edge from gaping away from the body. A stay will also keep fabric from stretching at foldlines on garment edges such as a front opening, zipper placket, or slashed pocket.

Stays are usually sewn to a single garment section and do not cross seamlines. One notable exception is a waistline or underbust stay, which is usually sewn in after the skirt is assembled and sometimes after the skirt and bodice are joined.

**1.** To apply a stay at an opening, mark its position on the right side of the garment during the fitting, before stitching the seam. When removing fullness, pin out a small dart—or series of small darts if there's a lot of fullness—indicating the amount to be eased.

**2.** With the dart(s) pinned and the garment still on the body, measure the length for the finished stay. This length will vary, depending on how easily the fabric can be eased,

## STAYING A SEAM

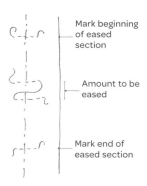

Mark beginning of eased section

Amount to be eased

Mark end of eased section

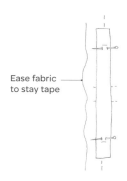

Ease fabric to stay tape

the fabric grain, the garment design, and the amount to be eased; but the stay should always be a little longer than the section being stayed. The excess can be trimmed away later.

**3.** After the fitting, if a dart was pinned out, mark its width by thread-tracing a crossmark on the seamline at each dart leg.

CLAIRE'S HINT *Charles Kleibacker would leave a connecting thread between the crossmarks to avoid confusion with nearby thread tracings.*

**4.** Press a ¼- to ½-in.-wide strip of preshrunk silk organza or chiffon selvage, plain-weave tape or seam binding, and pencil mark the finished length of the stay on the strip.

**5.** Wrong side up, center the stay over the seamline, aligning and pinning the matchpoints on the stay and garment.

**6.** Pin the mid-point of the stay; distribute and pin any excess to be eased.

**7.** Use running stitches just inside the seamline to sew the stay in place. At the end, check the stay's length then anchor the thread.

**8.** Using the iron point and a damp press cloth, shrink out the ease. You can shrink some of the ease before pinning the stay on the garment and finish shrinking after it's sewn.

### FOLDED-EDGE STAY

A stay at a folded edge preserves the lines of a design, prevents the edge from stretching, and makes a softer fold.

**1.** With the wrong side up, fold the stay in half.

**2.** Use blindstitches to sew the folded edge to the garment fold. Do not pull the stitches tight. If the garment has a backing, use short running stitches to sew the stay to the backing.

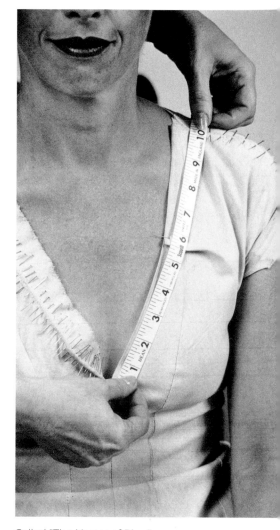

Called "The Master of Bias," Charles Kleibacker always used stays to control V-necklines and keep them from sagging and gaping when worn. On this toile from Kleibacker's workroom, a dart was pinned out on the left side of the neckline to make it fit snugly. On the right side, a stay was pinned in place and the dart's fullness distributed evenly along the edge.

(Photo courtesy of *Threads* magazine.)

tightly as possible. Fasten the threads by making a figure-8 around a pin at the end of the center row.

5. Hold the top of the gathered section in one hand. Use the other hand to pull the bottom sharply so the ridges—tops of the gathered folds—are parallel to one another.

6. Remove the pin holding the gathering threads and loosen the threads. Use a tapestry needle to stroke the gathers so they lie evenly side by side.

7. Adjust the gathered section to the desired length; fasten the threads in a figure-8 around a pin.

8. When sewing a seam at a waistband, armscye, cuff or yoke, fold under the seam allowance of the ungathered edge.

9. Right sides up, and the ungathered edge on top, align the seamlines and matchpoints; pin. Top baste the sections together for fitting.

10. After fitting, machine stitch or slipstitch the seamline permanently.

11. Trim the seam allowances to ½ in.; press first the band, then the gathered section, working carefully to press between the ridges to avoid setting creases.

12. To make a buttressed seam, turn the seam allowances toward the gathered section. Trim the seam allowances to ½ in. and press first the band, then the gathered section, working carefully to press between the ridges to avoid setting creases (see "Buttressed Seam," p. 221).

13. Overcast the seams.

## SEAMS WITH REVERSE CORNERS

Designs with gussets, square or pointed yokes, and shawl collars have seams with reverse corners, that is, an inward corner on one edge and an outward corner on the adjoining edge (see photo on p. 38). The Adrian jacket has decorative seams with reverse corners. At the inward corner, the seam allowance is clipped to the seamline so the seam can be stitched and pressed open. Since the seam allowance tapers to nothing at the corner, the seam cannot withstand stress. When these seams are used on decorative godets or shawl collars, their weakness is not a problem. But on seams such as

### REVERSE CORNER

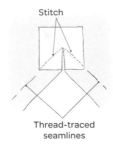
Stitch

Thread-traced seamlines

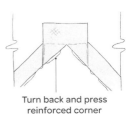
Turn back and press reinforced corner

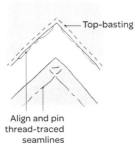
Top-basting

Align and pin thread-traced seamlines

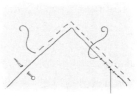
Slip baste or fell stitch

gussets and yokes that will be subjected to stress when the garment is worn, the corner must be reinforced.

There are a variety of ways to reinforce an inward-corner seam. The simplest method is to back each garment section at the outset with a lightweight, firmly woven backing fabric, like silk organza or chiffon. To reinforce the seamline to withstand more stress, face the inward corner.

1. Thread-trace the seamlines.

2. To face the corner, cut a 2-in. square of silk organza or silk chiffon; center it over the corner on the right side of the garment section so the grainline of the square is parallel to one seamline; baste.

3. Use short machine stitches to sew just inside the seamline, beginning and ending 1 in. from the corner.

4. Clip the corner up to the machine stitching.
CLAIRE'S HINT *When clipping, I use my best scissors with very sharp points; position the points exactly where I want the clip to be and close the scissors.*

5. Turn the facing and seam allowance to the wrong side; press lightly.
6. Trim away the excess reinforcing fabric, and overcast the clipped edges with tiny stitches.
7. Right sides up and the inward corner on top, align and pin the seamlines and matchpoints; top baste the sections together.
8. Slip baste the seam.
9. Remove the top-basting and reposition the sections with right sides together and the faced corner uppermost. Using short stitches, begin at the corner and stitch away from it for about 1 in. on the seamline. Lengthen the stitch and finish the seam.
10. Finish the corner by repositioning your work so you can begin at the corner. Again stitch away from the corner, using short stitches.
CLAIRE'S HINT *By starting the seam at the corner and sewing away from it, you'll get a sharper corner and eliminate the shifting and mismatching of edges that might otherwise occur if you stitch toward the corner.*

11. Fasten the threads at the corners with tailor's knots, remove the bastings and press the seam toward the section with the inward corner. If the fabric is bulky, press the seam open so you can flatten the seam allowance on the outward corner.

## SEAMS WITH REVERSE CURVES

A seam with a reverse curve joins an outward curve on one garment section with an inward curve on another section, as shown in the top photo on p. 10. The seam can either be decorative, or it can be functional, as in the case of a princess fitting seam.

Although the seamlines joining a pair of decorative inward and outward curves are the same length, the raw edges of their seam allowances are different. On the inward curve it's

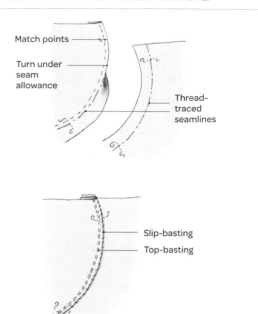

Match points

Turn under seam allowance

Thread-traced seamlines

Slip-basting
Top-basting

shorter than on the outward curve. Successfully joining these two curved edges requires some manipulation—the more intricate the curve, the more the edges have to be manipulated. Since seams in couture are first thread-traced, matched and basted with right sides up, these seams are easier to sew than they would be otherwise.

### Stitching Reverse Curves
1. Thread-trace seamlines.
2. When stitching a decorative seamline, first turn under the seam allowance on the outward curve; baste about 1/8 in. from the folded edge.
3. Right sides up and the folded edge on top, align and pin the seamline and matchpoints; top baste the sections together. Slip baste.
4. Remove the top-basting so the sections can be repositioned with right sides together for machine stitching. Stitch.
5. Remove the bastings, trim the seam allowances and press the seam open, clipping the inward seam as necessary to make it lie flat.
6. Round any clipped corners, and when overcasting the edges, overcast the clips as well.

Attributed to Emanuel Ungaro, this 1960s dress is one of my favorites. The insets are cut on the same grain as the dress so the reverse corner seams are sewn with two bias edges. The jacket is cleverly designed to show the insets when the dress and jacket are worn. A view with the jacket is on p. 186.

(Photo by Ken Howie. Author's collection.)

**Stitching Fitting Seams.** Fitting seams such as a princess seam or a sleeve-cap seam are frequently uneven in length. Once joined, the excess fabric on the longer edge shapes the design.

1. Ease-baste and shrink the longer edge to control the fullness before basting the two edges together.
2. Complete the seam like a plain seam.

## BRACED SEAM

A braced seam is a plain seam with a bias strip of lightweight, crisp interfacing such as silk organza, sewn over the seam allowances to hold them open. Intended for fabrics that are difficult

### BRACED SEAM

Running stitches

to press crisply without marring the garment itself, the braced seam produces a smooth, flat seamline.

1. Right sides together, stitch a plain seam and press it open.
2. Measure the width of the pressed-open seam. Cut a bias strip this width to make the brace.
3. Center the brace over the seamline and pin.
4. Use running stitches to sew the brace edges to the garment seam allowances.
5. Finish the edges.

## Darts

A dart is a stitched fold that shapes the fabric to the contours of the body. When positioned at the edge of a garment section such as a skirt, the dart can taper to a point at one end or be released to form a dart tuck. When placed in the middle of a garment section, such as a dart below the bust on a jacket, both ends taper.

Unlike the darts in ready-to-wear and home sewn garments, which are pressed to one side, darts in haute couture are pressed open or balanced to prevent a ridge. Most darts are stitched on the wrong side of the garment to hide their bulk, but "stand-up" darts are stitched on the right side for decorative effects—a treatment Valentino frequently used. To avoid disrupting a patterned fabric, darts can also be sewn as appliqué seams (see p. 50 and the photo on the facing page).

In haute couture, darts are used less often than in ready-to-wear and whenever possible are converted to ease (see p. 60). Nonetheless, couture garments certainly use darts and occasionally they're in unusual places. For example, horizontal darts are sometimes used on the hem allowance to raise the hemline. On slips and underpinnings, which need

Appliqué seaming can be used to stitch a dart. On the right side of this sample, the tulip was cut to lap over the dartline and appliquéd in place with tiny fell stitches. If it had been stitched in the usual manner as with the dart on the left side, the tulip would have had an ugly straight line at the stitching.

(Photo by Taylor Sherrill. Author's collection.)

to fit the bust closely, horizontal darts extend from a center-front seam to the bust.

## STITCHING A DART

When stitched properly, a dart is barely visible on the right side of the garment.

1. Thread-trace the stitching lines. If the dart is long or shaped, mark any matchpoints with crossmarks.

2. Right sides together, baste the dart with short even-basting stitches, tapering the stitches to the point.

3. To prepare the dart for a fitting, fold the basted dart into position and top baste. If there are no corrections after the fitting, remove the top-basting.

4. Wrong side up, lightly press the dart flat and machine stitch precisely on the basted lines.

5. Secure the thread ends at the point with a tailor's knot, remove the bastings; press the stitched line.

6. Carefully clip the dart open, stopping about

¼ in. from the point. If the dart is wide, trim it to 1 in. on each side of the stitched line. If the dart is too narrow to cut open, arrange the dart like a box pleat so that it is centered over the stitched line; baste the center so the dart will not shift when pressed. Or balance the dart using the directions on p. 60.

7. Open the garment and spread the darted area over an appropriate pressing cushion to shape the dart to fit the body.

8. Open the dart with your fingers and, with the iron point, press just the stitched line firmly with a sharp up-and-down movement. If necessary, insert a tapestry needle into the dart point to press it smoothly.

CLAIRE'S HINT *Pressing over the needle keeps the fabric centered over the stitched line and prevents the dart from becoming crooked at the tip end. Press the entire section, shaping it to fit the body and overcast the dart's raw edges.*

### Double-pointed Darts

1. When pressing double-pointed darts, stretch the folded edge of the dart at the widest point so it will fold back smoothly.

2. If the fabric is cotton, linen or another fiber without much give, clip the dart before pressing it.

If the dart is too narrow to be cut open, balance it with a strip of fabric (see p. 60).

### Backed Darts

1. To sew darts on a garment with a backing, apply the backing to the fabric wrong side.

2. Baste the dart centers together and work the two layers as one.

3. After the darts are stitched, check to be sure the backing is not too tight. If it is, remove the bastings at the edges of the garment section and rebaste so both layers lie flat.

**Interfacing Darts.** Eliminate extra bulk on interfacings by adapting the instructions for lapped or abutted seams to make the darts. On the Yves

Saint Laurent jacket on p. 172, the interfacing dart take-up was cut away and the dart edges were catchstitched to the jacket dart.

## BALANCED DART

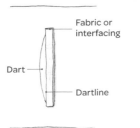

Fabric or interfacing

Dart

Dartline

**Balanced Darts.** On a balanced dart, a strip of fabric is sewn and pressed in the opposite direction from the dart fold to balance its bulk. This technique is particularly useful for sewing small darts on bulky fabrics that ravel, although it's rarely used on lightweight fabrics.

1. Baste the dart.

2. Use self-fabric or an interfacing similar in weight to the garment fabric to cut a strip on the lengthwise grain twice the width of the dart and about 1 in. longer.

3. Center the strip over the basted dart.

4. Double-baste through the strip to keep the strip from slipping, stitch permanently.

5. Remove the bastings and press the dart in one direction and the interfacing strip in the other.

## CONVERTING DARTS TO EASE

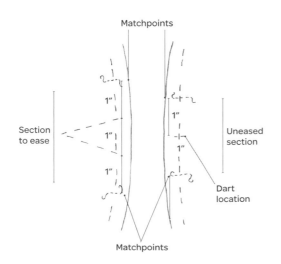

Matchpoints

Section to ease

1"

1"

1"

1"

Uneased section

Dart location

Matchpoints

By converting darts to ease, you can avoid disrupting the fabric pattern or the style lines of the garment. The waist dart on the right has been converted to ease on the left side; the excess was shrunk away with a steam iron. Notice that the dart on the right is positioned between two prominent stripes to create a flattering line.

(Photo by Susan Kahn.)

## CONVERTING DARTS TO EASE

In home sewing and luxury ready-to-wear, the practice of converting small darts to ease is often used at the elbow and back shoulder. In couture, darts are converted much more extensively to preserve the uninterrupted lines of a design. And sometimes they're converted in unconventional places to refine the garment's fit. This technique is frequently used on skirts to eliminate some or all darts, to prevent gaping décolleté necklines, to tighten the back armscye on tailored jackets, to replace elbow darts on sleeves, and to replace the bust darts from the armscye. It works best on fabrics that can be shrunk easily.

In these directions, the dart is marked when the toile is fitted, and the technique can also be adapted to commercial patterns.

1. During the fitting, pin a small dart anywhere it's needed or indicated on the pattern. Generally, the

dart must be relatively small and positioned at an edge or a seamline.

2. Remove the garment and mark the location of the dart.

3. Remove the bastings and lay the garment flat.

4. On the wrong side, mark the dart stitching lines with chalk and measure its width at the seamline.

5. On the section with the dart, measure and mark the dart's width on each side of the marked dart so the section to be eased is three times the width of the dart. For example, if the dart is 1 in. wide at the seamline, measure 1 in. above the dart and 1 in. below it, making the eased section 3 in.

6. On the undarted section, measure and mark the dart width above and below the stitching line of the dart location, so the uneased section is twice the width of the dart. For example, if the pinned dart is 1 in., the eased section will be 3 in. and the undarted section will be 2 in.

7. Shrink out the fullness, ease and shrink the longer section to fit the adjoining section smoothly (see "Eased Seams," p. 53).

8. Complete the eased seams.

# Pressing Techniques

Pressing is such an important priority in couture sewing that many workrooms I visited had more irons than sewing machines. Pressing occurs throughout a design's construction—from shaping and molding garment sections before joining them, to pressing seams and edges during and after their shaping or sewing, to the final pressing of a completed garment.

The pressing tools I saw in couture workrooms are similar to many you may already have. An industrial steam iron with an outside water tank was generally used in tailoring workrooms, while a dry iron was used in dressmaking workrooms. Sometimes, however, a regular domestic iron was the only one used. The issue is not the brand or type of iron you have, but how you use it.

## PRESSING TOOLS

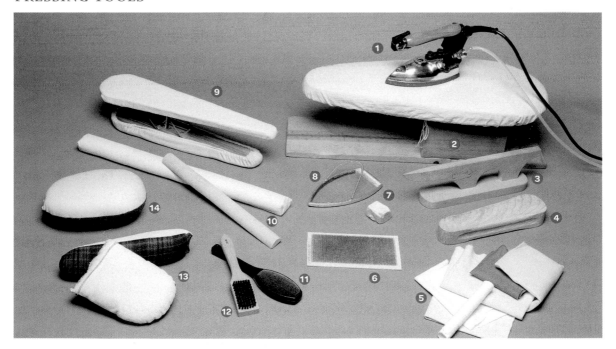

Steam iron (1), pressing stand (2), point presser (3), clapper (4), an assortment of pressing cloths in cotton, wool, silk (5), needle board (6), soap (7), Teflon® iron shoe (8), sleeve board (9), seam stick (10), lint brush (11), spotter's brush (12), pressing pads (13), large pressing pad or ham (14). (Photo by Susan Kahn.)

# Interfacings and Backings

**USED MUCH MORE EXTENSIVELY** in haute couture than in luxury ready-to-wear and home sewing, interfacings and backings are generally natural-fiber fabrics sewn to the interior of a garment to help shape and support the design. More malleable than synthetic and fusible materials, these natural-fiber fabrics can be applied to part or all of a garment section.

By contrast, linings, which are generally silk, serve for aesthetics rather than durability. Although almost always used on tailored jackets and coats, linings are used much less frequently in couture than in luxury ready-to-wear for dresses and evening gowns since they add an unnecessary layer that may wrinkle or distort the garment's drape.

The distinction between an interfacing and a backing is somewhat blurred. They both help shape a garment, but a backing (sometimes called an underlining or mounting) usually lends body to the fabric itself, while an interfacing helps control or produce the shape of the garment. An interfacing is never used for modesty, but a backing is often applied to make a fabric opaque or change its color. Both backings and interfacings can duplicate the garment section or just a portion of it.

Traditional couture interfacing and backing fabrics include hair canvas, silk organza, China silk, handkerchief linen, organdy, muslin, cotton flannel, lamb's wool, net, tulle, crinoline, and self-fabric. I've also seen more luxurious fabric used, like fine Egyptian cotton, faille, silk taffeta, charmeuse, and chiffon. I've found one stiffener, horsehair braid, used in several interesting ways—on the front edges of a Dior jacket, as the skirt backing for a Nina Ricci evening gown, and as the support for one of Hardy Amies's off-the-shoulder wedding dresses.

Choose a backing or interfacing fabric by deciding how much support the interior architecture of the garment needs—the more support required, the stiffer the backing or interfacing (or both). To make a selection, try draping the garment fabric over the support material and examine the results: Does it hang stiffly or fall gently from your hand? Does it overwhelm the garment fabric? The support fabric can be crisper than the garment fabric, but it should not be heavier. Experiment with various support fabrics to find the effect you want.

Known for blurring the boundaries between art and fashion, Roberto Cappucci often experimented with structure and over-the-top designs. Fabricated in black silk taffeta, the ruffle on this beautiful piece is lined with fuschia and stiffened with very rigid crinoline. It outlines the hem, then spirals around the body to the top of the dress back.

(Photo by Taylor Sherrill. Author's collection.)

## CLAIRE'S HINT
*I frequently cut backing and interfacing on the bias because they provide the support I want but they don't hang as stiffly.*

Other essential pressing tools include an ironing board or pressing table, point presser, sleeve roll, seam stick or seam board, large pressing pad or tailor's ham, a clapper and point presser, lint brush, and an assortment of pressing cloths in cotton, linen, wool, and silk to press various types and weights of garment fabrics. Optional tools I use regularly are a needleboard and a tailor's brush. Designed for pressing velvet, a needleboard is very expensive; but it will last forever—mine is about 75 years old. The tailor's brush is a stiff brush about 2 in. by 4 in.

Pressing successfully is not difficult, but it requires some experimentation because there are no set formulas, and it's not uncommon for two people to press the same fabric differently. The key to getting professional results is understanding the essential elements of pressing—heat, moisture, and pressure—and how they work together and affect the fabric. For general pressing techniques and more information on pressing specific fabrics, see *Claire Shaeffer's Fabric Sewing Guide* in the Bibliography on p. 244.

The amount of heat, moisture, and pressure needed for successful pressing depends on the fiber content, weight, thickness, and texture of the fabric. Cotton and linen fabrics need more heat than woolens, silks, and synthetics. Thin fabrics are more easily damaged by excessive heat than thick fabrics, even when both have the same fiber content. No matter what the fabric, pressing without a press cloth—or with a very thin one—requires a cooler iron than pressing with a regular or thicker press cloth.

Many fabrics become more malleable when pressed with both moisture and heat. You can apply moisture with a steam iron, damp pressing cloth, or sponge. Steaming with an iron is both the easiest and most unpredictable method since it may leave waterspots. The damp press cloth and sponge are much more dependable and versatile since you can use them directly on fabrics that do not waterspot. For fabrics that do waterspot, cover them first with a dry press cloth; then apply the damp press cloth or sponge.

To dampen a press cloth, wet one end and wring it out. Then fold the cloth so the wet end wraps around the dry section and press it to distribute the moisture evenly. To dampen a sponge or dauber, dip it in water and shake it so it's wet but not dripping. Then rub the wet end over the area to be pressed.

Most pressing requires some pressure, but the amount needed varies with the pressing task and fabric. For flattening seams and edges or reducing bulk on heavy fabrics, apply more pressure than for pressing lightweight or napped fabrics. You can apply pressure with several tools—an iron, clapper, bristles or handle of a tailor's brush, or your fingers. And you can vary the pressure by using different pressing surfaces. For pressing pockets, buttonholes, hems, appliquéd seams, and textured fabrics place the garment section wrong side up on a softly padded surface or a needleboard to avoid flattening it or causing pressing imprints. For a hard, crisp press at seamlines and edges, use an unpadded hardwood surface.

Always test-press on fabric scraps first. Make sample darts, seams, and hems, then experiment with various amounts of heat, moisture, and pressure, and with different press cloths and pressing tools to determine which work best for your fabric and design.

Whenever possible, press from the wrong side. When pressing from the right side, use a press cloth to protect the surface. When pressing large sections or uncut yardage, check to be sure the grain is straight. To avoid stretching the fabric when pressing, slide the iron only with the lengthwise grain, and do not move the fabric or garment section until it's cool and dry.

Press at every stage of construction. Press flat areas on flat surfaces and shaped sections over a pressing cushion or curved board that duplicates the shape of the body. Press small garment sections before applying or joining them to other sections. Press darts well before joining the section to other sections. Press all seams and darts before crossing them with another line of stitching.

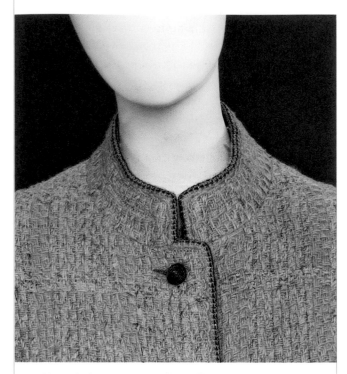

Many designers cut standing collars on grain—sometimes the straight grain, sometimes the crossgrain—to create a more pleasing design. The collar on this Chanel jacket is cut on the straight grain. The upper edge was shrunk, and the lower edge stretched.

(Photo by Taylor Sherrill. Author's collection.)

Before pressing seams and darts, check the fit and examine the stitching. If it's not perfect, correct it before pressing. Remove all bastings and thread tracings. Press the seam or dart flat in the direction it was sewn to "marry" the stitches. When pressing heavy or bulky fabrics, turn the seam over and press again. To avoid making unwanted impressions on the right side, place the seam wrong side up on a seam roll, point presser, or seam stick so you can press just the stitched line. Then, using your fingers, a pin or the iron tip, open the seam without applying pressure.

Press the seamline firmly with the iron point, using steam or a damp press cloth if needed.

For flatter, sharper edges, clip, notch, and grade seams properly. Press enclosed seams open before trimming them and turning the section right side out. To flatten the edge after it's turned, place it on a firm surface, then fill the edge with steam, and cover it with a clapper. If the edge is bulky and doesn't flatten easily, spank it once or twice with the clapper to beat the steam out. Do not move the section until it's dry.

Avoid overpressing. You can always press again, but well-set creases, unwanted wrinkles, shines, and scorches may be impossible to remove. If you overpress and the seam or dart shows on the right, place the section wrong side up on a needle-board or large piece of hook and loop tape. Fill the fabric with steam; turn it right side up and brush with tailor's or fabric brush. Repeat until the seam impression is removed.

## Shrinking or Stretching the Garment

The ease with which you can shrink or stretch fabrics when pressing depends on the fiber content, weave, and the grain of the garment section or edge to be shaped. Wools, wool blends, and loosely woven materials shrink and stretch more easily than silk, cotton, linen, synthetic, or closely woven fabrics. Bias sections and edges are easy to shrink (and stretch), while the lengthwise straight grain is more difficult.

### SHRINKING

Although the technique for shrinking fabric is familiar to many home sewers, it's used much more extensively in couture and bespoke tailoring than in home sewing. Shrinking is used most commonly to reduce excess fullness when shaping sleeve caps, easing skirts to waistbands, controlling flared hems, tightening an armscye or converting darts to ease. It can also be used to restore a stretched edge, such as a neckline.

1. Begin by ease-basting as for an eased seam (see p. 53); pull up the basting threads until the edge is the desired length.

2. Wrong side up, press with a steam iron or with a dry iron and a damp press cloth. Moisten or steam the garment section and apply heat. As the fabric

shrinks, use finger pressure, then press with the iron. When the surplus fabric has been removed, use a dry pressing cloth and a cooler iron to press the fabric dry.

**Shrinking Within a Section.** Shrinking within a garment section is slightly more difficult than shrinking at the edges, but the technique can be used to remove fullness at the waist or under the

To shrink an edge, pull up the ease basting and fill the edge with steam. Pat it with your hand; then apply pressure with the iron. To avoid pressing pleats, shrink a small amount, pull up the ease, baste again, and shrink some more. Lift the iron and repeat until the entire section has been shrunk. Use a dry iron and press cloth to press the section dry. When shrinking with the right side up, cover the fabric with a press cloth (not used here in order to show the fabric).

(Photo by Susan Kahn.)

bust so the garment will conform to the body contours.

1. When the garment has a backing, stitch the darts in the backing material before basting it to the shell fabric.
2. Baste the sections together. The shell fabric will bubble over the darted backing.
3. Baste around the bubble since you want to control the shrinking.
4. Steam the shell fabric and finger-press to remove as much of the excess as possible. Then cover with a damp press cloth and shrink some more.
5. Continue until the excess is shrunk out.

## STRETCHING

Stretching a garment section to conform to the body will be a new technique for most home sewers. It's used to straighten and lengthen inward curves and to transform straight edges into outward curves. Frequently used in tandem with shrinking, stretching can also be used at the top or bottom of waistbands and the front edge of an upper sleeve.

1. Begin with the section wrong side up. Dampen the edge with steam, a moistened press cloth, or a sponge, depending on the fabric.
2. As you press, hold one edge of the fabric with one hand and use the iron as a weight to stretch the edge into the desired shape. Check your work often to be sure you don't overstretch it.

# 4

# Edge Finishes

Three finishes are used extensively in couture: hems, facings, and bindings. The choice of edge finish depends on many things—the shape of the edge being finished; its position on the garment; the type, design, and fabric of the garment; current fashion trends; and the preferences of the individual wearer and designer. For example, if the lower

The opening on this Dior jacket from the late 1990s is finished with an extended facing for the jacket front and a separate facing for the lapel/collar.

(Photo by Ken Howie. Author's collection.)

edge of a dress is straight, it might be completed with a hem, facing, or binding. However, if this edge is asymmetrical, curved, scalloped, or otherwise unusually shaped, it will require a facing. Even when the edge is visually the same on the neckline and hem, the two different edges are likely to require slightly different finishes to accommodate the curve at the neckline and the weight of the fabric at the hem. Hems, facings, and bindings are all edge finishes, but each has a slightly different function.

Hems are used on the lower edges of a garment or garment section (like a sleeve) and may help the garment hang attractively by adding weight to the edge. Facings, on the other hand, are most often applied to the upper and vertical edges of a garment. Bindings can be used on

**HEM**

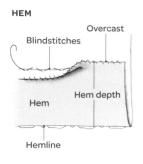

Blindstitches
Overcast
Hem
Hem depth
Hemline

**FACING**

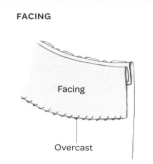

Facing
Overcast

**BINDING**

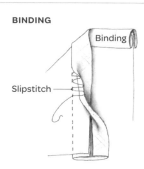

Binding
Slipstitch

upper, lower, or vertical edges, but they are used more often to replace facings rather than hems.

Cut as an extension of the garment section, hems can be wide or narrow, depending on the design, the hem location, and the fabric weight and/or transparency. Hems can even be finished with a separate facing, but this treatment is generally reserved for unusually shaped hems.

Facings can be cut as separate sections and sewn to the garment to finish curved or shaped edges. Or, when used on straight or slightly curved edges, they can be nothing more than a wide hem allowance, in which case they are called extended facings. Both hems and facings are visible on only one side—usually the underside—of the garment.

Bindings, by contrast, are separate strips of fabric that encase the garment edge and finish both sides of the garment attractively.

In couture, the cost of labor and materials takes a back seat to the desired results, so edges are not always finished with the simplest method or the one most common to ready-to-wear construction or home sewing. Whatever the finishing method, hems, facings, and bindings can be sewn entirely by hand or machine, or a combination of both. The hand work visible on the finished product, however, is only a fraction of the hand work used to finish the edges of the traditional couture garment.

# Hems

Before a customer's first fitting, the hemline is marked with thread-tracing so the hem can be folded under and basted in place. This enables the fitter and the client to consider the overall effect of the design and its fit. After the fitting, the basting is removed so any necessary alterations can be made and the vertical seamlines stitched permanently. The garment length might be adjusted at this stage with new thread tracing. The process is repeated for the second fitting, when the final hemline is usually established.

## PLAIN HEM

Sometimes called a "couture hem" or "blind hem," the plain hem is the simplest hem. It's the most commonly used because it's the flattest and easiest to sew. Whether the lower edge of the garment with a plain hem is wide or narrow, the vertical seamlines in the hem are on the lengthwise grain and the hem allowance has no excess fullness.

After the hemline is thread traced, the plain hem is made by folding and basting the hem allowance to the wrong side of the garment; the raw edge is overcast, folded under, or bound to prevent raveling and is secured inconspicuously by hand near the upper edge. Properly finished, the hem is completely invisible on the garment outside.

## HANGING A HEM

The process of establishing the finished garment's length is called "hanging a hem." Whether the skirt is straight or full, the goal is to create the illusion that the hemline is parallel to the floor. To create this impression, many designers finish the skirt ½ in. longer at center back than at center front to account for the contours of the body.

1. Thread-trace the hemline on each garment section.

2. Baste the garment together, pin and baste the hem in place for the first fitting. Baste first about ¼ in. above the hemline and then baste again about ¼ in. below the hem's raw edge; lightly press the hem fold.

3. Try on the garment; match and pin the opening closed.

4. Examine the hemline to see if it appears level and parallel to the floor. Use a yardstick to check the distance from the floor to the garment hemline at center front, center back, and the side seams.

5. To lengthen or shorten a level hemline, just mark the new hem length with one or two pins. Remove the basting, but not the thread tracing. Spread the garment on a table; measure and mark the new hemline in a second color an even distance from the original thread-traced hemline.

6. If the original hemline is so uneven that it needs to be completely remarked, release the bastings during the fitting, but do not remove the original thread tracing. Measure the hem parallel to the floor and mark it with very fine pins or needles set horizontally to keep them from falling out. Pin up the hem so the folded edge is ½ in. below the pin at center back and ¼ in. below the pin on each side seam. The sections between these points should be pinned smoothly. Examine the altered hemline to see if it looks level; if necessary, continue to correct it until you're satisfied with the results.

7. When hanging a floor-length skirt, it's difficult to measure close to the floor. To make the task easier, pin-mark a guideline below the fullest part of the hip parallel to the floor, about 12 in. from the floor and use this as a marking guide for the hemline. Mark the finished length at center front.

8. Remove the garment and lay it on a table, measure the distance between the two pins at the center front; use this measurement to mark a new hemline below the pinned guide.

## The Hemming Process

The garment style and fabric weight influence the hem depth. For straight skirts sewn from medium-weight fabrics, the hem is usually 2½ in. to 3 in. deep. In general, heavy or stretchy fabrics and full skirts (including those with pleats, gathers, or flare) require narrower hems, from 1 in. to 2 in. On garments sewn from transparent fabrics, the hem depth is visible and becomes an integral part of the design. It's usually very narrow on these garments, but if the skirt is straight and gathered, but unflared (like a dirndl), the hem depth can be as much as one-third of the skirt length on sheer special occasion dresses.

Once the hem depth is established, the actual hemming process begins.

1. Wrong side up, fold up the hem on the thread-traced hemline; baste ¼ in. above the hemline.

CLAIRE'S HINT *If the fabric is heavy or bulky, I reduce the seam allowances on the shell fabric—but not on the backing since it is lightweight and provides a buffer for the seam allowances.*

2. Wrong side up, place the skirt on an ironing board or pressing stand.

CLAIRE'S HINT *I like using a pressing stand on a table so the table will support the skirt weight. If you don't have a pressing stand, place a table next to the ironing board.*

3. Press the folded edge of the hem firmly. To avoid stretching the hem and to prevent rippling, don't

### REDUCED BULK OF SEAM ALLOWANCE IN HEM AREA

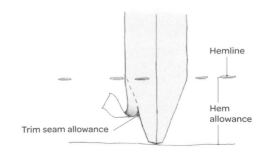

Hemline

Hem allowance

Trim seam allowance

## PLAIN HEM FOLDED, PINNED, AND BASTED FOR STITCHING

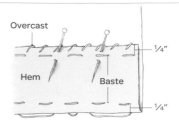

Overcast

Hem

Baste

¼"

¼"

slide the iron along the hemline, which is on the crossgrain. Instead, lower the iron onto the fabric, press, then lift the iron and reposition it.

4. Continue pressing, working your way around the entire hem. When pressing with steam or a damp press cloth, press a second time without moisture to dry the hem section before moving on to the next (see "Pressing Techniques," p. 61).

5. Mark the hem depth with chalk. With wrong side up and the hem toward you, measure the finished hem depth from the fold. If the upper hem is to be finished with a folded edge, add ¼ in. to the desired finished depth. Trim away any excess above the chalked line.

6. Finish the raw edge appropriately (see "Seam Finishes," p. 44).

7. Pin the hem flat against the garment, setting the pins on an angle and with the heads away from you. Baste about ¼ in. below the pinned edge. When the garment is backed, pin the hem only to the backing layer.

8. Right side out, spread the garment on the table with the hem toward you.

9. If the fabric doesn't wrinkle easily, pick up the hem of the top skirt layer, hold it perpendicular to the table and fold it back at the basting so the garment is folded right sides together.

10. If the fabric creases easily, work on the bottom layer of the skirt, leaving the hem flat on the table and folding back just the upper hem edge, instead of the entire hem allowance. (See "The Hemming Process," p. 69.)

11. Using a fine needle and matching thread, anchor the thread into the hem allowance. Hold the folded-back edge in place with one thumb while securing the edge with a fairly loose stitch. The stitches should hold the hem in place but not be tight enough to show. If the garment is backed, try to avoid sewing through the backing to the garment fabric (see "Hemming Stitches," p. 35). CLAIRE'S HINT *If the garment is made of a heavy fabric use blind catchstitches, and work from left to right.*

12. Complete the hem and remove all basting threads. With the skirt wrong side up, press the hem carefully, stopping just below the top of the hem allowance to avoid creating a pressing imprint on the garment right side. Press the skirt itself, sliding the tip of the iron between the hem and the garment. Examine the right side of the garment. If there are any basting imprints, cover the hem with a self-fabric or woolen pressing cloth and steampress to remove them.

## PLAIN HEM VARIATIONS

On flared designs such as gored, trumpet, A-line, and circular skirts, the raw hem edge is the widest part of the skirt. The excess fullness caused by the

## TWO WAYS TO HOLD GARMENT FOR HEMMING

**HEMMING FABRICS THAT DO NOT WRINKLE**

Blindstitches

**HEMING FABRICS THAT WRINKLE**

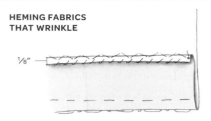

⅛"

## EASE THE FACING TO THE LINING

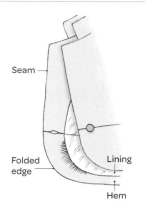

Seam

Folded edge

Lining

Hem

flare is concentrated near the seamlines. If this extra fabric is not eliminated or controlled, the garment will not hang properly, the hem will not lie flat against the skirt, and the excess bulk may show through to the outside of the garment.

The simplest method for controlling fullness on a curved wool hem is to shrink out the excess fullness with heat and moisture. The curved corners on a bouclé wool Balenciaga jacket shown above were finished in this manner. Folding small darts into a hem is another effective means of controlling the fullness when fabric cannot be shrunk. Although the wrong side of the hem will not look as neat as a hem allowance shrunk with easing, the hem will hang attractively when the garment is worn. This method of controlling fullness is more likely to be used on a lined garment.

Some cottons, linens, silks, and other fabrics, like the velvet dress shown at right, however, cannot be shrunk effectively, and the fullness in a curved hem of these fabrics would have to be handled with dressmaker techniques including small darts in the hem or using the hemming stitches themselves. Darting would be used on crisp fabrics, while eliminating fullness with hemming stitches would be preferable for lighter-weight fabrics.

### Controlling Fullness.

1. Fold the hem to the wrong side on the thread-traced hemline; baste ⅛ in. from the folded edge. The excess fullness will cause the hem to ripple.
2. Wrong side up, press just the folded edge without pressing over the ripples on the hem allowance.
3. Measure and mark the hem allowance so it's even; trim to reduce the depth.

CLAIRE'S HINT *I generally trim to 1 in. to 1½ in. It's tempting to reduce it more; but since the hem allowance provides weight, a very narrow hem will change the way the skirt drapes.*

4. Match and pin the seamlines on the hem and skirt. Smooth and pin the hem against the garment wrong side, working from the front and back centers to the seamlines. As the skirt begins to flare, the excess fullness will form ripples perpendicular to the hemline.
5. Pin the hem allowance to the garment, setting the pins at right angles to the edge and

This bias-cut dress from the 1930s drapes softly at the neckline. The smoothness of the drape belies the garment's excess fullness, which has been skillfully controlled on the hem allowance. In addition, the dress fastens with two zippers at the shoulders, an underarm zipper, and buttons and loops at the wrist.

(Photo by Taylor Sherrill. Author's collection.)

Inset: On the inside, the stitches have been carefully placed between the ripples.

(Photo by Taylor Sherrill. Author's collection.)

from 1 in. to 3 in. apart—the tighter the curve, the closer the pins. The excess fullness will stand up in small ripples between the pins. To avoid distorting the hang of the garment, keep the ripples perpendicular to the hemline.

6. Baste near the top of the hem allowance without flattening the ripples. Using blindstitches, sew the hem between the ripples.

**Double-stitched Hem.** When the fabric is heavy, the weight of the hem will pull on the hemming stitches, causing them to show on the right side.

DOUBLE-
STITCHED HEM

A simple solution is to hem the garment twice or three times—first at the midpoint of the hem allowance depth, then near the finished edge.

1. For a double hem, mark the hem depth and place a row of basting stitches midway between the hemline and the upper finished edge. For a triple hem, divide the hem allowance into thirds.

2. Use blindstitches or blind catchstitches to hem the garment at the basted line.

3. Baste and hem again at the top of the hem allowance as you would normally.

## INTERFACED HEM

Hems interfaced with bias strips add body to the lower garment, reduce wrinkling, create smoother hemlines, and prevent visible breaks at the hemline.

If you wish to add body to the garment, the best interfacing fabrics include traditional woven, non-fusible interfacing materials such as hair canvas, muslin, wigan, silk organza, and silk shantung. For a soft, padded hemline, try lambswool, wadding (cotton batting), and cotton flannel are good choices. For more padding, choose wadding, polyester batting, or polyester or wool fleece. The best choice for a very crisp hemline is horsehair braid or crinoline.

To determine the width of the interfacing strip, first consider whether you want a soft or crisp edge and whether the garment is to be lined or unlined. For a soft edge, cut the interfacing to overlap the hemline ½ in. to 1 in. For a sharper edge, cut the interfacing just wide enough to meet the hemline.

On unlined garments, the interfacing should be concealed within the hem, with the upper edge of the interfacing ½ in. below the top of the hem allowance. On lined garments, the interfacing can be any width, though it is usually at least 3 in. wide so it will extend at least ½ in. above the hem allowance to act as a buffer between the garment and hem, and keep the hem edge from showing on the garment right side. Generally, interfacings on the hems of special-occasion dresses, which are usually longer than regular daywear, are 10 in. to 12 in. wide, while those on daywear will be from 2 in. to 4 in. wide. However, there are always exceptions: The hem interfacing on some of Yves Saint Laurent's famous trapeze dresses for Dior, shown on p. 127, had interfacings as wide as 20 in. to help shape the skirt. The design silhouette, fabric weight, and the skirt length all determine how wide the hem, and consequently its interfacing, should be.

1. Cut enough bias strips to interface the hem's entire length.

2. Spread the garment on the table wrong side up; pin the interfacing on the garment so it laps the hemline ½ in.

CLAIRE'S HINT *I piece the strips as I go by lapping the ends ½ in. and joining them with short running stitches.*

**SOFT-EDGED HEMLINE**

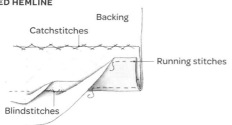

Backing

Catchstitches

Running stitches

Blindstitches

**FLARED HEMLINE**

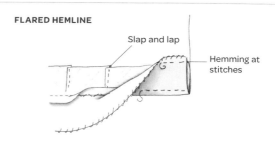

Slap and lap

Hemming at stitches

3. Use catchstitches to sew the upper edge of the interfacing to the backing or vertical seams.

4. At the hemline, attach the interfacing lightly to the garment with long running stitches or by folding the interfacing at the hemline and securing it with widely spaced blindstitches. If the garment is backed, catch it to the backing but not the garment. When the vertical seamlines are closely spaced, I don't sew the interfacing at the hemline.

5. On lined garments; use catchstitches to sew the top of the interfacing to the garment or its backing. To complete the hem, fold and baste it in place. Use catchstitches or running stitches to sew the hem to the interfacing.

6. If the skirt is flared, shape the interfacing when you lay it on the garment by slashing the strip slightly and lapping out small darts. If you're using horsehair braid on a flared skirt, however, instead of slashing the edge, pull up the edge thread and ease.

7. For a wider interfacing, pin a second interfacing strip to the first. I frequently use two 4-in.-wide interfacing strips on jacket hems so the interfacing will begin just below the waist. Generally, it isn't necessary to catchstitch the top of the first interfacing to the garment.

**Horsehair Braid Hem.** Unlike traditional interfacing materials, horsehair braid is too stiff to fold and lap at the hemline. Wider horsehair braids have a string along one edge so it can be pulled up to fit the edge of a flared skirt smoothly.

1. Use 2-in.-wide horsehair braid.

2. Align the edge with the hemline; use blind-stitches to sew it permanently.

3. At the end, lap the ends of the horsehair braid ½ in. Cover the cut ends with seam binding or ribbon.

4. Use catchstitches to sew the upper edge of the horsehair braid to the seams.

5. Shape the horsehair braid as needed on a flared hem by pulling up the edge thread.

6. Turn up the hem allowance and complete the hem.

## NARROW HEMS

The narrow hem has several variations—the hand-rolled hem, pin hem, felled hem, and several types of blouse hems. The hand-rolled hem and felled hem are among the most useful. On couture garments, narrow hems are usually sewn by hand, while on luxury ready-to-wear and home-sewn clothing, they are often machine stitched. Narrow hems are softer and more supple than machine-stitched ones.

CLAIRE'S HINT *Regardless of which narrow-hem style you choose, carefully check the length of the garment before trimming away the excess fabric since you cannot lengthen a hem that's too short.*

**Hand-rolled Hem.** Hand-rolled hems are used frequently on lightweight silks and wools, and on chiffons and organzas. They are not suitable for heavyweight fabrics or lightweight materials with weave variations, embroidery, metallic threads, or beading because the edges are uneven and will be difficult to roll smoothly.

The thread on a hand-rolled hem is almost completely hidden within the roll.

There are three types of facings: extended, separate, and bias. Two of these—separate and bias—are cut independently of the garment from self- or contrast fabric, or lightweight lining fabrics. The extended facing is cut as an extension of the garment section like a plain hem.

The extended facing is nothing more than a ½-in. to 5-in. hem, generally sewn like a plain hem (see "Plain Hem" on p. 68). When the garment edge is on the lengthwise grain, the extended facing duplicates the shape and grain of the edge it faces. When the edge is slanted on a bias, or has a slight curve, the facing cannot duplicate the grain and must be eased, stretched, mitered, or clipped to fit the edge smoothly.

The extended facing is used extensively in couture because the folded edge is flatter and more supple than the seamed edges of separate and bias facings and consequently drapes better.

The separate facing duplicates the shape of the edge it faces and often the grain as well. This facing is used on necklines and on edges intended to have a crisp, constructed look; it is also used on scalloped hems.

The bias facing is a strip cut on the true bias. Since it doesn't duplicate the grain of the edge it faces, this facing must itself be shaped to fit the edge. Bias facings are made from lightweight fabrics and produce a narrow, inconspicuous look.

In couture, more than one type of facing is often used on a single garment or even on a single edge. The dress shown at left has extended facings on the front neckline and back opening with separate facings on the back neckline. Similarly, the jacket shown on p. 66 has a separate facing on the upper half of the front edge and an extended facing on the lower half of this edge.

Before applying any kind of facing, examine the garment's fit to determine whether the edge needs to be held in or stabilized with a stay tape (see p. 54) or interfaced (see p. 73).

## SEPARATE FACINGS

Separate facings can be applied by hand or machine. Both types of applications are used in couture, while only machine applications are used in ready-to-wear. These directions are for applying the facing by hand.

Facings can be cut from the original garment pattern if the edge was not changed during the fitting process, or the garment itself can serve as a pattern. When the garment is used as a pattern, use the thread-traced neckline to establish a corresponding stitching line on the facing. A finished neckline can also be used as a guide when applying the facing by hand.

Neck facings can be cut in several shapes. Two of the most popular are the traditional circular shape, which measures an even width from the

This 1950s design from Hardy Amies features a scalloped neckline, a dropped waist, and a full skirt. The neckline is finished with separate facings.

(Photo by Ken Howie. Author's collection.)

## SHAPED FACINGS

| CIRCULAR FACING | RECTANGULAR FACING |
|---|---|
| 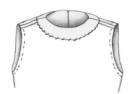 | 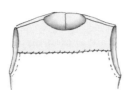 |

edge, and a rectangular shape, which extends into the armscye seams. When the larger shape is used, the facing edges can be anchored at the armscyes, to hold them smoothly in place. The facing shadow may also be less obtrusive with the larger shape, depending on the design. The obvious disadvantage of the larger facing is the additional fabric introduced into the shoulder area, which may give the garment a bulky appearance.

One solution for reducing some of this bulk is to relocate the seamlines on the facing ½ in. to 1 in. from their original positions. In couture, the seams on facings are not always aligned with the corresponding garment seamlines, as they are in ready-to-wear and home sewing.

These directions are for the less familiar rectangular facing. They can easily be adapted for a smaller facing or a lining.

1. Use the garment fabric or a lighter, firmly woven material for the facings. Begin with a large rectangle about 16 in. wide by 7 in. long for the front facing and two smaller ones about 8 in. wide

This silk print dress was designed by Cristobal Balenciaga in the 1950s. A wide facing finishes the neckline and armscyes. It is made of ribbon and finished with ribbon at the top and bottom. The dress had a wide waist stay originally, which was removed.

(Photo by Taylor Sherrill. Author's collection.)

by 6 in. long for the back facings. Adjust the sizes as needed for different garment sizes.

2. Finish the garment neckline before making the facing pattern. Tape or interface the edge as needed. Trim the seam allowance to ¾ in. Turn under the seam allowance; pin. Baste a generous ⅛ in. from the edge.

3. Wrong side up, place the neckline over a pressing cushion; steam and finger-press the edge. With your fingers, gently try to flatten the raw edge. If necessary, trim the edge to ¼ in. or ⅜ in. for firmly woven fabrics and slightly wider for less stable materials.

CLAIRE'S HINT *To minimize the seam allowance's tendency to curl around the neckline curve, snip shallow cuts into the raw edge every in. or so as needed to make the neckline seam allowance lie flat (see "Bias Facings" on p. 78). Don't clip through the basting stitches around the neck edge.*

4. Use loose catchstitches to sew the edge of the garment's seam allowance to the backing or interfacing. If the garment has neither a backing nor interfacing, sew carefully so the stitches do not show on the right side.

5. Cut a rectangle for each section to be faced. Before proceeding, I examine the bulk at the shoulder seams. If it's thick, I relocate the facing seams to redistribute the bulk.

6. Wrong sides together, match and pin the grainlines of the garment and its facing at center front.

7. Hold the neckline curved, as it will be when worn and smooth the facing in place, pinning as you go.

8. At the shoulder seams, smooth the front facing over the seams so the seam allowances are flat. Pin; then trim away the excess at the shoulders and neck edge, leaving ½-in. seam allowances on the facing.

9. Pin the back facing(s) in place. At the shoulders, trim and turn under the raw edges; pin and slipstitch.

10. At the neckline, trim away the excess, leaving a ½-in. seam allowance.

**MAKING FRONT FACING**

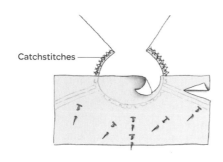

Catchstitches

**MAKING BACK FACING**

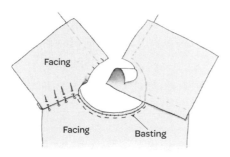

Facing

Facing    Basting

11. Wrong sides together, pin the facing to the garment. Turn under the raw edge so the facing is 1/16 in. to 1/4 in. below the garment edge and does not expose the clips on the garment seam allowance; pin.

12. With the facing toward you, baste the facing in place and press lightly. Use fell stitches or slipstitches to sew the facing to the neck edge.

13. Remove all bastings and press lightly.

## BIAS FACINGS

A bias facing is shaped, rather than cut, to duplicate the edge it faces. Well adapted to garments with soft edges, this facing is frequently used on blouses and dresses, and on lightweight silk and cotton fabrics. In couture workrooms, self-fabric is used if the garment is sewn from lightweight fabric, but if the fabric is heavy, lining can be used instead. Designer Mainbocher frequently used narrow chiffon facings for necklines, armscyes, and hems.

Bias facings are narrower, smoother, and less conspicuous than separate facings. Often cut from silk chiffon or organza as well as self-fabric, they may require less fabric. Bias and separate facings are generally more comfortable to wear next to the skin and sometimes more economical to sew. There are two disadvantages to these facings: the garment edge is rarely interfaced and may not be as smooth, and since the bias facing is usually slipstitched to the garment, it can be difficult to prevent the stitches from showing on the garment outside.

Most bias facings are finished to about 3/8 in. to 1/2 in. wide, but they can be as narrow as 1/4 in. on a jewel neckline and as wide as 2 in. at the waist of a skirt. Generally, the wider the bias facing, the more difficult it is to shape to a curved edge.

1. Before applying a bias facing, finish the garment edge. Fold the seam allowance to the wrong side and baste 1/8 in. to 1/4 in. from the edge. Clip as needed to make the edge lie flat. Wrong side up, press.

2. Measure the garment edge to be faced; cut a bias strip several inches longer, or join several strips to get the length you need. For a 1/2-in.-wide facing, cut the strip 1 in. wide for straight edges and 1 1/2 in. wide for curved edges.

3. On a straight garment edge, begin wrong sides together. Fold one long bias edge under 1/4 in.; align the folded bias edge with the basting, 1/8 in. to 1/4 in. below the garment edge. Pin.

4. For a shaped edge, press the bias; stretch slightly, and shape the strip to smoothly fit the edge. Wrong sides together, fold the bias edge under 1/4 in.; align the fold with the basting and baste.

### BIAS FACING

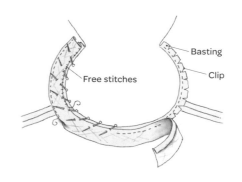

Basting

Clip

Free stitches

5. Wrong side up, place the edge over a pressing cushion; press just the edge and the bias strip. The facing should lie smoothly against the wrong side of the garment. If it doesn't, release the basting and try again.

CLAIRE'S HINT *I cover the section I'm pressing with a satin-faced organza press cloth. This allows me to see the section and protects the garment.*

6. Using slipstitches or fell stitches, sew the facing to the seam allowance.

7. Trim the bias to an even ¾ in. wide. To finish the bias, fold under ¼ in., pin, and baste.

8. With a very fine, short needle, make loose slipstitches or fell stitches to sew the edge to the garment. If the garment is backed, catch the backing but not the garment.

9. Remove the bastings and press lightly.

### Armscye Bias Facing

1. Finish the armscye using the directions above.

2. Beginning at the underarm, fold under the end and baste the bias around the armscye.

CLAIRE'S HINT *I apply the bias to the front armscye first because the deeper curve is more difficult to shape than the back; then I smooth it over the shoulder and around the back armscye.*

3. To finish the ends, turn under the remaining end; slipstitch the folds together.

4. Complete the facing using the directions above.

CLAIRE'S HINT *A neckline without an opening is very similar to an armscye, I begin at the left shoulder seam and work toward the front neckline because the front is more difficult to face due to a deeper curve.*

### Worth's Corded Facing.
Charles Frederick Worth frequently used a corded bias facing in a contrast or matching fabric to finish the edges of bodices. From the outside, the facing looks like a corded piping; from the reverse, it resembles the narrow bias facing described above.

1. Begin by finishing the edge using the bias facing directions above.

Fabricated in cloth of silver with cut and uncut velvet flowers, the waist edge of this Worth design from 1860 is finished with corded piping. This signature detail has two separate rows of piping. The first is cut with a narrow seam allowance and sewn in place; the second is cut so one seam allowance is wide enough to make a narrow bias facing on the wrong side.

(Photo by David Arky, courtesy of the Museum of the City of New York, gift of Miss Sarah Diodati Gardiner.)

2. Cut the bias 1 in. to 1¼ in. wide.

3. Wrong side up, place a very small cord on the bias ¼ in. from one edge.

4. Wrap the bias over the cord; baste close to the cord.

5. Wrong sides together, place and pin the facing on the garment so the cording shows just above the edge; baste. Using small running stitches, sew it permanently at the basting.

6. To finish, turn under the bias facing edge ¼ in.; fell stitch permanently.

CLAIRE'S HINT *If the edge has a corner, I miter the corner when I apply the facing and sew the fold flat with fellstitches.*

7. Remove the bastings.

# Bindings

An elegant finish suitable for nearly every edge, a binding is made by stitching a strip of fabric to the right side of an edge, wrapping it around the edge and securing it neatly on the underside. Often finished so they are attractive on both sides of the garment, bindings are frequently used on transparent fabrics, double-faced fabrics, and on reversible and unlined garments.

To shape and sew bindings to curved edges easily, most fabric bindings are cut on the true bias (at a 45° angle to the lengthwise grain). But if the garment edges are straight or almost straight, bindings can be cut on either the crossgrain or lengthwise grain to enhance the design. These directions focus on bias-cut bindings.

Most bindings are finished about ¼ in. wide; on very lightweight fabrics they can be as narrow as ⅛ in., and on bulky or heavy fabrics they can be as wide as 1 in. They can be made with either a single-layer, open strip of fabric or with a double-layer, folded strip. Obviously, bindings sewn from a double layer are stiffer and thicker because they contain more fabric, an advantage when the binding fabric is lightweight or when you want a sharply defined edge. When the binding fabric is heavy or bulky or the garment edge is designed to hang softly, a single-layer binding is more suitable.

Generally, bindings are not applied until the appropriate interfacings and backings have already been applied, the garment fitted, and all corrections made. On lined couture garments, the binding is frequently applied first by hand or machine, and the raw edge is covered by the lining.

## CUT AND STITCH THE BIAS STRIP

If you lived in Italy, you would visit your favorite *merceria*, or sewing-notions store, when you wanted to trim a design with bias bindings. There you would find a large assortment of fabrics already cut with one edge on the bias. After you chose your fabric, a salesperson would cut a parallelogram for you, which would be ready to be cut into bias strips. Unfortunately, bias is not sold like this in the

# Finishing Corners

**WHEN A FACING AND HEM MEET** at the corner of a jacket or coat opening, or skirt or sleeve vents, the bulk must be reduced for a smooth finish, either hemming the lower edge, trimming away some of the hem at the corner, and hemming the vertical edge, or by mitering. These directions are for a garment or garment section where the lining will cover the raw edges.

## MITERING A CORNER

**1.** Thread-trace the foldlines for the facing and hem.
**2.** Turn under and press the facing and hem using the thread tracings as a guide.
**3.** Mark where the raw edges meet with a pin.
**4.** Chalk-mark at the miter seamline from the pin to the corner on the hem.
**5.** Unfold the hem; chalk-mark the facing from pin to corner.
**6.** Fold the corner on the chalked lines; baste, backstitching at the corner. Press and trim to ¼ in.
**7.** Fold the facing and hem in place so the folded edges match; baste.
**8.** Baste the miter flat against the garment. Slipstitch; press lightly.
**9.** On an acute angle, the chalked and basted lines will form a wide

## MITERING A CORNER

**MAKING A RIGHT ANGLE**

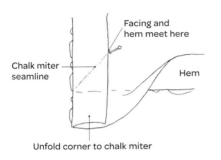

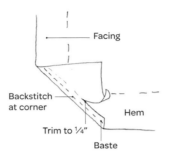

**MAKING AN ACUTE ANGLE**

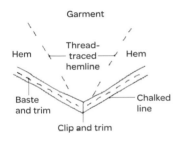

**MAKING AN OBTUSE ANGLE**

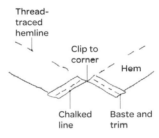

## HEMMING A CORNER

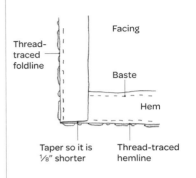

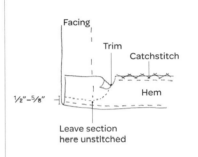

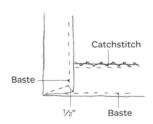

"V" from the corner. Clip to the corner and trim away the excess.
**10.** On an obtuse angle, the chalked and basted lines will be shaped like an inverted "V." Clip the seam allowance to the corner.

### HEMMING A CORNER

**1.** Thread-trace the foldlines for the facing and hem.
**2.** Wrong side up, turn under the hem using the thread tracings as a guide; baste. Press.

**3.** Turn under the facing, tapering the bottom of the facing from the corner to ⅛ in. shorter than hem; baste. Press lightly.
**4.** If the fabric is bulky, release the basting for the facing; trim.
**5.** Catchstitch the hem.
**6.** Baste the facing in place with the edge ½ in. tapered above the hemline; baste. Press lightly.
**7.** Hold back the lower edge of the facing; blindstitch to corner.
**8.** Catchstitch the raw edge of the facing to the hem.

CLAIRE'S HINT *When finishing the corners on flaps, pockets, and waistbands, after the corners and seam allowances are catchstitched, I apply the lining with wrong sides together.*

Americas; and, even though I've looked in stores in France and England, I haven't found it there either.

**Establishing True Bias.** Establishing true bias is particularly important because the strips must be cut exactly at a 45° angle or the finished bindings will ripple, twist, and pucker. The best way to establish the true bias is with a right triangle—a drafting tool that has two sides of equal length with a 90° angle in between.

1. Spread the fabric on the table. Mark the lengthwise grain about 1 in. from the selvage.
2. Straighten the fabric so the crossgrain is perpendicular to the lengthwise grain.

## MARKING BIAS

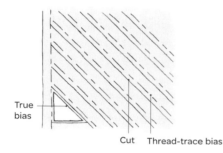

True bias

Cut     Thread-trace bias

3. Align one short side of the triangle with the grain. The other side will be on the crossgrain, and the long edge in between will mark the true bias.
4. Mark parallel lines on the bias first with chalk, then with thread tracing to mark the stitching lines. For single bindings, mark the strips 2 in. wide; and cut ¼ in. from the thread tracings. For double bindings, mark the strips about four times the finished width plus two ½-in. seam allowances; cut midway between the thread tracings.

**Join Bias Strips.** When the binding is applied prominently, such as on a neckline or lapel, try to avoid seaming the bias. For longer edges, join as many strips as needed for your length.
1. Trim all ends of the bias strips diagonally so they are on the desired grain—usually the lengthwise grain. When the fabric has a prominent cross-rib

## JOINING BIAS

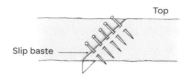

Top

Slip baste

or horizontal stripe, the seam will be less noticeable if the seam is parallel to the stripe or rib.
2. Right sides up, turn under ¼ in. at the end of one strip. Align the grainlines and pin it to another strip; slip-baste at the fold. Repeat until all the strips are basted together.
3. Refold the basted strips with right sides together; sew the seams with very short machine stitches (20 stitches/in.). Remove the bastings.
4. Press the seams flat, then open. Trim away the extended seam ends and trim the seams to ⅛ in.
5. To prepare the garment, thread-trace the seamline; then thread-trace a guideline for the binding seamline ¼ in.—or the width of the finished binding—below the seamline. Before proceeding, compare the neckline to the pattern to be sure they're the same. Don't trim away the seam allowance. The first thread-tracing marks the finished edge of the garment; the second marks the stitching line for sewing the binding.

Although bindings can be applied to almost any edge, the directions given here are for applying single and double bindings to a neckline, where they are most often sewn.

## NECK EDGE PREPARED
## FOR A BINDING

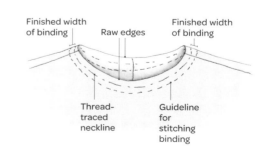

Finished width of binding    Raw edges    Finished width of binding

Thread-traced neckline    Guideline for stitching binding

## SINGLE BINDING

The couture method of applying a single binding has several advantages over the regular home-sewing method. It's worked right sides up, allowing you to see the binding as you shape it to fit the edge. It can also be made entirely by hand rather than by machine, which results in a softer finish. To determine the most suitable width for the finished binding, experiment with fabric scraps until you arrive at a size you like, then cut the strips.

1. Thread-trace the garment edge, and cut the bias strips so that the width of each strip is six times the desired finished width of the binding plus ½ in. (To make a finished ¼-in.-wide binding, for example, cut a bias strip 2 in. wide.) Press the strip, stretching it slightly lengthwise. Fold under one long edge of the bias ¼ in., regardless of the desired finished width, and baste ⅛ in. from the fold.

2. Working with the right sides up, align and pin the folded bias edge to the garment so it barely laps the binding seamline. To apply the bias smoothly to a neckline, hold the folded edge of the strip taut when pinning it in place.

3. Top-baste through all layers close to the folded edge and slip-baste the strip to the garment. Then remove the first row of basting that holds the

binding flat, unfold the strip so the right sides are together, and machine stitch over the basted line. Trim the seam allowance at the neckline, remove any bastings, and press lightly.

4. Fold the binding toward the neckline and finger-press the binding seam. Wrap the binding around the neckline's raw edge and finger-press again. Pin-baste the binding in place on the wrong side of the neckline, setting the pins just below the binding. Measure the binding width. If it is more than ¼ in., the finished neckline will probably be too tight. If this is the case, unpin the binding and trim the seam as needed to keep the finished binding width at ¼ in.

5. Fold the raw edge under so that the folded edge touches the seamline. If the folded edge overlaps the seamline, unfold the bias and trim it as needed to make a folded edge the width you need. Baste and then permanently fell or slipstitch the folded edge to the stitched line. Remove the bastings and press lightly.

6. Some binding fabrics are too bulky to produce a binding that looks the same on both sides. If the design has a lining that can be applied over the binding raw edge, bulk can be reduced. Sew the binding in place by hand with short running stitches. Then trim it ¼ in. below the seamline and apply the lining to cover the raw edge.

7. When binding outward curves, for example on collars and pockets, trim away the garment seam allowance. Ease the folded edge of the binding to the seamline so the bias is smooth at the raw edge. Then proceed as for neckline curve.

## DOUBLE BINDING

American couturier Charles Kleibacker had an unusual method for applying a double binding, which he used to finish and trim the edges of his lace designs and to sew wide bias bands in the place of skirt hems. He laid the bias strip flat on the table and applied the garment to the bias strip, instead of the reverse. Working this way makes it easier to control the bias binding and it produces fantastic results.

### SINGLE BINDING

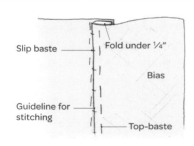

Slip baste

Fold under ¼"

Bias

Guideline for stitching

Top-baste

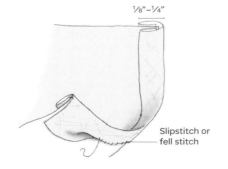

⅛"–¼"

Slipstitch or fell stitch

## DOUBLE BINDING

**PREPARING BINDING STRIP**

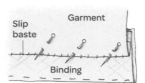

½" seam allowance

Baste ⅛"

2x binding width

Fold

**SEWING GARMENT TO BIAS STRIP**

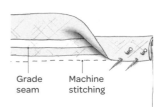

Slip baste

Garment

Binding

**FINISHING BINDING**

Grade seam

Machine stitching

Because the finished binding for this application method will consist of at least seven layers, the weight and bulk of the binding fabric are particularly important and must be taken into account when deciding the width of the finished bias. Medium-weight fabrics such as 4-ply silk and silk linen are suitable for bindings ranging from ¼ in. to several inches wide. For bindings as narrow as ⅛ in., lightweight crepes, chiffon, and organza can be used.

The instructions here are for a finished ¼-in.-wide binding. They can be modified to make a very narrow ⅛-in.-wide binding or one that's several inches wide.

1. Cut the bias strip four times the finished width plus two ½-in.-wide seam allowances. For a finished binding ¼ in. wide, cut the strip 2 in. wide.

This narrow bias facing was frequently used by Mainbocher instead of a wide facing. Made of silk chiffon, it is lightweight, inconspicuous, and easy to apply.

(Photo by Author, courtesy of the Museum of the City of New York.)

2. Wrong sides together, fold the strip in half lengthwise and baste about ⅛ in. from the fold.
3. Place the strip flat on the table with the fold toward you. Using chalk, mark a line an even distance from the folded edge and equal to twice the finished width. For a ¼-in.-wide binding, mark ½ in. from the fold. Baste through both layers on the chalked line to mark the seamline.
4. On the garment, thread-trace the finished edge and the seamline for the binding, spread the garment flat on the table right side up with the edge to be bound toward you.
5. Using the thread-traced seamline as a guide, fold under the garment edge ¼ in.; pin.

On a neckline or concave curve, the turned-under edge is shorter than the garment section. To do this neatly and without stretching the neckline, I clip as needed and fold under a small section at a time.
6. Match and pin the folded edge of the garment to the binding seamline on the bias strip (the one farther from the folded edge of the bias strip). Baste the garment to the binding, using a small fell stitch or slip-basting. Reposition the layers with right sides together. Machine stitch over the basted seamline. Remove the basting and press lightly.
7. Trim away the original thread-traced seam allowance on the neckline to reduce bulk. Wrap the binding around this raw edge. The folded edge of the binding should just meet the stitched line on the wrong side, and the finished binding should measure ¼ in. wide. If it doesn't, trim the garment edge a little more. If the binding is wider on a neckline edge, it may be too tight and uncomfortable to wear.

8. Grade the seam allowances as needed. Pin the binding in place.

I set the pins at an angle with the heads toward the neckline so it's easy to baste over them.

9. Use fell stitches to sew the folded edge to the stitched line.

## FINISH BINDING ENDS

Bindings often begin and end at garment openings, such as neckline plackets and zipper closures. For a smooth, inconspicuous finish, fold the ends of the binding to the wrong side before wrapping the binding around the edge.

1. Complete the opening and trim away any excess bulk before beginning the binding. Pin the bias to the garment, allowing a 1-in. extension of the bias strip on each side of the opening.

2. Stitch the strip to the right side of the garment and fold the end of the bias strip at the opening to the wrong side.

3. Trim the folded end to about ½ in. and sew it with a catchstitch to the wrong sides of the bias strip and garment. Repeat for the other end. If the opening has a hook, eye, or button loop, sew it in

place now so the end will be hidden between the layers of the binding.

**Seaming Bias.** On couture and good-quality ready-to-wear garments, bindings applied to edges without openings (for example, circular necklines, armholes, sleeve edges, and skirt hems) usually have the ends seamed on grain. Before beginning such bindings, decide where to locate the seam so it will be as inconspicuous as possible on the finished design. On necklines, the seam is usually deemed least conspicuous at the left shoulder; on armholes and the edges of sleeves, under the arm; and, on hems, at the left side seam.

1. Prepare a bias strip that's long enough to allow for a 4-in. tail on each end of the strip. Pin the bias strip to the garment. Fold back one tail on the lengthwise grain with wrong sides of the bias together and pin it in place. Repeat for the other end so the folded edges meet.

2. Slip-baste the folds together. Unpin the bias about 1 in. on either side of the basted seamline so you can stitch the basted seam easily, or use a short backstitch to sew the seam by hand. Press the seam open and trim the seam allowances to ¼ in.

3. Repin the bias to the edge and complete the binding, which encases the raw edges of the seam.

### FINISHING BINDING ENDS

**AT AN OPENING**

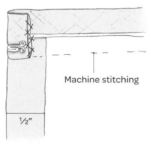

Machine stitching

½"

**ON EDGE WITHOUT OPENING**

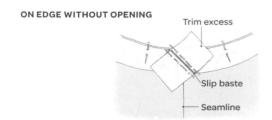

Trim excess

Slip baste

Seamline

This narrow bias binding on a chiffon blouse is from Yves Saint Laurent's Russian collecion. A narrow metallic braid was then applied to the silk charmeuse.

(Photo by Author, courtesy of the Museum of the City of New York.)

# 5

# Closures

The word "closure" refers to both an opening or placket in a garment and to the fastener that joins an opening. Closures can be inconspicuous or ornamental. They can be located in seamlines or in slashes in the garment. They can be lapped or abutted, straight or shaped, visible or invisible, and even wiggling and winding in a seemingly haphazard fashion within the garment's design.

Plackets can extend 2 or 3 in. from a garment edge or run the entire length of a garment. They can be located at the upper or lower edge of a garment section or within the body of the garment. They can be closed with any type of fastener, including zippers, hooks and eyes, snaps, or buttons with buttonholes or button loops.

In couture, the type of closure a garment will have, even when it's inconspicuous, is planned long before construction begins. The choice of closure depends on the garment's design and function, its fabric, the desired effect, and the closure location. For example, a bound buttonhole would rarely be used on a sheer fabric, and buttons would generally be avoided under the arm.

Designed by Marc Bohan for Dior, this beautiful evening gown has a very convoluted placket that, when fastened, completely obscures the zipper. If you look closely, you can see the zipper pull about 2 in. below the neckline.

(Photo by Brian Sanderson, courtesy of FIDM Museum at the Fashion Institute of Design & Merchandising, Los Angeles, CA; gift of Mrs. Alfred Bloomingdale, Spring/Summer 1992.)

garment design. Usually fastened with buttons and buttonholes, snaps, or zippers, these plackets can be lapped to produce a fly opening or abutted to make an inverted pleat.

**Fly Placket.** A favorite of many designers, the fly placket is frequently used on blouses, dresses, and suit skirts. Some fly plackets are topstitched, while others are left plain. The underlays, however, are made by hand and fastened with buttons and buttonholes or occasionally with snaps.

1. To plan the placket, decide first if the edge will be topstitched. If so, cut the extended facing ¼ in. to ½ in. wider than the finished width of the topstitching. Otherwise, cut the facing 1½ in. to 2 in. wide. Finish the facing and overcast the edge. Topstitch the garment section if planned.

2. For the underlay on a blouse or dress, cut a rectangle on the lengthwise grain 3 in. longer than the opening and 4 in. wide.

3. Right sides together, fold the underlay lengthwise. Baste, stitch the long raw edges ¼ in. from the edges. Overcast the edges at the sides and bottom.

4. Turn the underlay right side out; press.

Designed by Yves Saint Laurent in the 1970s, the bodice on this attractive dress fastens with a fly or concealed placket to the waist.

(Photo by Taylor Sherrill. Author's collection.)

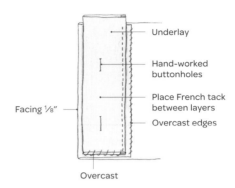

Underlay

Hand-worked buttonholes

Facing ⅛"

Place French tack between layers

Overcast edges

Overcast

5. Assemble the blouse and finish the hem; don't finish the neckline. On the underlay, mark the buttonhole locations and make hand-worked buttonholes.

6. Wrong side up, place the underlay on the facing so the facing shows about ⅛ in. at the front edge; baste. Using short running stitches, sew it permanently.

7. Use short thread tacks between buttonholes to join the underlay to the facing layer only.

8. Finish the neckline with a facing or collar. Remove all bastings.

## MULTIPLE PLACKETS

A multiple placket is composed of two or more plackets located at the same or nearby positions on different layers of the garment. Double, triple, and occasionally even quadruple plackets are a necessity for a design with a built-in foundation. The design of multiple plackets runs the gamut from a pair of simple center-back or underarm zippers on a dress and accompanying slip to far more convoluted combinations like the trio I saw on a Lanvin evening gown with a draped surplice bodice over an attached silk slip. The slip itself fastened under the arm with hooks and eyes. The left front bodice fastened to the slip with hooks and eyes at center front, and the right bodice similarly attached to the left bodice. Since the surplice edge was irregular, the hooks and eyes wiggled and wound from neckline to waist to create an invisible closure.

Fabricated in silk chiffon, this Valentino blouse from the mid-1980s has a double placket to accommodate a close-fitting underblouse and a pleated overblouse. The underblouse is closely fitted and fastens with a zipper. The overblouse fastens with small chiffon-covered snaps that allow it to drape softly.

(Photo by Taylor Sherrill. Author's collection.)

# Button Closures

Button closures are often an intrinsic part of a garment's design. They can serve as decorative accents as well as utilitarian fasteners and can be made from all kinds of materials.

Buttons can be used with a variety of buttonholes. Bound, hand-worked, and faced buttonholes, as well as button loops, are commonly used in couture. The choice depends on the garment's style, function and fabric; the desired finished effect, the location, and the designer's preference. Sometimes the choice is straightforward, and sometimes not. Generally, bound buttonholes are used on soft feminine designs such as afternoon and cocktail dresses. Hand-worked buttonholes are most often used on fine lingerie, traditional menswear-tailored designs, and skirts. In-seam buttonholes are frequently used on structured garments and crisp

fabrics. Faced buttonholes are reserved for unusual shapes, furs, and imitation-fur fabrics.

## MARK THE BUTTONHOLE

Regardless of the style of buttonhole you choose, the garment should be carefully prepared before you actually sew the buttonhole. All buttonholes should be identical in length and width, spaced evenly, and located an equal distance from the garment edge unless it's a novelty design. The garment should always be interfaced appropriately before buttonholes are made. If it's not, it won't maintain its shape, and the buttonholes won't wear well.

The thread-traced lines marking the garment centers are particularly important when fitting garments with button closures. They are always matched and pinned for each fitting so the closures are accurately positioned.

1. Measure the button's diameter and thickness.
CLAIRE'S HINT *To measure the diameter, I wrap a narrow strip of selvage, tape, or ribbon around the button, and pin the ends together. After removing the button and without unpinning the strip, I measure the distance between the strip's fold and the pin and add ⅛ in., since buttonholes, when worked, tend to shrink a little. This is the measurement I use to make a sample buttonhole.*

2. Slip the button through the sample buttonhole. If the buttonhole is the least bit tight, it won't wear well. Once you have determined the buttonhole length, thread-trace horizontal placement lines to indicate each buttonhole location and vertical lines to mark the ends of the buttonholes (see the drawing on p. 93).

## BOUND BUTTONHOLES

A bound buttonhole has two fabric welts that meet at the opening. This buttonhole is sewn in two separate steps: the first step finishes the buttonhole on the right side of the garment, and the second step finishes it on the inside or facing side. There are various methods for making bound

## MARK AND BASTE FLY ZIPPER

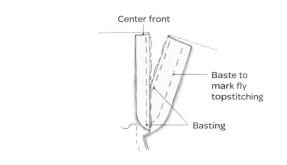

Center front

Baste to mark fly topstitching

Basting

## STITCH OPENING

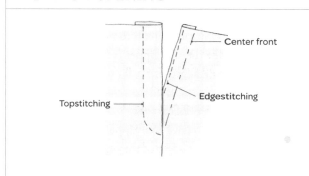

Center front

Edgestitching

Topstitching

## SEW ZIPPER TO UNDERLAP

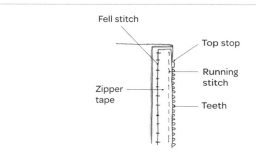

Fell stitch

Top stop

Running stitch

Zipper tape

Teeth

## SEW ZIPPER TO FLY

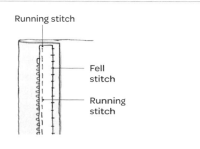

Running stitch

Fell stitch

Running stitch

zipper foot; and when fabrics are thick, the zipper placket is more secure than when it is stitched by hand. These directions are for a fly opening, but they can be adapted easily for any zipper. Since the fly opening is rarely altered, the zipper can be set before the first fitting.

1. Prepare the opening.

Turn under, baste, and press the opening's seam allowances. Mark the stitching lines on the overlap with basting so the layers will not shift when topstitched.

2. Select the thread and machine stitch length to correspond with other topstitching details on the garment. Stitch the fly opening as marked. Remove the bastings; press.

3. Position the folded edge of the placket's underlap close to the zipper teeth, with any excess zipper at the bottom of the opening length, and baste the zipper in place. Close the zipper and baste the garment together at the center front to position the zipper on the underneath side of the overlap.

4. Turn the garment wrong side up and baste the zipper on to the overlap facing. Sew the zipper permanently by hand with short running stitches strengthened by an occasional backstitch.

# Hooks and Eyes and Snaps

Hooks and eyes and snaps are frequently used instead of zippers in couture. Available in several sizes, hooks can be used with a straight or round metal eye, round ring, or a thread bar, which is less conspicuous but considerably weaker.

## HOOKS AND EYES

For skirt closures, the French prefer a fastener that's similar to the large coat hooks available in America. Since this hook is flat between the eyelets, it can be sewn to the wrong side of the waistband before the facing or lining is applied. The facing or lining can then be sewn in place by hand so only the hook itself (not the eyelets) is exposed.

1. Use mercerized cotton or machine silk thread that matches the garment; wax the thread for strength.

2. To be sure the hooks and eyes are aligned correctly, sew the hooks first; then sew the eyes.

3. When the hooks will be covered by a facing or lining, sew the end and the eyelets with backstitches. When the eyelets on the hooks and eyes will not be covered, use blanket stitches to sew around the eyelets. When making a thread eye, follow the directions for thread bars on p. 36.

For added security when sewing hooks at a placket on a waist stay or corselette, alternate the hooks and eyes so each side of the opening has both hooks and eyes. To make them less noticeable on delicate fabrics such as chiffon, lightweight metallics, and lace, bend the hook so the two eyelets are on top of each other.

## SNAPS

Snaps are even less conspicuous than hooks and eyes because they are easy to cover with fabric, but they're not nearly as strong. Used on lapped edges in couture, they are usually combined with another fastener or used on loosely fitted designs and on overskirts. When used on coats and jackets, they are generally covered with a lightweight lining fabric in a matching color.

1. Sew the snap ball to the overlap using a single strand of thread; secure the thread and make several stitches in the first hole without sewing through to the outside of the garment. After the last stitch in the first hole, run the needle between the fabric layers to the next hole. Repeat until all holes are sewn.

2. To mark the location for the snap socket, rub the ball with chalk and arrange the garment in the snapped position. Firmly press the two edges together to mark the socket's position. Sew the socket in place the same way as the ball.

3. You can use a hanging snap instead of a hook and eye at the top of a zipper placket as well as on other openings. Sew only one hole of the socket to one side of the opening; sew the ball to the facing on the other side.

### Covered Snaps

1. Cut two circles of lining fabric twice the diameter of the snap. Knot the thread and overcast the edge of one circle.

2. Place the ball facedown on the circle; pull up the thread. Sew across the back of the snap several times to flatten the fabric. Fasten the thread securely and repeat for the snap socket.

3. Snap the two sections together to make the hole at the center of the snap socket.

SNAP

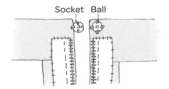

Socket   Ball

# PART TWO

# Applying
## Couture Techniques

On this pale pink princess-line dress from Chanel, the double-corded trim was appliquéd to the neck edge and armscyes. Notice the princess seaming that begins at the neck point.

(Photo by Ken Howie. Author's collection.)

# Skirts & Pants

WHETHER LONG OR SHORT, straight or full, skirts have historically made fashion news. One of the most controversial styles was French couturier Paul Poiret's hobble skirt, which he introduced in 1910. It was so narrow—only 12 in. wide below the knees—that to avoid splitting the seams, a woman wore a hobble garter, or strap of fabric that held the ankles

From the early 1950s, this stunning skirt by Mainbocher is pleated with a shaped yoke to flatter the figure and fit smoothly under the suit jacket, which is shown on p. 147. Like many Mainbocher designs, the fabric is a wool tweed and showcases his attention to detail; the yoke is applied to the pleats by hand.

(Photo by Ken Howie. Author's collection.)

together. By contrast, Christian Dior's New Look skirts, designed about in 1947, were so full that some required as much as 25 yds. of fabric.

A variety of silhouettes came and went in the decade after the New Look, but all skirts remained relatively long. In 1957, in his first collection at the House of Dior, Yves Saint Laurent shortened skirts and raised the waistline, paving the way for the miniskirt, which dominated the 1960s. In addition to the mini, the 1960s saw long romantic skirts traditional ethnic designs, and maxiskirts.

Loose trousers, on the other hand, weren't included in haute couture collections until 1911, when Poiret showed Turkish trousers with limited success. In 1964 the pants revolution began in earnest, when André Courrèges presented pantsuits featuring narrow pants with hems that curved into slits in the front and dropped below the heel in back.

Three years later, Yves Saint Laurent introduced two important trendsetters: the smoking suit and the daytime trouser suit, a feminine version of the man's business suit. He later introduced the culotte suit in 1968 and the safari suit in 1969.

When examined on the inside, couture skirts and pants are relatively easy to identify. The greater part of a skirt or pair of pants is often sewn by hand, including zippers, overcast seams, pleats, darts, waistline finishes, and hems on the lining as well as on the garment itself.

# Waistbands

Only three techniques are used extensively in couture for finishing the waist edges of skirts and pants: the self-fabric band, the faced band, and the faced edge, which does not have a band. Appropriate for lined or unlined skirts, the faced waistband is finished with a lining fabric facing or grosgrain ribbon applied by hand. This versatile method is suitable for a variety of waistband designs, fabrics, and figures, and can be easily adapted for pants (see p. 121) and applied to patch pockets, belts, tabs, and even facings.

### PREPARE THE WAISTBAND

Sewn from the same fabric as the skirt, the waistband can be cut on the lengthwise grain or crossgrain if the fabric pattern is being matched. It's rarely cut on the more easily shaped bias, except when it matches the blouse fabric and a bias cut is unnoticeable. Most finished bands are 1 in. to 1¼ in. wide. They can fasten with lapped or abutted ends. Use these directions for self-fabric and faced bands.

1. To determine the finished length of the band, measure your waist and add 1-in. ease.

CLAIRE'S HINT *I use a muslin strip instead of a tape measure; pin it around my waist; and sit down to be sure it's comfortable. Then I measure the strip.*

2. Thread-trace the band's finished length and desired width on a large fabric scrap, leaving at least ½-in. seam allowance on all sides and 3-in. extra length, if you plan to lap the ends.

Thread-trace all matchpoints and guidelines at garment centers, side seams, and the foldline for a self-fabric waistband. When planning a lap on the skirt back, I place the underlap on the right back.

3. Cut the interfacing the width and length of the finished band. If the fabric is medium- to heavyweight, choose a crisp interfacing material like hair canvas, tailor's linen, Petersham, woven belting or grosgrain ribbon. For lightweight fabrics, select woven belting or grosgrain ribbon. If the band is wide or shaped, the interfacing should be crisper than for a straight, narrow band. If one layer of interfacing isn't crisp enough, use two or more layers.

CLAIRE'S HINT *I use hair canvas scraps and quilt two layers together using zigzag stitches with rows spaced about ¼ in. apart.*

4. Wrong side up, baste the interfacing to the band.

### SELF-FABRIC BAND

Sometimes called a regular or one-piece waistband, the self-fabric band is used on light- and medium-weight fabrics.

SELF-FABRIC BAND

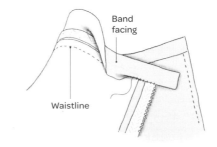

Band facing

Waistline

1. Using the directions on p. 161, apply the interfacing to the thread traced band. Catchstitch the edges of the interfacing to the band.

2. Wrong sides together, fold the waistband on the foldline. Use steam to shape the band for a smoother fit, stretch the upper edge so it's long enough to fit smoothly around the rib cage. To create a longer line for a short-waisted figure, stretch the bottom of the band so the top edge sits at the waistline.

3. Right sides together, align the matchpoints on the band and skirt; baste. Machine stitch and trim the seam to ½ in.

4. Remove the bastings and press the seam toward the band.

5. Right sides together, fold the band on the fold-line, baste the ends without catching the skirt. Stitch.

6. Press the seams open, trim, and turn the band right side out.

7. To finish the band, turn under the raw edge like a blouse cuff and fell stitch the folded edge to the seamline.

CLAIRE'S HINT *On many Balenciaga skirts, the waistband seam allowance is not turned under; instead, it is trimmed away to reduce bulk and the raw edge is overcast by hand. Then the edge is sewn to the seamline. If the band has a lap, the trimmed section is sewn to the band's seam allowance on the lap.*

## FACED WAISTBAND

The faced waistband is smoother and thinner than the self-fabric waistband. It is shaped and sewn almost completely by hand.

1. Using the directions on the facing page, apply the interfacing to the thread traced band. When

Here you can see the inside of a faced waistband on a skirt from Yves Saint Laurent. Lined with silk charmeuse and interfaced with hair canvas, the band is comfortable to wear and very thin.

(Photo by Author.)

sewing on wool and hair fibers, press to marry the fibers of the interfacing and fabric.

2. Wrap and pin the seam allowances around the interfacing and baste them in place for the fitting. Don't worry about the bulk at the corners.

3. Use steam to shape the band for a smoother fit, stretching the upper edge so it's long enough to fit smoothly around the rib cage.

4. Baste the band to the skirt for the fitting. If the band rolls, the interfacing is not crisp enough, the band is too tight, or the fabric is unusually bulky. Lengthen the band so it's comfortable using some of the 3-in. lap.

5. After the fitting, mark any corrections with contrasting thread. Remove the band.

6. Release the bastings holding the seam allowances in place at the ends and lower edge. Remove just enough of the bastings at the top of the band to release the ends. Trim the interfacing so it extends only 2 in. beyond the opening and does not extend into the end seam allowance.

7. Right sides together, baste the lower edge of the band to the skirt, aligning the seamlines and matchpoints; stitch. Remove the basting and press the seam flat, then open and press the waist seam toward the band.

CLAIRE'S HINT *When the fabric is bulky, I clip the skirt seam allowance about 1 in. from the end of the band.*

8. Grade the skirt seam allowance so the raw edge is about ⅛ in. below the raw edge of the band seam allowance.

9. On most light- and medium-weight fabrics, the corners of the band can be finished neatly without mitering. Baste next to the interfacing at the ends. Taper the end seam allowances so they won't show when the ends are folded under. Trim away a small triangle at the end of the interfacing. Trim at the center so they don't overlap; press.

10. Fold under the ends of the band, baste them in place and press again. Spank the ends briskly with a clapper to flatten them. Trim away any stray threads and sew the ends securely with small

## FITTING AND SHAPING PANTS

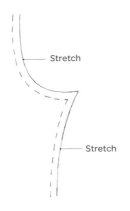

Stretch

Stretch

13. Turn the legs wrong side out and press the seams open.

14. Turn the legs right side out, lay one pants leg flat on a lightly padded pressing board with the inseam uppermost. Smooth the leg from the creaselines toward the crotch so the excess fullness is near the inseam. Press the front crease from waist to hemline.

On tailored pants, press the back crease on the grain, stopping at the crotch or about 3 in. below the crotch. On dressy pants, don't press a back crease. Leave the pants leg on the pressing board until it dries completely. Repeat to press the remaining leg.

CLAIRE'S HINT *When pressing hard-to-crease fabrics, I rub the wrong side of the crease with a bar of Ivory soap and press again; the soap works as a temporary adhesive and sets the crease more firmly.*

15. Baste and sew the crotch seam. The crotch seam is stressed more than most seams on a garment. To prevent ripping on English bespoke trousers, the back crotch seam is handsewn with backstitches to build stretch into the seam so it lasts for the life of the garment. Use a waxed, double thread.

16. Press the crotch seam flat, then press the upper part of the seam open. The curved section can be pressed flat or open.

CLAIRE'S HINT *When pressing the seam open, I trim the curved section to ½ in. Using the iron, I stretch the raw edges as much as possible. With one leg stuffed into the other, fold the seam allowances back against the inside of the pants. Press the crotch seam again.*

## HEMS AND CUFFS

Straight pants are usually considered more attractive when they are about ¾ in. shorter in front than in back. If the front is long enough to cover part of the instep at the side, the front crease will probably have a break. Although this is acceptable, you may prefer to avoid a break by adjusting the hem length so the fronts just skim the instep. A break at the back crease is far less acceptable than one at the front and should be eliminated.

1. For a shaped hem, thread-trace the hemline so the front is straight and the back curves down over the heel. Measure and mark the hem allowance 1½ in. to 2 in. wide; trim away any excess.

CLAIRE'S HINT *Since the hem allowance is sometimes shorter than the edge it finishes, I stretch the raw edge at center front so it can be turned back smoothly. If it won't stretch enough, I clip the hem allowance and overcast the clipped edges. At center back, I shrink out the excess hem allowance and, when this isn't possible, I make a small dart and sew it flat.*

2. Fold the hem in place, and baste ¼ in. from the edge; press and overcast the edge (see p. 70.)
3. Baste again at the top of the hem allowance; and blindstitch permanently.

**Hems on Lightweight Fabrics.** Pants made of lightweight fabrics frequently don't have enough weight to hang smoothly. This can be corrected by adding cuffs, placing weights in the hems; and if the hem has been finished, adding a hem or heel stay.

Bespoke tailors leave a 5-in. hem allowance just in case the client wants cuffs. When adding cuffs, make the hem allowance ¼ in. narrower than the finished cuff width so the hem can be finished with a catchstitch and the edge will not need overcasting. Anchor the finished cuffs inconspicuously at each seamline with a ⅛-in. thread chain between the cuff and pants (see p. 37).

# Belt and Hanger Loops

**BELT LOOPS ARE FREQUENTLY** used in couture on sport skirts and tailored trousers. They are used less often on dressy skirts. Most belt loops are finished ¼ in. to ⅜ in. wide and ⅜ in. to ½ in. longer than the band width. Generally, skirts have a loop at the top of each vertical seamline; and pants have loops at the center back, side seams, and tops of the front and back creases.

## LIGHT- AND MEDIUM-WEIGHT FABRICS

**1.** Cut a fabric strip 1½ in. wide and 3 in. long.

**2.** Right sides together, fold the strip lengthwise; stitch a generous ¼ in. from the fold. Press the seam open and trim it to ⅛ in.

**3.** Use a tube turner or a tapestry needle and buttonhole twist to turn the loop right side out. Center the seam on the underside; press.

**4.** Topstitch the loop if desired.

**5.** Repeat for additional loops.

## HEAVY OR BULKY FABRICS

**1.** Cut the fabric strip ⅝ in. wide and 3 in. long.

**2.** Wrong side up, fold the long edges to meet at the center; baste and press.

**3.** Using catchstitches, sew the raw edges together permanently.

**4.** Topstitch the loop; press.

## HANGER LOOPS

Hanger loops are used on better ready-to-wear, as well as haute couture garments—usually at the waistlines of dresses with heavy skirts; and on strapless, halters, and one-shoulder designs; skirts, and pants. Designed to reduce wrinkling and damage when the garment is hung for storage, the loops vary in location depending upon the garment style, but many are located at the side seams.

**1.** Cut a piece of lightweight lining 1½ in. wide and 8 in. long. For special-occasion dresses, cut the fabric strip as long as needed so the loops can be attached at the waist and support the hung garment without wrinkling the bodice.

**2.** Using the directions for lightweight belt loops, stitch and turn the loops.

**3.** Position the seamline at one edge; press.

**4.** Turn under the ends and hand sew them to the inside of the garment about ½ in. from the seamline. On strapless gowns, attach the ends at the waist. Make a thread bar about ½ in. from the upper edge to hold the strap. To hang, thread the hanger loop through the thread bar; then place it on the hanger.

### BELT LOOP

Trim seam to ⅛"     ⅜"

---

Unfortunately, the need for extra weight at the hems may not be apparent until the pants are finished. To correct this problem, a heel stay can be sewn to the hem allowance. Most are sewn to the back of the pants, but they can be sewn on the front as well. In addition to adding weight to the cuff, the heel stay will protect the hem from wear.

To make the stay, cut a self-fabric strip 6 in. long and 2 in. wide. Wrong side up, fold the long edges to the center; press. Overcast the ends. Place the stay on the back hem allowance just above the hemline. Fell stitch the stay in place without stitching into the pants.

# 7

# Blouses & Dresses

DRESSES, AND BEFORE THEM, robes and gowns, have been worn by women since the mid-14th century. Blouses (or, more accurately, shirts) became part of women's wardrobes in the 17th century, when women adapted men's fashions for riding. In the first half of the 20th century, blouses were worn primarily for sports and leisure or as an integral part of an ensemble.

This dress from the 1960s skims the body attractively. Attributed to Emanuel Ungaro, it was worn with a matching jacket, shown on p. 186. The dress has a square armscye and funnel neck. The neck area has been interfaced with hair canvas to maintain its unusual shape.

(Photo by Ken Howie. Author's collection.)

Then in the late 1940s, Givenchy created a collection of mix-and-match separates for Schiaparelli's Paris boutique.

As costume historian Robert Riley noted in his catalog for the 1982 exhibition "Givenchy, 30 Years" at the Fashion Institute of Technology in New York City, the designer's notion that a lady could travel for extended periods without transporting a lot of clothing changed the wardrobes of women of all classes.

At first glance, couture dresses and blouses may be difficult to distinguish from luxury ready-to-wear. Yet on closer inspection, you'll find differences, among them, hand-worked or bound buttonholes (never machine-stitched), hand-sewn zippers, and matched fabric patterns at seamlines, darts and pockets, sometimes even when the fabric is a single-color jacquard weave on couture.

And you will notice that couture dresses are unlined—a common practice in couture since linings add bulk and may adversely affect the drape of the garment. You will also immediately see all the handwork on a couture garment, including hand-stitched seams, hems and facings, and raw edges beautifully finished.

You might also find that the couture garment is backed (usually in silk) and a variety of details have been employed, such as stays, lingerie straps, French tacks, silk-covered shoulder pads, hip pads, and bust enhancers.

## Dressmaking Basics

Today the vast majority of couture blouses and dresses are made in the dressmaking workroom of the couture houses, where the staff specializes in sewing silks and other soft fabrics. More tailored dresses, such as the Dior trapeze dress, shown on the facing page, are made in the couture house's tailoring workroom.

Blouses and dresses are more difficult to sew than most skirts for several reasons. Their design is usually more complex, and fitting the upper torso is much more demanding than fitting the lower torso—unless, you are fitting pants.

Blouses and dresses are usually made from lighter-weight fabrics than skirts. They require more skill to sew and rarely drape like the muslin toile. Unlike wool, which is often used for skirts, many dress and blouse fabrics cannot be shaped with heat and moisture because they are more firmly woven, less elastic, and less able to shrink or stretch.

Blouses and dresses frequently rely on backings or underpinnings to establish and preserve their silhouette. Backings add body and stability to lightweight and fragile fabrics, which consequently hold their shape better and are less stressed at seamlines. Backings also serve as a buffer between the shell fabric and seam, hem, and facing edges; they keep these edges from showing on the right side of the garment. Cut to duplicate each of

the main sections of the garment, the backings are immediately basted to the wrong side of the corresponding garment sections. When the garment is assembled, the two fabrics are handled as one.

Underpinnings like slips, petticoats, pantaloons, corselettes, and waist cinchers provide support for the design and control the figure. The small sampling in this chapter of couture dressmaking techniques for underpinnings is intended to supplement, not replace, standard pattern guides.

## Fitting Blouses and Dresses

Fitting the toile is one of the first tasks because many changes are difficult, and sometimes impossible, to make after the garment fabric is cut. You can slash, lap, dart, and otherwise adjust a toile as much as needed before you cut into the garment fabric.

When fitting a dress with a seam at the waist, fit the bodice and skirt separately, using the fitting principles found on p. 116. If the design has shoulder pads, make and baste them in before you begin fitting. At the fitting, remember that blouses and dresses have more ease than the basic sloper bodice.

When fitting a blouse or dress without a seam at the waist, fit the toile using the basic principles described on p. 128 for fitting a bodice. Avoid overfitting the toile, which may destroy the lines of the design.

## Backing the Garment

Backings lend support to a blouse or dress. The backing fabric can be soft and its effect subtle, as in the silk Dior dress on p. 131. The silk charmeuse backing gently supports the garment design. Or the backing fabric can be crisp and add body, as it does in the trapeze dress designed by Yves Saint Laurent for Dior in 1958 (see the facing page). In this dress, several layers of crisp backing are combined with an interfacing.

When backing a blouse or dress, select the backing fabric carefully. It shouldn't be heavier

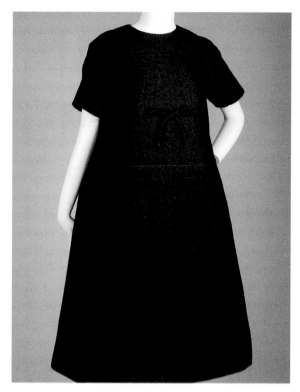

The "Trapeze" design was introduced by Yves Saint Laurent in 1958 in his first collection for the House of Dior. The clean, crisp lines of this afternoon dress are supported by silk organza backings and a specially designed slip.

(Courtesy of the Chicago History Museum.)

select organza, marquisette, shantung, taffeta, handkerchief linen, traditional interfacings, or hair canvas. Self-fabric, if it's neither bulky nor heavy, can also be a good choice. Experiment by matching your garment fabric with various backings until you are happy with how it drapes. Although the backing won't show, don't be tempted to choose an inexpensive material.

1. Preshrink all backing and shell fabrics before cutting; most can be preshrunk by pressing them wrong side up with a steam iron. For backing fabrics such as silk organza, China silk, handkerchief linen, or cotton batiste, soak the fabric in a basin of warm water and hang it to air dry to prevent later shrinkage.

2. Cut the backing and shell fabrics. If the shell fabric is crisp, or if the shell and backing fabrics are similar in elasticity, such as silk jacquard and silk charmeuse, cut the backing and shell the same. If the shell fabric is elastic, like wool, cut the backing a little wider than the garment and ease in the excess fullness. This prevents the backing from restricting the elasticity of the shell fabric.

3. To cut the backing, use either the toile or garment sections as a pattern. Mark the garment centers, stitching lines, hemline, and matchpoints on the backing with a tracing wheel and dressmaker's carbon.

CLAIRE'S HINT *I use a large piece of white dressmaker's carbon and a stiletto tracing wheel. Tape the tracing carbon to a large piece of cardboard so the fabric is clearly marked.*

4. Wrong side up, place the garment on the table; place the backing on top; match and pin the centers together.

5. If you don't plan to full the backing, match the seamlines precisely.

6. When fulling in backing, adjust and pin it so its vertical seamlines are about 1/8 in. inside the thread traced corresponding seamlines on the garment. This is the measurement to begin with if you are unsure of how much to full in the backing.

than the shell fabric, but it can be crisper if your design calls for a more exaggerated silhouette. Its drape should be similar to that of the shell fabric so it doesn't restrict the hang of the design, and it should be firmly woven to avoid seam slippage when the seams are stressed. Since the backing often lies next to the skin, it should be a fabric that absorbs perspiration, feels luxurious, and is comfortable to wear.

Fine fabrics and couture construction deserve high-quality backings. Natural-fiber fabrics like silk muslin, chiffon, China silk, silk crepe, charmeuse, silk gauze, fine cotton batiste, and voile are good choices for soft, draped designs. To add crispness to the silhouette without adding bulk,

# Fitting the Bodice Toile

**IF YOU'VE ALREADY PERFECTED** the fit of a skirt by using a toile, you understand basic fitting principles (see "Fitting the Skirt Toile," p. 116). Although the bodice is more complex in design than a skirt and the upper body is slightly more difficult to fit than the lower body, the basic principles still apply. Garment centers are centered on the body and are perpendicular to the floor, designated crossgrains are parallel to the floor, and the side seams should divide the figure attractively. When all these fitting points are correct, the garment

is said to be balanced. If you are sewing a dress, you must deal with balancing two areas of the garment: the skirt, whose balance is determined by the way it sets at the waistline; and the bodice, whose balance is established by the way it sets at the shoulders.

These directions focus on a simple, close-fitting bodice; they can be modified for more complex designs.

**1.** Add 1-in. seam allowances at garment centers, then cut the toile bodice front and back.

**2.** Mark all matchpoints, seamlines, and darts with a pencil or tracing wheel. Mark the crossgrain at the cross-chest and cross-back lines, and the bustline. The cross-chest and cross-back lines are located at the narrowest part of the chest where the arm joins the body. The bustline is located at the base of the underarm and may not actually be at the bust point. I mark both sides of the fabric.

**3.** Baste the darts and assemble the bodice; don't baste the sleeves into the armscyes.

**4.** Wrong side up, baste a narrow piece of selvage at the waistline, distributing the fullness as needed.

**5.** Put the bodice on, matching the center fronts, pin. Adjust the garment so the garment centers are centered on the figure.

**6.** Check the size. Is it too large or small? Too long or short?

**7.** Check the width at the front bust and waist, the back bust and waist, across the chest, and across the back. When fitting a basic bodice for a master pattern, there should be at least 2 in. of ease at the bustline and 1/2 in. at the waist.

**8.** Check the center front and center back length. A large bust and rounded shoulders will require extra length on the bodice. If either front or back is too long, you will have horizontal wrinkles above the waist.

When fitting a strapless bodice, the center front is on grain and perpendicular to the floor; the crossgrain between the bust points is parallel to the floor.

(Photo by Taylor Sherrill, Author's collection.)

## MAKING TOILE BODICE

Depending on the figure, it can be too long above or below the bust.

**9.** Check the shoulder seam length.

**10.** Check the front and back neckline width and depth, and look for diagonal wrinkles. For example, if the back neck is too narrow, the bodice front will have diagonal wrinkles pointing toward the shoulder point.

**11.** Evaluate the fit. The bodice should fit smoothly.

➤ The underarm seam should be straight and divide the body pleasingly. For a large bust, the underarm seam will be too far forward. For a large back, the seam will be too far back. In both instances, diagonal wrinkles will point toward the problem.

➤ The shoulder seam should be straight and inconspicuous from the front and back. On most figures, it will begin behind the ear

and end at the armscye on the center of the shoulder.

➤ The armscye seam should be in line with the front and back arm creases and extend ¼ in. to ½ in. at the shoulder. It should fit the body smoothly without gaping or binding, with the underarm about ½ in. below the armpit. Beginning at the cross-chest line, there should be a small fold of fabric extending downward from the armscye on the front, with a similar fold at the cross-back line.

➤ The darts should appear straight and shape the fabric to fit the body smoothly. On the front, they should be an appropriate length for the bust and point to the crown of the bust.

**12.** Begin making corrections by eliminating looseness in the bodice or by letting out any seams or darts that are too tight.

**13.** Correct the length if necessary.

**14.** Use the balance lines as a guide to correct the bodice. Begin with the crossgrains at the cross-chest and cross-back to determine the slope of the shoulders. If the crossgrain droops as it nears the armscyes, you have sloping shoulders. If it curves up instead, your shoulders are square. If only one end of the crossgrain line droops and the center front seam swings toward the other side, you have one low

shoulder. The shoulder slope can generally be corrected by taking up or letting out the shoulder seams until the crossgrain line is again horizontal.

**15.** Another common fitting problem is rounded shoulders, but the same principles apply. If the crossgrain at the bustline curves upward at the center back, your shoulders are rounded, and you need to add extra length at the center back. After adding length to the center back, you'll need to shape the fabric to fit the shoulder roundness. To do this, increase the fullness on the back shoulder by adding a shoulder dart, or increasing its size, or increasing the ease, or both until the crossgrain at the upper back is straight. For a very rounded back, add a yoke seam that can be fitted more closely at the armscyes.

**16.** Analyze the relationship of the front to the back. Look at the marked crossgrains and the lengths of the front and back bodice. When the garment fits the shoulders properly, it will not shift when the body moves, even when the garment is worn unbuttoned.

**17.** Once the bodice is balanced, check the armscye again.

**18.** Fit the sleeve (see p. 147).

**FULLING A BACKING**

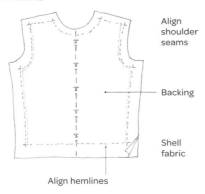

Align shoulder seams

Backing

Shell fabric

Align hemlines

**HOLDING SHORT A VERY CRISP BACKING**

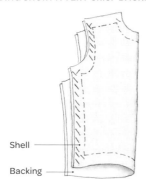

Shell

Backing

CLAIRE'S HINT *The amount of fulling required depends not only on the weave and elasticity of the shell and backing fabrics but also on the width of the garment sections. Wide garment sections need more backing than narrow sections. To check, after I've pinned the backing, I hold the sides of the sections firmly and stretch; the added fullness should disappear. If it doesn't, I repin with less fullness; if it is too tight, I repin with more fullness.*

7. Once the fullness is adjusted, use the thread traced seamlines on the bodice as a guide to baste the sections together on the vertical seamlines.

8. If you're using a very crisp backing material, such as hair canvas, "hold it short." To do this, cut the backing slightly narrower than the garment sections so it will not buckle under the shell fabric. With the centers basted together, hold the shell and backing in the round with the backing on the inside to duplicate the way the layers will fit the body. Holding the layers this way, baste the vertical edges together with diagonal basting, then baste the vertical thread-traced seamlines.

9. Right sides together, pin and then baste the backing and garment sections on horizontal seamlines, matching them exactly.

10. Repeat for all sections.

11. Baste the garment together and put it on the dress form or figure. Evaluate the way the shell and backing drape together, making certain there is no tightness or buckling in either layer.

12. Assemble the garment, treating the two layers as one. When finishing hems and facings, sew the stitches into the backing, but not into the shell fabric.

# Underpinnings

A distinguishing characteristic of many couture dresses is an underpinning especially designed to maintain the garment's silhouette. For example, the underpinnings for each of the YSL for Dior trapeze dresses is slightly different. Some have a separate slip while others have the slip built into the dress. Each is designed specifically for a particular dress; but all have similar elements that can be adapted for other designs.

Designed by Pierre Cardin in 1987, this silk dress had deep armholes. To conceal the wearer's undergarments, an underdress was made from the same fabric and cut much higher. (Photo by Author.)

The base slip for the dress on p. 127 is made of plain-weave silk and closely fitted. It has several additional skirts of crinoline, net, and organza sewn to it. Each of the slip's extra skirts is hand sewn to the base slip with a running stitch, and the raw edges are flattened with catchstitches. The organza top skirt is applied about 2 in. below the waist. Pleats control the fullness at the top of the skirt to create an A-line effect. The machine-stitched 4-in.-wide hem encases horsehair braid.

The first underskirt is made of net, gathered at the top and sewn to the slip 1 in. below the organza skirt. The second underskirt is made of silk organza and sewn about 2 in. below the top of the net underskirt. The fullness in the top of this skirt is controlled by long darts, with the balance gathered in between.

This slip also has two organza panels applied to the upper back to maintain the trapeze silhouette. The panels were first gathered, and then finished with a binding at the edge before being handsewn to the slip.

Sleeveless dresses and blouses tend to expose undergarments or the braless body underneath, especially when the armholes are deep. To solve this problem, some designers accompany these fashions with a camisole or slip that has side panels made from the dress or blouse fabric. One such design by Cardin is shown on the facing page.

These underpinnings offer some useful ideas, but you'll have to create your own solutions. Before deciding on the construction specifics, decide the kind of underpinning needed. To do this, examine the design itself. What needs support? The bodice—all or just part of it? The skirt? The waist? Does the body itself need control to wear the design? Whatever the answers, there are probably several ways to create that support. To determine the best solution, experiment with a variety of ideas.

For a simple underpinning like the slip mentioned above, begin with a pattern for a slip, camisole, or even a simple dress. For more complex, body-hugging support, look to bra, bathing suit, and evening dress patterns as well as to your own wardrobe for ideas or solutions.

For complex underpinnings, begin with a muslin to develop the silhouette. As you work with various support fabrics and underpinning designs, you'll soon learn which combinations are most effective.

## Dresses with Waistlines

Dresses with waistlines range from understated, tailored garments to exuberant creations for summer afternoon parties. Whatever their design, they're all sewn by separately assembling the bodice and skirt, then joining the two at the waistline.

Designed by Marc Bohan for the Dior 1985 Spring/ Summer Collection, this elegant silk jacquard dress is completely backed with silk charmeuse. The edges of the surplice neckline are stabilized with a bias-cut organza stay.

(Photo by Susan Kahn. Author's collection.)

1. Wrong side up, center a ½-in.-wide organza stay on the thread tracing at the bodice waist. Baste, distributing the ease.

2. Baste a grosgrain fitting band to the skirt waist.

3. Before joining the sections, fit and mark them separately (preferably on a dress form), make any necessary corrections, and remove the grosgrain fitting band from the skirt.

4. Baste the bodice and skirt together with the garment centers and side seams aligned.

5. Baste the grosgrain fitting band in once more and fit the basted dress on the figure.

6. After the fitting, mark the bodice stay and fitting band with the finished length, seams, beginning and end of any fullness on the bodice or skirt, and perhaps even the dart locations so the fullness will not have to be adjusted again.

7. Remove the stay and fitting band so you can complete all vertical seams and darts on both the bodice and skirt.

8. Baste the stay into the bodice again; baste the skirt to the bodice. Right sides together, stitch the waistline seam; press lightly.

9. For a flat, inconspicuous waistline seam, turn the seam toward the bodice. To accentuate a full skirt with a buttressed seam, press the waistline seam toward the hem so the skirt will stand away from the bodice at the waist.

10. Trim the raw edges of an inconspicuous waistline seam to 1 in. Finish the waistline seams by overcasting the raw edges of the bodice and skirt separately.

11. Sew in the waist stay with running stitches.

## The Blouse/Skirt Dress

Many designers use the blouse/skirt dress because it controls the fullness, distributes the fullness at the waist, and keeps the shirt-tail tucked-in. The bodice and skirt can be the same fabric like the Yves Saint Laurent design shown above, or the dress can be fabricated with different fabrics to simulate the look of separates. The disadvantage of different fabrications is the blouse fabrics soil and deteriorate

The bodice and skirt of this Yves Saint Laurent dress were assembled separately, then joined at the waist with a waistband. The bodice opens at center front, but to reduce bulk; the skirt front opens at the side. Snaps on the waist of the bodice and the waistband are used to connect the two.

(Photo by Taylor Sherrill. Author's collection.)

more quickly than the skirt materials. The dresses can be assembled using several methods, but the most practical and easiest is to complete the blouse and skirt separately, and then sew them together by hand.

In these directions the blouse and skirt are joined at the waist like the YSL dress; then the seam allowances are interfaced with a grosgrain ribbon and covered with a binding.

1. Complete the blouse and put it on a dress form or the figure. Place a narrow linen fitting tape around the waist, pin the ends together.

2. Arrange the blouse fullness as desired; pin the tape to the blouse so the pins are parallel to the tape.

3. Remove the blouse from the dress form, mark the garment centers and seamlines on the tape.

4. Turn the blouse wrong side out; using the pins as a guide, thread-trace the waistline and unpin the tape.

5. Cut the waistband 3 in. wide and the desired length plus two seam allowances. Thread-trace the seamlines ½ in. from the edges. Cut a 1-in.-wide grosgrain interfacing the desired length.

## ATTACHING SKIRT TO BLOUSE

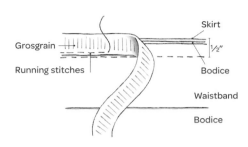

## SECURING THE GROSGRAIN

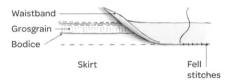

century (see one of her designs on p. 14). Her first designs, shown in 1907 over uncorseted figures with sandals or bare feet, shocked and infuriated many clients. A few appreciated the new freedom of these styles, which did not restrict movement even though they clung to the figure. It wasn't until after World War I, however, that Vionnet's innovative bias cut became high fashion. Two American couturiers, Valentina and Charles Kleibacker, were known for their classic bias dresses for day and evening. Both created designs to be worn without elaborate underpinnings.

6. Right sides together, pin and baste the skirt to the blouse, aligning the waistlines, garment centers, and side seams. Press lightly. Trim the seams to ½ in.

7. With the bodice on top, place the waistband on the seam; baste and stitch. Remove the bastings.

8. Align the edge of the grosgrain and the seam; use running stitches to secure the grosgrain.

9. Finish the ends of the band.

10. Wrap the band around the grosgrain; turn under the seam allowance, baste. Use fell stitches to finish the band.

CLAIRE'S HINT *On many blouse/skirt dresses the blouse and skirt are completely finished before they are joined. If the skirt has a band, the sections are sewn together at the bottom of the band with running stitches. If it has a facing, it is sewn together ¼ in. to ½ in. below the top of the facing.*

## Bias-cut Dresses

Only a few designers have been truly successful with bias creations, among them the legendary French couturier Madeleine Vionnet, who introduced the bias-cut garment at the turn of the

On this stunning bias-cut dress designed by Charles Kleibacker, the bodice is fitted with darts that are released at the waist to create the full flared skirt. The neck edge is finished with a narrow self-fabric binding. The fabric is a pebbly wool crepe.

(Photo by Gordon Munro, courtesy of estate of Charles Kleibacker.)

# Blouse Godets

Mainbocher to introduce enough fullness below the waist to accommodate the hips, this blouse has four godets—two in front and two in back.

**1.** On the blouse pattern, draw a new side seam on grain.

**2.** To determine the finished width of the godets at the hem, measure the distance between the new and old side seams at the hem.

**3.** Beginning at the waist, draw the location lines for the godets midway between the garment centers and new side seam. Measure the godet line from the waist to the hem.

**4.** To make the godet pattern, draw a triangle using the length of the godet line for the sides and the distance between the side lines for the base. If you need extra width at the hips, it's easy to make the triangle wider at the base.

**5.** Add seam and hem allowances to the godet.

**6.** Sew the godet.

(Photo by Author.)

---

Bias-cut garments are constructed with the bias hanging vertically, which makes these fashions more challenging to sew than traditional designs cut on the straight grain because the bias cut stretches more and is easily distorted.

Here are some useful tips I learned from Kleibacker for working with the bias:

➤ When making a muslin toile for a bias-cut garment, be sure the muslin for each garment section has a selvage edge. That edge will make it easy to align the grainlines when you lay out the toile on the garment fabric for cutting.

➤ Instead of folding the fabric lengthwise as you normally would to cut out two layers on the lengthwise grain, cut the unfolded fabric in two lengths long enough to accommodate your pattern.

➤ Mark the face side of each length with a cross-stitch in the upper right corner. Stack the two lengths with right sides together and the cross-stitches at one end. Smooth the stacked layers of fabric; and to prevent shifting, pin the layers together on all sides, setting the pins perpendicular to the edges.

➤ "Corner" the fabric so one end and long edge are aligned with one corner and long edge of the table; this ensures that the grainlines are at right angles.

➤ Slip large sheets of dressmaker's carbon under the fabric layers, and check to be sure the fabric is still cornered. Spread the muslin pattern on top of the fabric and pin the selvages on the muslin to the selvages on the garment fabric, allowing several inches between pattern pieces for seam allowances. Using weights or pins in the seam allowances, anchor the pattern.

➤ Transfer all stitching lines and matchpoints to the wrong side of the lower layer with a stiletto tracing wheel. As you wheel with one hand, hold the fabric layers flat with just the fingertips of the other hand (as if you are playing the piano). Roll the wheel in only one direction, and move your fingers frequently so you are holding the fabric next to where you are "wheeling," as it's called in couture.

➤ After you've wheeled the entire pattern, remove the muslin pattern, turn the two layers of fabric over so you can smooth and mark the second layer as you did the first.

➤ Lap-baste the garment centers and any other seamlines positioned with right sides together, so they are ready for stitching.

➤ Thread-trace the remaining stitching lines and matchpoints. To avoid catching the underlayer, slip a ruler in between the layers to separate them. Cut out the garment sections, leaving at least 1½-in.-wide seam allowances. When working with bias cut designs, some fabrics stretch much more than others; and the fabric lengthens, causing the garment to narrow. The extra wide seam allowances can be used to make it large enough.

➤ Machine stitch the dress only after it has been fitted, stretching the bias seams as much as possible as you sew so the garment will drape properly.

➤ Try to locate any zippers on the lengthwise grain rather than on the bias so they'll hang correctly without buckling. If this isn't possible, make a slashed opening for the zipper and bind the edges of the opening with bias binding (see p. 80).

## Blouse Designs

Blouses are usually designed to tuck in or be worn over the waistband of a skirt or pants. Many tuck-in couture blouses, like the Valentino design at right, have a seam at the waist and a separately cut section below the waist called a yoke. The yoke reduces bulk, controls the waistline fullness, and ensures a better fit. The yoke is generally made of fabric that is both lighter in weight and less expensive than the blouse fabric, for example, organza, China silk, or lightweight silk shantung. Most yokes are simple rectangles, darted to fit the waist and the upper hip. They're usually 4 in. to 7 in. wide and sometimes cut on the crossgrain so the selvage can be used at the bottom instead of a hem to further reduce bulk.

1. To make a blouse yoke, begin with a pattern for a close-fitting skirt. To use the yoke fabric selvage for a hem, place the top of the skirt front and back

pattern sections on the fabric the same distance from the selvage.

2. Using a tracing wheel and dressmaker's carbon, transfer the stitching lines at the top of the front and back pattern sections to the fabric. Remove the pattern and baste the yoke together.

3. Baste the yoke to the blouse for a fitting, make any necessary corrections, then permanently stitch and press the yoke and blouse. If you didn't use the selvage at the hem, finish the lower edge.

4. When a tuck-in blouse has a zipper, it usually extends 10 in. to 12 in. below the waist and several inches below the blouse hem so the wearer can step into the garment easily. Sometimes the zippers

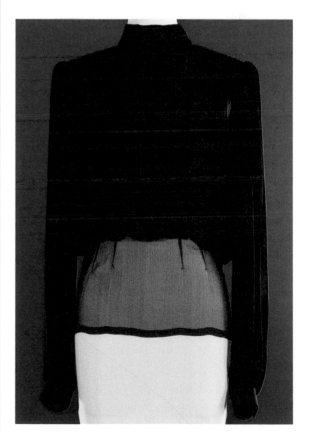

Designed by Valentino Garavani in the mid-1980s, this blouse has a seam at the waist with a fitted yoke. The yoke reduces bulk under the top of the skirt and prevents it from pulling out. For this design, it sets and preserves the drape of the bodice.

(Photo by Taylor Sherrill. Author's collection.)

are sewn in upside-down in place of a separating zipper since the latter are heavy and available in only limited lengths and colors (see p. 103).

## OVERBLOUSES

Frequently used with her classic suits, Coco Chanel's overblouses and tunics are always comfortable, even when they aren't high fashion. The blouse should hang smoothly without shifting toward the back or front of the body, and the hemline should appear parallel to the floor, except, of course, when the design's hemline is intentionally uneven. In couture, the drape of the overblouse is controlled with weights. Chanel used a variety of weights, including brass chains and circle weights. Other couturiers have weighted the blouse with wide hem allowances, bands, bindings, embroidery, ribbon or braid trims, and even pockets and buttons. Noted in the 1920s for his Grecian-inspired, long, pleated silk, column-like dresses, Italian designer Mariano Fortuny always used small glass beads as weights along the hemline of the blouse on his two-piece designs. More recent, Norell preferred silk-covered drapery weights, even though they had to be removed when the blouse was dry-cleaned. Many designs have a bias binding at the hem to weight it.

## SLEEVELESS BLOUSES AND DRESSES

Sleeveless designs were traditionally associated with casual dress and sportswear until American designer Mainbocher introduced haute couture to the bare armed suit blouse in the 1930s. Although Chanel liked this innovation for the comfort it offered, she wanted her suits to look as if they had long sleeves. She achieved this effect by creating separate blouse cuffs that were sewn or snapped into the insides of the jacket sleeves.

**Sleeveless Flange.** On both sleeveless blouses and dresses, Norell and Balenciaga favored an unusual front armhole shape, called a sleeveless flange. The shallow front armhole hugs the body at the top of the arm, while a fold of fabric extending from

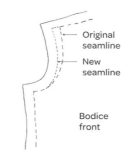

### RESHAPING ARMHOLE INTO SLEEVELESS FLANGE

- - - Original seamline

—— New seamline

Bodice front

the shoulder at the armscye covers the "crease" where the arm joins the body, one of the body's less attractive parts. On the Balenciaga, the sleeveless flange was used on both the front and back armholes.

1. To reshape the armscye, extend the shoulder seam on the pattern front 1¼ in.
2. Connect the end of the new shoulder seam with the armscye notch to create a shallow sleeve cap; add seam allowances to all edges as needed.
3. Repeat on the pattern back if you want a rounder, softer edge on the back armhole as well.
4. Finish the armscye with a facing or lining, then fold the extension under 1¼ in. and use catchstitches to sew it to the shoulder seam. The purpose is to create a flange with a small pleat at the armscye that covers the crease where the arm joins the body.

Used to flatter the wearer and cover the unattractive crease where the arm joins the body, flanges at the armscye were a favorite Balenciaga technique for sleeveless designs. The inside view of the flange shows its simplicity. The shoulder seam is simply extended, the armscye finished, and then the extension is folded to the inside.

(Photos by Taylor Sherrill. Author's collection.)

**Interfaced Armscye.** Any sleeveless design will be enhanced by interfacing the armscye with a bias strip to soften the edge without causing any "breaks"

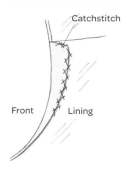

INTERFACING THE ARMSCYE

Catchstitch

Front    Lining

and to make the edge drape better. Using the same technique as for interfacing hems (see p. 72) you can create a softly rolled edge that's usually more attractive than a sharp, hard-pressed finish.

1. Depending on the amount of roll you want, choose an interfacing fabric like muslin, traditional interfacing fabrics, hair canvas, cotton flannel, or lambswool (listed here in order of the amount of roll they produce, from the least to the greatest), and cut a strip of interfacing 1½ in. wide.

2. After the facings are stitched and the seam is pressed and clipped, hand sew the strip to the seamline so it laps the facing ½ in. and the bodice 1 in.

3. Clip the strip as necessary so the edge will lie flat.

4. Fold the interfacing in place and secure it at the seams.

## Invisible Details

The construction details on the inside of a couture garment are among its most important secrets. These details represent the finishing touches that imperceptibly keep necklines from shifting or gaping, help pleats hang as designed, make waistlines fit smoothly, and generally hold the garment in place on the body.

### PERFECT NECKLINES

A well-made neckline that lies precisely as the designer intended is a hallmark of couture construction. There are many ways to achieve this end, from small weights to elaborate harnesses, and the design of the neckline determines the approach needed to tame it.

**Weights and Boning.** A draped cowl neckline can be held in place with small weights covered with plain-weave silk or organza and sewn with a small French tack to the inside fold of the drape. A deep V-shaped neckline will lie smoothly if anchored at the deepest point of the V with a boning stay.

1. Stabilize the neckline early in its construction to eliminate any gaping (see p. 54).

2. Sew a narrow silk tube about 4 in. long.

3. Insert a 3-in. piece of polyester boning or a man's shirt stay into the tube.

Short polyester stays like those used on men's shirts, here on a dress by designer James Galanos, were inserted into self-fabric tubes, which could be tucked into the wearer's bra when worn.

(Photo by Author.)

4. After the neckline is finished, sew one end of the tube to the facing about ¼ in. below the neckline.

5. When the garment is worn, the bottom of the anchor slips into the bra and the neckline clings to the body.

**Elastic Stays.** An elastic stay can also be used to tighten necklines, such as the sweetheart neckline on the evening gown on p. 138, or hold an off-the-shoulder neckline in position. This stay is a piece of elastic held in a thread casing of catchstitches.

These directions are for applying the elastic stay at a neckline.

1. Facing side up, pin a piece of braided elastic—the kind that narrows when stretched—to the neckline facing without stretching it.

2. Use catchstitches to make a casing over the elastic.

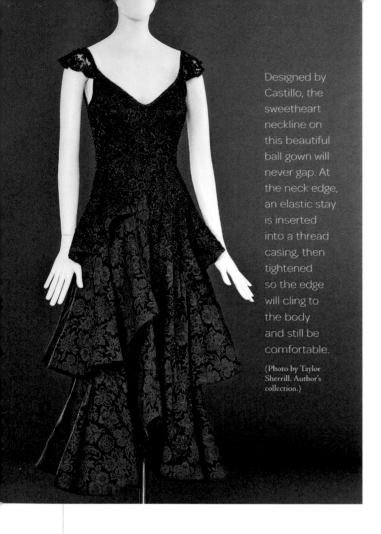

Designed by Castillo, the sweetheart neckline on this beautiful ball gown will never gap. At the neck edge, an elastic stay is inserted into a thread casing, then tightened so the edge will cling to the body and still be comfortable.

(Photo by Taylor Sherrill. Author's collection.)

## CONTROLLING AN OFF-THE-SHOULDER NECKLINE

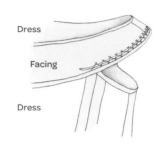

## CONTROLLING A SQUARE NECKLINE

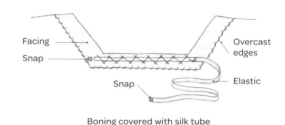

Boning covered with silk tube

3. Baste one end of the elastic to the facing so it won't pull out.

4. Pull up the other end of the elastic so it is about 1 in. shorter than the length of the neckline. Baste the end of the elastic to the neckline facing and cut the elastic, leaving an extra 2-in. tail. Since it is basted, the elastic length can be adjusted at the next fitting and the fullness adjusted.

5. After the fitting, trim the elastic ends. Use catchstitches or whipstitches to sew them securely to the facing.

CLAIRE'S HINT *If the elastic needs to be replaced at a later date, remove the old elastic and sew a short length of buttonhole twist thread to the end of the new elastic to thread it through the casing.*

**Square Neckline Control.** Use an elastic stay to control a square neckline and keep it from gaping. One of the advantages of this stay is that the

neckline will be held smooth at the front and the back can be loose.

1. Cut the elastic long enough to extend from one front corner of the neckline around the back to the other front corner.

2. Sew one end of the elastic to the facing at one corner; sew a snap socket to the other corner. Sew the snap ball to the free end of the elastic.

3. If the neckline sags a little despite the elastic, use a piece of polyester boning to keep it smooth. Cut the boning 1 in. longer than the neckline width, insert it into a narrow silk tube and catchstitch the tube to the neckline facing ¼ in. to ½ in. below the neckline.

**Harnesses.** Designs with deep décolletés, low-cut necklines, or wrapped surplice designs are more difficult to control, particularly when they are not close-fitting. To solve the problem, low-cut couture blouses and dresses have harnesses that attach to a narrow waistband. The specific design of the harness varies with each neckline, but they usually have a band that snugly fits the waist or under the bust. The shoulder straps extending from the waistband are either sewn to the garment shoulder seams or held in place with lingerie guards to keep the garment from shifting when it's worn.

I first saw a harness on a YSL evening blouse with deep décolleté at center front and back. To control the neckline, silk straps were sewn to a waist stay. On the front, two straps were placed to form a triangle from the waist to the shoulder, bypassing the bust. On the back, one of the front straps continued to the back waist. At the shoulder, they were held in place by a lingerie guard.

Designed by Oscar de la Renta, this two-piece silk matelassé dress was inspired by a 1961 Balenciaga design. It has a graceful surplice wrap in the back and a soft blouson in the front.

(Photo by Taylor Sherrill. Author's collection.)

Another much simpler harness was on a dress by American designer Valentina. The harness consisted of two long straps attached at the shoulders. Made of seam binding, the straps crossed in front at the bust and tied in the back at the waist.

The harness on the Oscar de la Renta dress, below, is similar to one I saw on a Balenciaga. The dress surplice back wraps loosely; without the harness, it would fall open and shift off the shoulders.

1. To determine the amount of grosgrain needed, you'll need two straps and one waist stay. For the straps, measure the length from your back waist to the shoulder; multiply by two; add this measurement to your waist measurement. Add ¼ yd. for seam allowances and finishing the ends of the waist stay.

2. Make the waist stay using ½-in.- or 1-in.-wide grosgrain. To finish the ends, see p. 140.

3. Pin and baste the straps on the back of the stay about 3 in. from center back, letting the ends extend about ½ in. below the stay.

4. Wrong side up, place the harness on the bodice. Pin the straps to the shoulder seams. Don't cut the straps too short at the shoulders so they can be lengthened if needed.

5. At the fitting, check the strap length. Adjust as needed.

6. Turn under the ends of the straps at the shoulder seams and waist stay. Use fell stitches to sew them at the shoulder seams. Use whipstitches at the bottom of the waist stay and catchstitches at the top.

The harness—also inspired by the Balenciaga design—which prevents the bodice from falling off the shoulders, is easy to see when the back is opened.

(Photo by Taylor Sherrill. Author's collection.)

# Finishing Ends on the Waist Stay

**1.** Mark the stay 2 in. from the end for the hooks and 4½ in. for the eyes.

**2.** To finish the hook end, fold under the stay at the marked point.

**3.** On a 1-in.-wide stay, sew two hooks, placing them about ⅛ in. from the folded end.

**4.** Fold under the end; slide the folded end under the hooks to cover the eyelets. Fell the end and whipstitch the edges together.

**5.** To finish the eye end, fold under the stay at the marked point; sew the edges together for ½ in.

**6.** Align the eyes with the hooks and sew them to the stay so they extend ⅛ in. beyond the folded edge.

**7.** Fold the end back on itself for 1 in. with right sides together to make a 1-in. underlap beyond the marked foldline.

**8.** At the end of the underlap, fold the stay with wrong sides together. To finish, fold the raw edge under ½ in., fell it in place and whipstitch the folded edges together.

**9.** To finish a waistline or underbust stay on a garment with a side closure, place the hooks on the left front of the stay. For a garment with a center closure, place them on the right back.

**10.** Use running stitches or short French tacks to sew the stay into the garment.

## FINISHING STAY ENDS

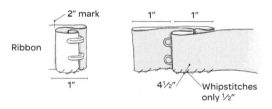

## More Stays

In addition to elastic stays and harnesses, other types of stays used in couture garments include waist stays, underbust stays, and pleat stays. While elastic stays stretch, waist and underbust stays anchor the garment in the desired position on the body. Pleat stays allow you to reduce the bulk of the garment while stabilizing this decorative detail.

### WAIST STAY

Sometimes called an inside waistband or Petersham, a waist stay generally ensures a better fitting and more comfortable dress. It eases the strain at the zipper on close-fitting garments, supports the weight of a dress's full or heavy skirt, and controls the fullness on a blouson bodice. It also controls the hang of dresses without waistline seams to create a smoother line on the figure. For most daytime dresses, a ½-in.- to 1-in.-wide grosgrain stay is suitable. On evening gowns, the waist stay can be 1-in.-wide grosgrain or several inches wide and made of faille with stays (see p. 222).

1. Begin by cutting the grosgrain about 7 in. longer than the waistline measurement of the garment. With the garment wrong side up, align the bottom of the grosgrain with the seamline and pin it to the seam allowances.

2. Beginning and ending 1½ in. from the garment opening, baste the center of the grosgrain to the seam.

3. After the fitting, finish the stay ends neatly, as described in the sidebar, above.

4. Sew the grosgrain permanently with short running stitches. If the dress doesn't have a waistline seam, sew the stay to the vertical seams using short French tacks.

## UNDERBUST STAY

An underbust stay is often made of elastic instead of grosgrain ribbon. The elastic allows it to move with the body while holding the bodice securely in place. Sometimes encased in a silk tube, the stay is held in place by a series of thread chains placed on the inside of the bodice at the center front, side seams, and darts.

---

### UNDERBUST STAY

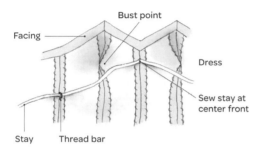

1. Begin with ¼-in.- to ⅜-in.-wide elastic. Cut the ends the same length as the underbust measurement of the wearer.
2. Finish the ends with a hook and eye.
3. On the inside of the bodice, make the thread chains for the stay at the side seams (see p. 37) just long enough for the elastic to slip through. For a closer fit at the bustline, sew the elastic to the garment midway between the bust points and locate the thread guides as needed to guide the elastic under the bust.

## PLEAT STAY

A pleat or fullness stay ensures that the pleat or fullness hangs softly in its intended position without being held by any stitching. Such a stay was used to secure the pleat at the armscye on the Balenciaga gown at right, a treatment that would work equally well for a daytime design. The inside

A look inside the Balenciaga dress reveals a simple silk tube anchored at the neckpoint and on the armscye. Notice that the stay is shorter than the garment section to create the pleat at the armscye. At the top of the sleeve cap, the edge is finished with a wide extended facing; at the underarm, a separate facing is used.

(Photo by Irving Solero, courtesy of the National Museum of Fashion at the Fashion Institute of Technology, New York, gift of Mrs. Ephraim London.)

Designed in 1965 by Balenciaga, the silk gazar gown has a graceful pleat at each shoulder held in place on the inside of the garment by a pleat stay (inset). This design relied on the cut, the fabric's characteristics, and the wearer's movements for the intended effect: When the wearer walked, the raised front hem allowed the skirt, lined with self-fabric, to fill with air and billow out to form a cone.

(Photo by Irving Solero, courtesy of the National Museum of Fashion at the Fashion Institute of Technology, New York, gift of Mrs. Ephraim London.)

view of the bodice shows the simplicity of the stay. I've used this stay on several designs that had pleats or shirring in the shoulder area to keep the fullness from "falling off" the arm.

On other designs, a small triangular stay was used instead of the tape.

1. To make the stay for each pleat, sew a ¼-in. tube 2 in. longer than its finished length (see "Stitching Tube," p. 98).

2. Wrong side up, pin one end of the strap at the shoulder point and the other at the armscye. CLAIRE'S HINT *Experiment with the length and placement until the pleat drapes as you want.*

3. Trim the ends of the strap, leaving ¼ in. at each end. Turn under the ends and sew them securely.

### CROTCH STAY

A crotch stay is a simple, functional means of anchoring a tuck-in blouse to prevent it from riding up. Similar to a body suit, a crotch stay keeps the blouse hem from pulling out.

1. To sew a crotch stay, begin with the blouse on the figure and determine the needed length of the stay by measuring from the back hem of the blouse through the legs to the front hem.

2. Cut two strips of elastic this length. Insert the elastic strips into narrow silk tubes about 2 in. longer than the elastic.

3. Stretch the elastic and sew the ends to the tube ends.

### CROTCH STAY

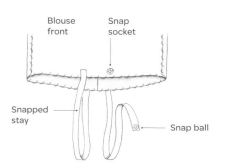

Blouse front    Snap socket

Snapped stay

Snap ball

4. Sew one end of one strap to the inside hem of the blouse, about 1 in. to the right of the center back, and the end of the other strap about 1 in. to the left of center.

5. Sew the ball half of a snap to the other end of each strap and the corresponding snap socket to the inside hem of the blouse, positioning the sockets similarly to the right and left of center front.

## Shoulder Pads

The shoulder pads used in dressmaking are generally softer and thinner than those used in tailoring. They're sometimes shaped irregularly to fit an unusual neckline, and they're always covered

Shoulder pads can be any shape you want. To create a strong shoulder for a blouse like the one shown on the facing page, left, small shoulder pads have been fashioned with a cut-out to fit around the blouse's bateau neckline.

(Photo by Taylor Sherrill. Author's collection.)

with fabric when not concealed by a lining. The pads themselves are made and shaped on a dress form in the same way as tailored shoulder pads.

1. For each shoulder pad, cut a piece of lining about 12 in. square; mark the true bias at the center.

2. Before removing the pads from the dress form, align the bias with the armscye edge of the pad; smooth and pin the lining fabric over the pad.

3. Remove the pads from the dress form; wrap the lining around the pad. Pin a dart in the center of the underside to remove the excess fullness; smooth and pin the fabric on the underside.

4. At the edge of the pad, use running stitches to sew the layers together. Trim away the excess, fell

Fabricated in silk charmeuse, this beautiful Yves Saint Laurent blouse from the 1980s has a bateau neckline. The bodice of the blouse is lined, but the sleeves are not. The band at the waist is interfaced with hair canvas.

(Photo by Taylor Sherrill. Author's collection.)

In a couture atelier, dress shields are often sewn from silk lining or backing fabric. For sleeveless designs, they're often made from self-fabric so they will be inconspicuous at the underarm. Here, the dress shields were added later and made from flesh-colored silk to make them inconspicuous.

(Photo by Susan Kahn. Author's collection.)

stitch the dart flat, and overcast the edges of the silk by hand.

5. Mark the front of the shoulder pad with a cross stitch, and baste it into the garment for fitting.

6. To secure it permanently, use blindstitches to sew it to the shoulder seam and the armscye for about 1 in. on each side of the shoulder point.

7. Use short French tacks to sew the corners to the armscye seam.

CLAIRE'S HINT *Valentino used elastic stays on the shoulder pads to control necklines. The elastic is inserted into a narrow silk tube, and the ends are sewn to the front and back of the shoulder pad to form a loop that fits snugly, but not tightly, under the arm. The exact placement of the elastic depends on the design, but it's usually in line with the armscye. Surprisingly, these stays are neither uncomfortable nor unattractive, and I've used them on several loose-fitting designs with excellent results.*

# Dress Shields

Dress shields fit inside the garment at the underarm and protect the garment from perspiration. Made from the lining or backing fabric, they're about 5 in. wide and 5 in. long, with an inward curve at the top. For greater protection, they can be made double, with mirror-image sides

so one side extends into the sleeve; or they can be interfaced with cotton flannel for extra absorbency; and they can be covered with self-fabric.

1. Draw the shape of the shield you want and add ¼-in. seam allowances to all the edges.

2. For a pair of shields, cut four sections from the blouse or lining fabric.

3. Right sides together, stitch all edges, leaving a 1-in. opening on one side.

4. Trim the seams to ⅛ in.; turn the shield right side out.

5. Close the opening with slipstitches; press.

6. Use running stitches to sew the shields into the garment so they can be removed for laundering.

CLAIRE'S HINT *For sleeveless designs, I make the shields from self-fabric and position the shield so it extends ⅛ in. above the armhole to catch the perspiration before the garment does.*

7. For double shields, cut eight sections; join each of the two pairs at the armscye. Line and finish the shields as above.

# 8

# Sleeves

ALTHOUGH THERE'S AN ENDLESS VARIETY of sleeve styles and silhouettes to choose from, there are only two basic categories of sleeves: set-in sleeves, made separately and sewn to the bodice at the armscye; and sleeves cut as an integral part of the bodice. This latter group includes kimono, dolman, batwing, and raglan sleeves. While both sleeve types are used in haute couture, this chapter focuses on the separately cut, set-in sleeve because it's more difficult to fit and sew successfully. Designer methods for sewing cut-on sleeves are quite similar to traditional home-sewing techniques.

Set-in sleeves are known by a variety of names that describe their silhouette—bell, bishop, cap, lantern, leg-of-mutton, puff, shirt, and tulip. The sleeve cap, or top, can be set smoothly into the armscye (armhole) of the bodice, or it can be gathered, pleated, tucked, or draped. The bottom of the sleeve can be finished with a self-hem, separate facing, binding, cuff, or casing. But whatever the style and cut, the general method for hanging, or fitting, and sewing all set-in sleeves is fundamentally the same.

Designed by the English couturier Lachasse in the late 1940s, this garment is a testament to the influence of Dior's New Look. Like Dior's "Bar" design, the hips are padded to make the waist look smaller. Lapped seams are used on the front and the sleeves are finished with an intricate double-cuff design.

(Photo by Ken Howie. Author's collection.)

## Basic One-piece Fitted Sleeve

Before exploring how to fit and sew a set-in sleeve, let's look at the anatomy of a fitted sleeve. When the sleeve is laid flat, the grainline runs the length of the arm from the shoulder point, or highest point on the sleeve cap, to the back of the wrist. Above the elbow, the grainline is located at the sleeve center. Below the elbow, the grainline and sleeve center move apart.

The vertical grainline is used as a guide for marking the horizontal lines of the biceps, cap, and elbow. The biceps line connects the top of the underarm seam and marks the crossgrain. It defines the base of the sleeve cap and the top of the sleeve body.

The capline is located on the crossgrain midway between the biceps and the shoulder point.

The cap is wider and higher in front than in back to accommodate the shoulder joint, which juts forward. The cap is scooped out more on the front than the back to allow the arm to move forward without binding at the front of the armscye. The cap back underarm curve is just deep enough to allow the arm to swing forward without ripping the seam.

The cap height is affected by the length of the shoulder seam and height of the shoulder pads—two details influenced by changing fashions. Whatever the fashion, the shorter the shoulder seam then the higher the sleeve cap; and the longer the seam, the lower the cap. To accommodate a

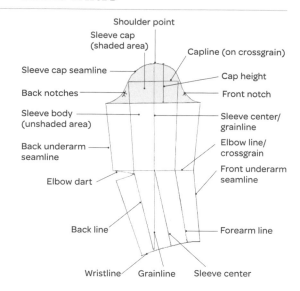

shoulder pad, for example, the sleeve cap has extra height.

The sleeve cap seamline outlines the top of the cap. Designed to fit the outward curve of the shoulder, the length of this seamline is 1 in. to 2 in. longer than the armscye of the bodice and must be eased in when the bodice and sleeve are joined. Generally located on the sleeve cap seamline about ¾ in. below the capline, the balance marks or matchpoints (notches on commercial patterns), are used to indicate the beginning and end of the ease on the upper part of the sleeve cap. The balance marks are only guides, and are frequently changed when the sleeve is fitted.

The elbow line is marked on the crossgrain level with the elbow. The elbow dart shapes the fitted sleeve to follow the curve of the arm and provides fullness to allow for bending the elbow. Sometimes the elbow dart is converted to ease.

The other vertical lines on the sleeve are the front and back underarm seamlines, the forearm line and the back line. The forearm line marks the center of the sleeve front and extends from the front end of the capline to the wrist. The back line marks the center of the sleeve back and extends from the other end of the capline through the point of the

This Adrian jacket has a one-piece sleeve, which was used more often on tailored designs in the 1940s and '50s than it is today. The sleeve is shaped with two darts at the elbow. On many designs, the darts are converted to ease so they are less conspicuous.

(Photo by Taylor Sherrill. Author's collection.)

This dressmaker suit by Mainbocher has a close-fitting two-piece sleeve. It was worn with the skirt shown on p. 108. (Photo by Ken Howie. Author's collection.)

3. Baste the elbow dart closed. Baste the underarm seam. Turn under the hem and baste.

4. Fit and machine stitch the bodice. Baste shoulder pads in place. It's important to have a variety of pads on hand to experiment with when fitting and never fit a garment without them.

5. Try on the garment and slip the sleeve over your arm. Anchor the shoulder point of the sleeve temporarily to the bodice so the grain at the sleeve center hangs perpendicular to the floor. Set a pin at a right angle to the seamline without folding under the sleeve's seam allowance. Don't be concerned if the shoulder point isn't pinned exactly to the shoulder seam on the garment.

6. Extend the arm; fold the sleeve seam allowance under at the underarm. Match the underarm seamlines of the sleeve and bodice; pin them together. With the arm down and relaxed, adjust the cap so the capline is horizontal and the sleeve falls in a gentle vertical column. Pin the ends of the capline to the bodice without folding the seam allowance under. Since you're hanging the sleeve for a particular figure, the matchpoints that were transferred from the pattern may not match. If the capline bows upward at the sleeve center, the cap is too short. In that case, release the pin at the shoulder point and repin so the capline is level and the sleeve is balanced.

7. Beginning at the underarm, fold the sleeve seam allowance under and pin the sleeve front to the armscye seamline. Stop at the marked capline and repeat on back of the sleeve.

elbow dart to the wrist. The back line is frequently used to locate sleeve vents, cuff openings, darts, and extra length for full sleeves.

## PREPARE, HANG, AND FIT THE SLEEVE

These directions are for hanging a basic, full-length sleeve on a toile or garment. The advantage of hanging sleeves on the toile is that, unlike the garment fabric, the muslin can be marked quickly and easily with a pencil.

1. Cut out the sleeve with 1-in. seam allowances, except at the top of the cap seamline; cut it with a 1½-in. allowance.

2. Thread-trace all seamlines, elbow darts, and matchpoints. Mark the grainline and sleeve center, beginning at the shoulder point and continuing the length of the sleeve. Mark the crossgrain at the capline, bicep, and elbow.

### SLEEVE TO SHOULDER POINT

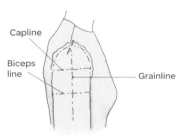

Capline

Biceps line

Grainline

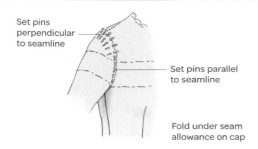

Set pins perpendicular to seamline

Set pins parallel to seamline

Fold under seam allowance on cap

8. Before pinning the top of the cap, check the grainlines again to be sure the sleeve is balanced. Remove the pin at the shoulder point and fold under the sleeve seam allowance at the top of the cap. Ease and repin the top of the cap to the bodice, setting the pins perpendicular to the folded edge. The cap probably will not lie flat between the pins because you haven't shaped the sleeve cap to control the fullness.

9. Check the sleeve length. It should end just below the wrist bone when the arm is held down at the side. Bend the arm; the sleeve should be long enough so it doesn't pull away from the wrist. Check that the elbow dart points toward the elbow.

Next check the underarm seam. It should end at the wrist at the center of the palm. Swing your arms forward and, bending them at the elbows, place each hand on the opposite shoulder. The bodice back and sleeve cap should be wide enough to allow mobility. Correct and repin any of the above sleeve points as needed.

10. When hanging a fabric sleeve, examine the sleeve to determine whether the fabric has enough body to support the sleeve shape. If the sleeve seems limp, it can be completely backed after you've fitted it, or backed just above the elbow, or in part or all of the sleeve cap. When working with plaid, striped, or patterned fabrics that require matching, draw the fabric pattern at the bodice shoulder onto the sleeve cap so you can accurately match the patterns when cutting the garment fabric. At the House of Valentino, a fabric scrap with the

appropriate pattern is basted onto the muslin toile so the patterns can be easily matched.

11. Once the fit is checked, remove the toile or garment and mark the bodice and sleeve carefully before unpinning. Mark any changes made on the seamlines of the sleeve or bodice. Indicate new matchpoints as needed at the shoulder point and capline, and again midway between the two. If the underarm bodice and sleeve seams don't match those on the bodice, decide which should be repositioned and mark the new location.

12. Unpin the sleeve, remove bastings, and press the sleeve. Using a ruler and French curve, correct any irregular lines to true them.

# Cut and Shape the Sleeve

The success of the sleeves begins with the cutting and shaping before it is assembled.

1. Using the corrected toile sleeve as a guide, cut and mark the fabric sleeve. Cut the backing.

2. Baste the backing to the wrong side of the sleeve. Baste first with diagonal stitches at the center on the lengthwise grain. Fold the sleeve vertically and pin the thread traced seamlines to the backing. Baste the layers together on the seamlines.

3. Baste and stitch the elbow dart. Remove the bastings, slash the dart open and press. If the dart was converted to ease (see p. 60), shrink and shape the elbow area.

The muslin sleeve was fitted into the jacket; a scrap of the plaid was matched to the plaid on the jacket front and basted to the muslin cap. It isn't unusual to need a separate muslin for each sleeve.

(Photo by Author.)

Place the sleeve cap on a tailor's ham to shrink out the excess fullness. Cover the fabric with a damp cloth (not shown since it would obscure the sleeve) and press, allowing the tip of the iron to cross the seamline no more than 1 in.

(Photo by Susan Kahn.)

4. Baste and stitch the underarm seam; press it open. Finish the lower edge of the sleeve appropriately for the design.

5. To shape the sleeve cap, place a row of ease basting on the seamline between the matchpoints. Place a second row 1/8 in. above the seamline and another 1/8 in. below it. Measure the armscye and pull up the ease basting on the cap so the sleeve seamline is the same as the corresponding length of the armscye.

6. Right side up, arrange the cap on a tailor's ham. Cover the section with a damp press cloth and shrink out the excess fullness. When shrinking, work from the seam allowance inward, moving the iron no more than 1 in. over the seamline to keep from shrinking out too much fullness and distorting the hang of the sleeve. After shrinking, cover the sleeve with a dry press cloth and press until the cap is dry.

7. To preserve the shape and support of the sleeve cap, pin the sleeves to a pair of shoulder pads that have been sewn to the ends of a coat hanger or stuff the caps with tissue paper.

8. Set the sleeves aside until you're ready to sew them into the garment.

## SET THE SLEEVE

The process of setting the sleeve in haute couture varies from the one used in home sewing.

1. Complete the bodice and tighten the back armscye (see the facing page).

2. Right sides together, pin the sleeve into the armscye using the matchpoints as a guide. If you're right-handed, begin with the left sleeve, which will be easier to baste; if you're left-handed, begin with the right sleeve.

CLAIRE'S HINT *Many home-sewing instructions advise against putting ease at the top of the sleeve because it's difficult to ease smoothly on the crossgrain. In haute couture, a small amount of ease is added at the top of the sleeve so the cap will not fit too tightly over the seam allowances.*

3. Starting at the front matchpoint, baste along the seamline with short, even basting stitches across the top of the cap to the back matchpoints, under the arm, and back to the starting point. Distribute the ease with your thumb between the matchpoints as you baste. When matching plaids, stripes or other fabric patterns, begin with the garment on a dress form so that you can baste with fell stitches or slip basting from the right side. Be sure to keep the fabric patterns aligned. Remove the garment from the dress form and, working from the wrong side, even-baste the armscye seam a second time to make sure the layers are securely positioned.

4. Examine the sleeve to be sure it hangs correctly and to evaluate the ease and smoothness of the cap. The garment can be refitted on the figure, put on a dress form, or simply held over your arm by putting your fist into the sleeve cap with the garment shoulder over your forearm. Hold your arm forward so the garment hangs naturally. The sleeve should hang straight without wrinkling.

5. Baste the remaining sleeve into the garment so the bodice can be fitted on the figure; baste any shoulder pads in place. Check the fit of the sleeves and fine-tune as needed.

6. Examine the sleeve cap. It shouldn't have pleats or gathers at the seamline, and the cap should look smooth and free of dimples. If the basted sleeve has dimples, try to determine the reason. Dimples frequently occur simply because the sleeve head (see p. 156) hasn't yet been set. If the fabric is tightly woven and difficult to shrink, you can

use a thicker sleeve head, redistribute the ease so there's a small amount of ease—between ¼ in. and ³⁄₈ in.—in the underarm area, or make the sleeve narrower by sewing a wider seam at the underarm. To do either of the last two, remove the sleeve and rebaste. None of these solutions will significantly affect the hang of the sleeve.

## LOWERING A SLEEVE CAP

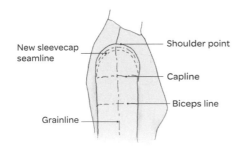

New sleevecap seamline
Shoulder point
Capline
Biceps line
Grainline

If all else fails, you can increase the seam allowance at the top of the sleeve cap to make the cap fit smoothly. This lowers the sleeve cap and is a particularly effective way to reduce unwanted fullness in a short sleeve, which requires less ease. Although the shortened cap will cause the sleeve to hang at an angle from the shoulder instead of falling vertically, and the crossgrain will not be parallel to the floor, these imperfections will not be noticeable in a short sleeve. If your sleeve is long, however, these problems will be more obvious.

7. Stitch the sleeve permanently. Most sleeves are set in by machine because the method is less expensive than hand sewing. However, at Huntsman, the most expensive bespoke tailor on London's Saville Row, the tailors set sleeves by hand since it is easier to control than machine stitching. To set the sleeve by machine, double-baste at the top of the cap to prevent the ease from shifting when you stitch. Machine stitch. To set the sleeve by hand, use full backstitches, which are more elastic than the machine lockstitch. Since the sleeve is securely basted, I prefer to stitch with the garment uppermost.

8. Remove the bastings and press the armscye seam flat, allowing the tip of the iron to lap the seamline only ⅛ in.

9. At the bottom of the armscye, press the seam flat—don't press it open. It should stand straight up to allow the sleeves to hang in an attractive vertical line. At the top of the cap, the seam can be turned toward the sleeve, pressed open, or balanced, depending on the desired result. When turned toward the sleeve, the seam creates a small ridge at the top of the sleeve. When pressed open, the cap is flat at the top; clip the bodice seam allowance to the seamline on both the front and back at the capline, to free the underarm seam. When working with a bulky fabric, balance the seam with a small piece of fabric at the top of the cap; press the fabric toward the garment and the seam toward the sleeve (see "Balanced Darts," on p. 60).

10. On unlined garments, finish the raw edges with overcasting or a narrow binding (see p. 44).

11. Sew in the sleeve heads and shoulder pads.

# Blouse Sleeve

Unlike the basic one-piece sleeve, the blouse sleeve with a cuff doesn't have an elbow dart. Instead, the lower edge of the sleeve is cut longer at the back to provide enough length for the elbow to bend. The length on the sleeve front remains shorter than in back so the sleeve doesn't droop over the hand. At the wrist, the sleeve is pleated, gathered or tapered to fit into the cuff, and a small placket is added so the cuff can be pulled over the hand.

On couture blouses, the sleeves are often cut so the cuff faces toward the front, instead of toward the floor, because this is the way the arm hangs. This blouse sleeve is from an Yves Saint Laurent blouse.

(Photo by Author.)

## RESHAPE WRIST EDGE OF BLOUSE SLEEVE

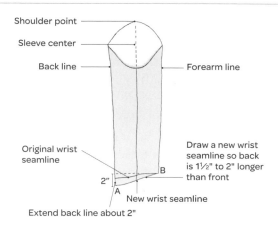

Shoulder point
Sleeve center
Back line
Forearm line
Original wrist seamline
Draw a new wrist seamline so back is 1½" to 2" longer than front
B
2"
A
New wrist seamline
Extend back line about 2"

## BLOUSE SLEEVE PATTERN SHAPING

On most commercial patterns, the sleeve wrist edge has a shallow S-curve. The sleeve will hang more attractively when this curve is exaggerated.

1. Pin the underarm seam together on the paper pattern.
2. Fold the sleeve pattern so the sleeve center and seam are aligned.
3. Square a line (that is, draw a right-angle line) from the forearm line to the back line. Extend the back line; mark point A 2 in. below the original wrist seamline. Mark point B on forearm line at the wrist.
4. Establish a new wrist seamline, beginning at the point A. Draw a gentle S-curve to point B.
5. Use the new pattern to cut the sleeves.

## TAILORED PLACKET

The opening of the tailored placket is finished with a wide band—the gauntlet—on the overlap and a narrow binding or a hem on the underlap. The gauntlet duplicates the grain of the sleeve and is generally finished about 1 in. wide and 3½ in. to 4½ in. long. The underlap binding is cut on the straight grain and finished ¼ in. wide and 1 in. shorter than the gauntlet upper edge. The upper end of the placket can be finished with a point or squared off; it usually extends about 1 in. beyond

the end of the opening. Unlike similar plackets on expensive ready-to-wear, the couture tailored placket is finished by hand without topstitching.

1. Thread-trace the opening. For a placket 1 in. wide by 4 in. long, mark the end 3¼ in. from the wrist seamline.
2. Cut the gauntlet 2¾ in. wide by 6 in. long. Cut the underlap binding 1¼ in. wide by 5 in. long.
3. Right sides together, align the edge of the underlap with the thread traced opening on the side nearer the underarm seam; baste ¼ in. from the thread-traced opening, stopping at the end of the placket.
4. Right sides together, align the edge of the gauntlet to the other side of the opening; baste ¼ in. from the opening, stopping at the end of the placket.
5. Machine stitch; tie the threads at the ends. Cut the slit open and clip straight or diagonally to the ends of the stitched lines.
6. Press both strips toward the opening; then wrap the underlap strip around the edge of the opening. Turn under the edge and fell stitch to the end (see "Fell Stitch," p.33).

## MAKING THE PLACKET SLIT

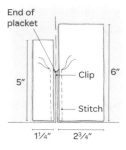

End of placket
Clip
6"
5"
Stitch
1¼"    2¾"

## FELL STITCHING THE PLACKET

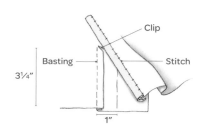

Clip
Basting
Stitch
3¼"
1"

7. To finish the overlap, baste a guide on the gauntlet 1 in. from the seamline. Fold the gauntlet with wrong sides together at the basted line so the gauntlet wraps around the edge of the opening; press lightly. Wrong side up, turn under the edge; pin. Fell stitch the gauntlet to the end of the placket.

8. To finish the point, begin with the sleeve right side up. Pull the gauntlet to the right side. Check to be sure the end of the underlap binding is on top of the sleeve and enclosed between the gauntlet and sleeve. Trim the underlap end to ¼ in.

9. Mark the gauntlet on both sides 4 in. from the wrist seamline; thread trace the sides of the point so they intersect at a right angle.

10. Fold and baste the end of the gauntlet to make the point, trimming as needed so the raw edges are hidden; baste. Using fell stitches, sew around the point and about ¼ in. down the sides.

11. Right sides together, stitch the underarm sleeve seam; press. Set the sleeve aside until you're ready to set the cuff.

### MAKING THE GAUNTLET

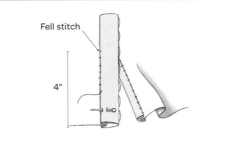

Fell stitch

4"

### FELL STITCHING THE GAUNTLET

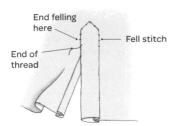

End felling here

Fell stitch

End of thread

## MAKE AND SET THE CUFF

Cuff styles range from very narrow straight bands to wide shaped cuffs, but simple barrel and French cuffs (with and without turn-backs) are the usual choice for classic shirts and blouses. Handworked and bound buttonholes, as well as button loops, are used to fasten barrel cuffs, while handworked buttonholes are generally preferred for French cuffs. The pattern for the barrel cuff included with most commercial patterns can be adapted easily to make a French cuff without a turn-back by replacing the button with a second buttonhole.

1. Cut out the cuffs; thread-trace the seamlines and foldline. Mark the button and buttonhole locations. Choose a lightweight interfacing such as silk organza, fine cotton batiste, or silk-weight interfacing. Cut the interfacing so it extends into the seam allowances and laps the folded cuff edge at the wrist by ½ in.

2. Wrong side up, baste the interfacing to the upper-cuff section, which will join the sleeve.

3. Divide the cuff wrist edge (excluding the seam allowances) into quarters so you can distribute the fullness evenly.

4. Divide the sleeve wrist edge into quarters.

CLAIRE'S HINT *I mark the sleeve center and align it with the underarm seam to mark the wrist seamline at the front and back folds. This distributes a little more fullness in the back of the sleeve than the front.*

5. Stitch two or three rows of gathers along the sleeve wrist seamline.

6. Right sides together, align the matchpoints and pin the cuff to the sleeve. Pull up and adjust the gathers on the cuff; baste.

7. Machine stitch the seam and trim to ½ in.

8. Remove the bastings and press the seam toward the cuff.

9. Right sides together, fold the cuff on the foldline, baste the ends without catching the blouse sleeve. Stitch.

CLAIRE'S HINT *Before stitching, I baste both cuffs, and turn them right-side out to be sure their shapes and ends are identical.*

## BASTE A CUFF

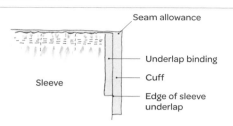

Seam allowance

Underlap binding

Cuff

Edge of sleeve underlap

Sleeve

## BASTE ENDS

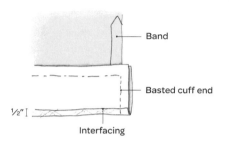

Band

Basted cuff end

½"

Interfacing

## FINISH A CUFF

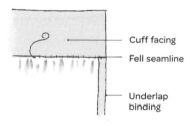

Cuff facing

Fell seamline

Underlap binding

10. Remove the bastings, press the seams open, and trim to ¼ in.

11. Sew the corners of the seam allowance to the interfacing with a catchstitch. Turn the cuffs right side out; press lightly.

12. Fold under the remaining raw edge; pin and baste. Fell stitch or slipstitch it permanently.

13. Remove the bastings and press.

# Tailored Sleeve

The principles for hanging and setting the basic one-piece sleeve can also be applied to the tailored sleeve. Generally used for coats, suits, and tailored dresses, the tailored sleeve differs in several ways

from a one-piece sleeve. First, it's cut with two or three pieces rather than one. It may also have a higher cap; the fullness for the elbow is built into the back seam. It may have a vent at the wrist, and it's usually lined. The sleeves on both the Yves Saint Laurent jacket on p. 172 and the Mainbocher jacket on p. 147 are excellent examples of tailored sleeves

The tailored sleeve is most often composed of two sections—an upper sleeve and a narrower under sleeve. The elbow, or back seam is located on the back of the sleeve, approximately midway between the sleeve center and underarm; and the inseam, or front seam, is located on the underside of the sleeve front about ¾ in. from the center of the underarm.

The tailored sleeve is basted and hung in the same way as the one-piece sleeve. If you make a toile, use the muslin as a pattern for cutting out the fabric and the lining. The sleeve lining should have a 1½-in. seam allowance at the cap and a 1¼-in. hem allowance at the bottom.

## THREAD-TRACED TWO-PIECE SLEEVE

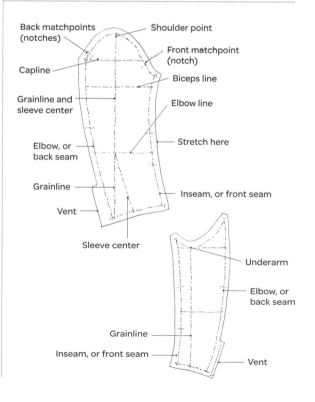

Back matchpoints (notches)

Shoulder point

Front matchpoint (notch)

Capline

Biceps line

Grainline and sleeve center

Elbow line

Elbow, or back seam

Stretch here

Grainline

Inseam, or front seam

Vent

Sleeve center

Underarm

Elbow, or back seam

Grainline

Inseam, or front seam

Vent

Most tailored sleeves have two pieces—an upper sleeve (the one with buttons) and a smaller under sleeve. The vent, if any, is located at the end of the back vent. These sleeves are on an Yves Saint Laurent jacket which you can see on p. 172.

(Photo by Susan Kahn. Author's collection.)

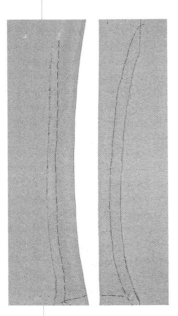

The tailored sleeve drapes more attractively when the front seam of the upper sleeve is shaped before it is joined to the under sleeve. On the sample, you can see the difference. The sleeve on the right was folded vertically. The fold is straight; the amount folded under is wider at the top and bottom than at the center. The upper sleeve on the left was stretched at the center before it was folded under. The fold is curved; the amount folded under is the same width at the top, bottom, and center, mimicking the shape of the arm itself.

(Photo by Susan Kahn. Author's collection.)

## SHAPE THE UPPER SLEEVE

Before assembling the sleeves, shape the upper sleeve so it will curve to the shape of the arm instead of wrinkling unattractively. To do this, stretch the shorter edge of the upper sleeve to fit the under sleeve.

1. Stack the right and left sleeves right sides together. Place the sleeves on the pressing table with the front seam away from you.

2. Dampen the curved edge of the sections at the elbow.

CLAIRE'S HINT *When working on wool, I use a damp sponge; on silks or other fabrics, I use a damp press cloth.*

3. Place the iron on the front seam at the wrist, press and stretch the edge. Turn the sections over and repeat. To determine when you've stretched the edge enough, make a vertical fold about ¾ in. from the seamline. The folded edge should curve nicely from top to bottom without wrinkling at the center (see the bottom left photo).

## ASSEMBLE THE SLEEVE

In couture, the tailored sleeve is lined before it's sewn into the garment. In dressmaking, the lining is not sewn in until the garment is almost complete.

1. Baste the sleeves together, then baste them to the garment for the fitting.

After the fitting, take out the bastings, lay the sleeve flat and make any corrections.

2. Machine stitch the front seam. Stretch the seam allowances as you press the seam flat; press the seams open. Fold the sleeve in half vertically and mark the foldline with basting.

3. With the sleeve wrong side up, smooth it flat on one side of the basted line; press to the basted line. Repeat on the other half of the sleeve.

4. Machine stitch and press the elbow seam, finish the vent if there is one, interface the sleeve hem, and hem the sleeve. Remove the bastings. If the sleeve has a vent, baste it closed.

5. Machine stitch the back seam; press.

## LINE THE SLEEVE

1. Right sides together, stitch the vertical seams on the lining; press.

CLAIRE'S HINT *I stitch them slightly narrower than the sleeve seams so the lining is a little larger than the sleeve since the lining material is often more firmly woven than the shell fabric, which is usually wool on a tailored jacket.*

2. To sew the lining in, begin with both the sleeve and lining wrong side out. Lay the sleeve on the table with the under sleeve down. Place the lining on top of the sleeve (under sleeve up) so the elbow seams are aligned. Align the matchpoints on the elbow and inseam seamlines. Pin the seams together.

## SET LINING TO SLEEVE

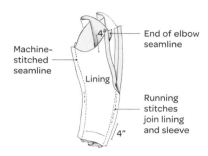

Machine-stitched seamline

4″ — End of elbow seamline

Lining

4″

Running stitches join lining and sleeve

Using running stitches, sew the lining and sleeve seams together, sewing close to the seamline and beginning and ending about 4 in. from each end of the seam. Keep the stitches loose so the lining will not distort the sleeve when the garment is worn.

3. Turn the sleeve and lining right side out, and arrange the lining inside the sleeve.

4. Using large diagonal basting stitches, baste the sleeve and lining together about 5 in. from the wrist and just below the cap.

5. At the wrist, trim the lining hem so it's ½ in. longer than the finished length of the sleeve.

6. Turn the sleeve wrong side out. Fold the lining under so the sleeve hem shows ½ in. to ¾ in. Baste ⅜ in. from the folded edge.

7. Hold the fold of the lining out of the way with your thumb. Sew the lining to the hem using a blindstitch.

8. Fold the top of the lining out of the way so you can set the sleeve.

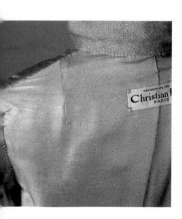

In haute couture, the sleeve lining is always sewn by hand, as on this Christian Dior coat from 1970. Hand-stitched linings often have excess fullness at the armscye and are not eased as smoothly as with machine stitching, a true sign of a hand-made garment.

(Photo by Susan Kahn. Author's collection.)

## BASTE LINING TO SLEEVE

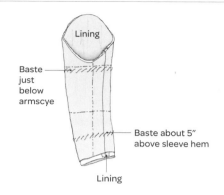

Lining

Baste just below armscye

Baste about 5″ above sleeve hem

Lining

## HEM SLEEVE LINING

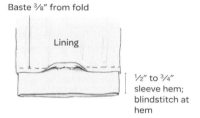

Baste ⅜″ from fold

Lining

½″ to ¾″ sleeve hem; blindstitch at hem

## FINISH THE SLEEVE LINING

After setting the sleeve, add the shoulder pads and sleeve heads (see p. 157) and line the body of the garment.

1. To finish the lining, hold the garment right side out; baste around the armscye of the garment on the seamline.

2. Bring the sleeve cap lining up into the sleeve cap. Smooth the lining and pin it to the sleeve about 4 in. from the top.

3. At the underarm, smooth the lining over the armscye seam without flattening the seam. Turn under the raw edge; pin the folded edge to the seamline. Trim as needed to remove excess lining.

4. At the top of the cap, smooth the lining in place. Trim away the excess lining, adjust the fullness, and pin. Baste the lining around the armscye about ⅛ in. from the folded edge. Using fell stitches, sew the lining permanently. Remove the bastings. The lining should be neat, but it will not be as smooth as a machine-stitched lining on ready-to-wear designs.

# Sleeve Heads, Boosters, and Interfacings

**MOST SLEEVES NEED SOME** support to maintain their shape. Couturiers often use sleeve heads, sleeve boosters, and interfacings for this purpose. A sleeve head or header is used to support a classic, eased sleeve cap, while a sleeve booster supports a full or exaggerated cap. Compared to a sleeve head, a booster is usually wider and fuller and extends farther into the sleeve cap. A sleeve interfacing duplicates the sleeve cap and can be used on a variety of sleeve types. All are used with or without shoulder pads but are sewn into the sleeve cap rather than the shoulder area of the garment.

Sleeve heads, boosters, and interfacings are made from a variety of fabrics from silk organza to hair canvas, depending on how light or crisp of a support is needed. They can be made with a single or double roll of fabric and can be wide or narrow. A single roll usually just fills out any "dimples" in a sleeve cap, while a double roll produces the effect of a full, well-defined cap. To decide which fabric to use and whether to make a single-layer or double-layer roll, first determine the effect you want to achieve.

## INTERFACING THE SLEEVE CAP

Although sleeves are rarely interfaced completely like the jacket front, a sleeve cap interfacing can provide minimal support to enhance the appearance, prevent the sleeve cap from collapsing, and fill out any dimples near the armscye seam. Interfacings, unlike sleeve heads and boosters are sewn into the sleeve before the sleeve is assembled.

**1.** Make a pattern for the interfacing using the sleeve pattern. Depending on the amount of support required and the shell fabric, the interfacing can extend just to the notches or as much as 2 in. below the armhole. Draw the grainline at a 45° angle to the sleeve center so the interfacing will be cut on the bias.

**2.** Wrong side up, place the interfacing on the sleeve cap; use diagonal basting stitches to baste the layers together at the center.

**3.** At the top of the cap, place a row of ease basting on the seamline between the notches. Place a second row ⅛ in. above the first.

**4.** Assemble the sleeve.

Here is an inside view of an Yves Saint Laurent jacket showing a hair canvas interfacing for the cap and a shaped lambswool sleeve header. The interfacing can be shorter and extend only to the middle of the cap. I usually cut it longer and trim it if needed later. Also, I cut the interfacing on the bias because it is easier to shape than the straight grain seen here.

(Photo by Greg Rothschild, courtesy of *Threads* magazine.)

## MAKING A SLEEVE HEAD

To make a sleeve head to preserve the shape of a flat, smooth cap, choose a lightweight material like silk organza, blouse-weight silk, or muslin, and sew a sleeve head with a single roll. For a subtle increase in the size of the sleeve head, use muslin, soft wool, lambswool, or hair canvas or wrap the sleeve head fabric around a piece of wadding.

**1.** Cut two bias strips about 8½ in. long and 1½ in. wide. For medium-weight wools, I use hair canvas, soft wool, or lambswool. For lighter weight materials, I use silk organza, China silk, or muslin.

**2.** Fold the strip lengthwise so one long edge is ⅛ in. wider than the other; using loose diagonal stitches, sew the layers together. Round the corners, so they don't curl or show on the right side.

**3.** Place the folded edge of the sleeve head on the armscye seamline so the wider side of the sleeve head lies against the sleeve. Adjust the sleeve head so it extends 5 in. into the back of the sleeve. Using blindstitches, sew the folded edge to the seamline stitches.

**4.** To support a high sleeve cap with a well-defined sleeve cap, choose materials like wadding, cotton batting, hair canvas, soft wool, or lambswool. Cut the bias strip 2½ in. wide and 8½ in. long. Make the sleeve head using the directions above. When using wadding or cotton batting, fold it with the fuzzy side out. Tear the cut edges with your fingers to feather them so they will not make a ridge.

**5.** Place the sleeve head at the top of the cap, but lap the folded edge ⅛ in. to ¼ in. over the seamline instead of aligning the fold with the seamline. Sew through all layers at the seamline with a running stitch, just catching the seamline. When the sleeve head is turned toward the sleeve, it will have a double roll.

## MAKING A SLEEVE BOOSTER

This booster will support the cap on most sleeves. For the cap on a more extended shoulder, make the booster wider and shape it like a football.

**1.** For each booster, cut a strip of lightweight silk on the crossgrain, 3 in. by 13½ in. Cut a bias strip of woven interfacing 1½ in. by 14 in.

**2.** Wrong side up, align one long raw edge of the interfacing to the silk; baste.

**3.** Right sides together, fold the silk strip in half lengthwise. Stitch a ¼-in. seam at the ends, rounding the corners. Trim away the excess at the ends.

**4.** Turn the booster right side out.

**5.** Gather the unfinished edge ¼ in. from the edge. Pull up the gathers to 7½ in.

**6.** Bind the gathered edges with chiffon or organza.

**7.** Using running stitches or blindstitches, sew the bound edge to the armscye seam.

## MAKING A SLEEVE HEAD

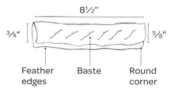

8½"

¾"          ⅝"

Feather edges     Baste     Round corner

## DOUBLE-ROLL SLEEVE HEAD

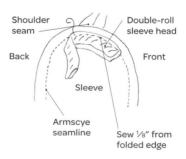

Shoulder seam          Double-roll sleeve head

Back          Front

Sleeve

Armscye seamline          Sew ⅛" from folded edge

## MAKING A SLEEVE BOOSTER

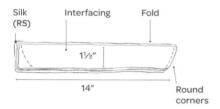

Silk (RS)     Interfacing     Fold

1½"

14"          Round corners

## SEW BOOSTER TO ARMSCYE

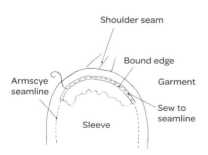

Shoulder seam

Bound edge

Armscye seamline          Garment

Sew to seamline

Sleeve

# 9

# Pockets

POCKETS CAN BE DECORATIVE as well as functional. During her comeback years, when Chanel was one of the reigning influences in the couture industry, she applied pockets lavishly to all types of garments from sportswear to formal wear. She designed pockets to be used, rather than just to decorate a garment. Many photographs of

If you look carefully, you can see the pockets on this suit designed by Chanel in 1967. The top of the pocket, collar, and back belt are trimmed with self-fabric, which has been cut apart and resewn. On the pocket trim, the navy color bars were resewn to create a design at the ends.

(Photo by Ken Howie. Author's collection.)

"la grande Mademoiselle," as Chanel was called, show her with her hands hidden inside her jacket pockets. This is not to say that all of her pockets were functional—some were merely artfully executed flaps.

Chanel's pocket designs, even when elaborately trimmed, were simple. By comparison, those of her contemporary, Elsa Schiaparelli, featured unusual shapes, with fanciful embellishments of beads, embroidery, and even metal springs. Designer Christian Dior sometimes used pockets to add roundness to the hips, which in turn made the waistline look smaller.

Whatever their shape or design, pockets fall into two basic categories: patch pockets and set-in pockets. The patch pocket is a "pocket bag" sewn to the outside of the garment, while the set-in pocket is a pocket bag sewn into a seam opening or slash, which rests unseen inside the garment.

Couturiers have much to teach us about pockets. In many instances, their techniques differ from those used in home sewing and in ready-to-wear construction, and are easy to apply to other design elements. For example, the directions for patch pockets and flaps can be applied to belts and tabs, and bound pocket directions can be adapted for zipper openings and bound plackets.

## Patch Pockets

Unlike pockets on ready-to-wear garments, patch pockets on couture designs are applied by hand. In fact, a hand-applied patch pocket is one of the identifying characteristics of a couture

This Paul Poiret simple coat from 1923 features two stunning patch pockets embellished with wool embroidery. Designed to flatter the figure, the pocket "straps" are embroidered on the coat and give the illusion of separate hanging pockets.

(Photo courtesy of the Chicago History Museum.)

garment, even though many such pockets are first topstitched to look as if they've been applied by machine.

Patch pockets usually consist of three layers: the pocket itself, interfacing, and lining, which usually match the garment lining. When the pocket is made of transparent or open-weave fabrics, it may also be backed to hide the construction details or to match other sections of the garment, or it may be cut with a self-fabric lining and an interfacing.

This type of pocket can be made before or after the first fitting. If the pocket shape and size is established before the fitting, the pockets are usually finished and basted in place for the fitting. If the pocket shape, size, or location is in question and to be determined at the fitting, or if the pocket and garment are patterned and require matching, cut a temporary pocket shape from a fabric scrap and baste it onto the garment for the fitting.

### POCKET CUTTING AND MARKING

These directions are for an interfaced patch pocket with a separate lining. They can be adapted for a flap or for an applied-welt pocket.

1. Cut a muslin pattern the size and shape of the finished pocket; don't add seam or hem allowances. CLAIRE'S HINT *When the fabric has a design that must be matched, I cut a pattern for each pocket so the fabric design can be marked on each pattern.*

2. Complete any seams on the garment that will be under the pocket. Thread-trace the pocket locations on the garment sections.
3. Right side up, place the pocket pattern on the thread tracing that marks the pocket's location. Draw the continuation of the grain or the color bars of the fabric pattern onto the muslin pocket. When the pocket stands away from the garment, match the pattern at the edge toward center front. Instead of drawing the fabric design on the pocket, pin a fabric scrap on it to use as a guide when cutting out.
4. Right side up, place the muslin pocket pattern on a large scrap of the garment fabric. Match the

design and grain on the pattern to those on the scrap; pin. Chalk-mark around the pattern, then thread trace. If there is a pair of pockets, repeat the procedure for the other pocket.

5. Add seam and hem allowances. Cut out the pocket.

CLAIRE'S HINT *When cutting out, I don't measure the width of the seam and hem allowances because I thread-traced the finished size, and the allowances don't have to be exact. I leave at least ½-in. seam allowances and a 1¼-in. hem allowance at the pocket opening.*

## INTERFACE THE POCKET

Interfacing the pocket will help it hold its shape. The interfacing material for a pocket is often crisper than interfacings used in other parts of the garment, and its weight should be appropriate for the weight and drape of the garment fabric. Muslin, linen, hair canvas, and crisp lining fabrics are all suitable for interfacing, as are knit and weft fusibles when an especially crisp finish is preferred. The interfacing can be cut on the lengthwise grain or crossgrain, or on the bias.

The interfacing size is determined by the type and the desired look. Generally, the interfacing is cut to the finished pocket size. Fusible interfacings can be cut to the finished pocket size or extend into the seam or hem allowance. When the interfacing extends into the seam or hem allowances, the pocket edges will be slightly rounded instead of sharply creased.

1. Cut a piece of pocket interfacing. I use hair canvas. It can be cut on the lengthwise grain or crossgrain, or on the bias. Since the crossgrain will have the least stretch at the pocket opening, the opening doesn't have to be stabilized. The bias is more supple and shapes to the body better.

2. Wrong side up, place the interfacing on the pocket with the top of the interfacing just below the pocket hemline. Using large diagonal basting stitches, baste the centers together.

To check the interfacing size, fold and pin the pocket hem and seam allowances over the edges of

## INTERFACING THE POCKET

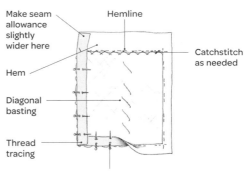

Make seam allowance slightly wider here

Hemline

Catchstitch as needed

Hem

Diagonal basting

Thread tracing

Fold and pin seam allowance

the interfacing, to be sure the thread-tracings are on the very edges of the pocket and invisible from the pocket right side. If the thread-tracings are visible from the right side, release the pins and trim the interfacing edges very slightly; repin and check again.

3. Release the pins so the pocket is flat. This is the first of three opportunities to topstitch the pocket. When topstitching, thread-trace a guide the desired distance from the finished edges; use a soft basting thread which breaks easily. It takes time to remove it but it isn't difficult. Or you can stitch next to the basted line.

4. Use catchstitches to sew the edges of the interfacing to the pocket wrong side. If the pocket is topstitched, skip this step.

5. Stabilize the pocket opening with a silk organza stay or seam binding. Steam-press the stay to shrink it. Center it over the thread traced foldline at the opening. Use running stitches to sew it permanently. Measure the pocket opening, including seam allowances, on the tissue pattern; and cut the stay this length

## FINISH POCKET EDGES

1. When the pocket has curved edges, ease-baste the seam allowance at the curves about ⅛ in. from the interfacing and again ¼ in. away. Pull up the ease basting so the seam allowance fits smoothly against the pocket, and shrink out the excess fullness (see p. 65). To avoid shrinking the pocket itself, place a

## FINISH POCKET EDGES

### CURVED CORNERS

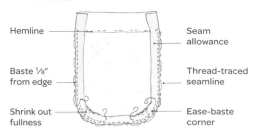

Hemline

Baste ⅛"
from edge

Shrink out
fullness

Seam
allowance

Thread-traced
seamline

Ease-baste
corner

### SQUARE-CORNER POCKET

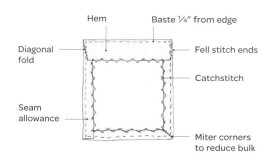

Hem

Diagonal
fold

Seam
allowance

Baste ¼" from edge

Fell stitch ends

Catchstitch

Miter corners
to reduce bulk

piece of brown paper between the seam allowance and the interfacing. Baste ¼ in. from the edges.

2. When the pocket has square corners, fold under the seam allowance at the bottom. Baste ¼ in. from the seamline and press. Fold and baste the side seam allowances.

CLAIRE'S HINT *To prevent the hem allowance from showing at the sides when it's folded back, I make a diagonal fold at the ends so the seam allowances in the hem are slightly wider than at the sides.*

3. Trim away the excess bulk at the corners and press the edges. When working with bulky fabrics, spank the corners with a clapper to flatten them.

4. Fold the hem at the top to the wrong side. Baste all edges of the pocket about ¼ in. from the edges. To reduce the bulk in the hem, clip the seam allowances on the foldline almost to the corners and remove a small triangle so the sides of the pocket hem can be tapered.

5. Wrong side up, press the edges and shrink out any excess fullness. Trim the seam allowances close to the basting to reduce the bulk.

6. Use catchstitches to sew the raw edges of the pocket to the interfacing if the pocket will not be topstitched.

7. This is the second opportunity to topstitch.

8. Press the pocket. Right side up, place the pocket on a tailor's ham or pressing pad that simulates the body's curve in the pocket area. Cover the pocket with a press cloth, and press to shape the pocket to conform to the shape of the body.

9. When making a pair of pockets, compare them to be sure they're identical. If the person for whom the garment is intended has an asymmetrical figure and one hip is larger than the other, the pocket for the larger side can be made slightly larger (up to ¼ in.); but when worn, the difference between the two pockets should be imperceptible.

## LINE THE POCKET

This lining technique with the wrong sides together can be applied for flaps, facings, and waistbands.

1. To line the pocket, cut a lining fabric rectangle on the same grain as the pocket and at least ¼ in. larger on all sides.

2. Fold under about 1 in. at the top of the lining; press.

3. Wrong sides together, place the lining on the pocket so the folded edge is about ¾ in. below the pocket top. Match the centers and baste them together with diagonal basting stitches. Fold under the remaining raw edges of the lining so they're ⅛ in. to ¼ in. from the edges, trimming the lining as needed to remove excess bulk; pin. Baste the lining to the pocket. Press the edges lightly.

4. Fell stitch the lining in place. Remove all bastings and press thoroughly, using a damp press cloth. This is the last opportunity to press the pocket before it's applied.

5. If topstitching the pocket, this is the last opportunity before it's applied.

## SET THE POCKET

Before setting the pocket to the garment, decide whether the garment should be stabilized with interfacing under the pocket or just under the opening. If the pocket is simply decorative or if the entire front is backed with interfacing, an interfacing stay may not be needed. But if the pocket is designed for occasional use and the front is not entirely interfaced, stay the opening.

1. Cut an interfacing stay on the straight grain about 2 in. wide and long enough so the ends of the stay can be sewn to the interfacing at the front opening and to a dart or seam at the side.

2. Wrong side up, baste the stay over the thread-traced opening. When you sew the pocket, you'll sew through the stay to secure it.

3. Right sides up, align the edges of the pocket with the thread-traced outline on the garment. Baste with a large "X" at the center; then use uneven basting stitches to baste an even ¼ in. from the edges.

### BASTE POCKET

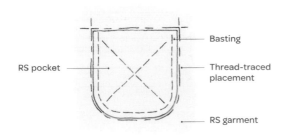

RS pocket

Basting

Thread-traced placement

RS garment

4. Examine the pocket. It can fit smoothly or stand away from the garment slightly but it should not be tight. If it looks tight, rebaste.

5. Wrong side up, use short running stitches or diagonal stitches to sew the pocket permanently. Use the basting as a guide to sew ⅛ in. from the pocket edge working carefully so the stitches don't show on the pocket face. If the pocket will be used frequently, sew two rows of diagonal stitches around the pocket.

6. At the top of the pocket, wrong side up, sew several cross stitches at each side for reinforcement.

7. Remove the bastings; press lightly using a press cloth.

# Set-in Pockets

There are two types of set-in pockets: the in-seam pocket sewn into a seam, and the slash pocket set into a slash. Unlike the single-layer pocket bag of a patch pocket, the pocket bag of a set-in pocket has two sections sewn together—an under pocket, which sets nearest the lining, and an upper pocket. On both couture and ready-to-wear skirts, an in-seam pocket often hides the skirt opening. However, couture skirts usually have zippers inside the pocket, while even very expensive ready-to-wear garments often do not.

## ZIPPERED IN-SEAM POCKET

These directions are for a lined skirt with an in-seam pocket in a side seam and a 7-in. zipper inside the pocket.

### Mark the Pocket

1. Cut out the skirt with a 1½-in. seam allowance on the side seams. Measure and mark the pocket opening 8 in. below the waistline thread tracing.

2. Thread-trace the seamlines and baste the skirt together.

3. Cut a rectangle 10 in. by 12 in. from lining fabric for the pocket bag.

4. Right sides together, stitch the seam below the pocket opening; knot the thread ends. Remove the basting.

5. With the skirt right side up, chalk a line on the front seam allowance 1⅜ in. from the side seam. On the skirt back, chalk and thread trace the zipper opening 1 in. from the seamline. Mark the bottom of the pocket opening 7¼ in. below the thread traced waistline.

6. On the skirt back, clip the seam allowance at the bottom of the opening to the seamline so you can press the seam open below the clip.

7. With the skirt front wrong side up, stabilize the pocket opening with a narrow strip of organza (see p. 101) Turn under the seam allowance at the opening and baste ¼ in. from the edge.

## INSEAM POCKET WITH ZIPPER

**MARK POCKET**

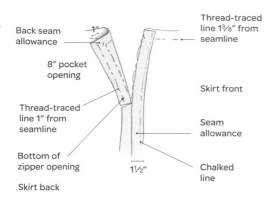

Back seam allowance

1"

8" pocket opening

Thread-traced line 1" from seamline

Bottom of zipper opening

Skirt back

1½"

Thread-traced line 1⅜" from seamline

Skirt front

Seam allowance

Chalked line

**BASTE SKIRT FRONT TO POCKET BAG**

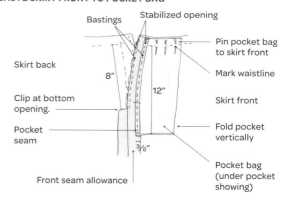

Bastings

Stabilized opening

Skirt back

8"

12"

Clip at bottom opening.

Pocket seam

Front seam allowance

3⁄8"

Pin pocket bag to skirt front

Mark waistline

Skirt front

Fold pocket vertically

Pocket bag (under pocket showing)

**PREPARE ZIPPER OPENING**

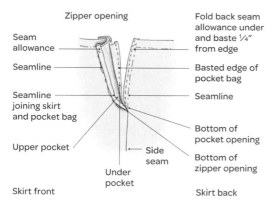

Zipper opening

Seam allowance

Seamline

Seamline joining skirt and pocket bag

Upper pocket

Skirt front

Side seam

Under pocket

Fold back seam allowance under and baste ¼" from edge

Basted edge of pocket bag

Seamline

Bottom of pocket opening

Bottom of zipper opening

Skirt back

**ATTACH SKIRT LINING**

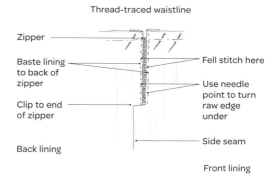

Thread-traced waistline

Zipper

Baste lining to back of zipper

Clip to end of zipper

Back lining

Fell stitch here

Use needle point to turn raw edge under

Side seam

Front lining

### Baste Skirt Front to Pocket Bag

1. Right sides together, match and pin one side of the pocket bag to the chalk-marked line on the skirt front seam allowance. Baste the pocket (this is the upper pocket) and skirt front together with a ⅜-in. seam. Stitch and knot the thread ends.

2. Remove the bastings. Press the seam flat, and then press it toward the pocket bag.

3. Turn under the opposite side of the pocket bag (the under pocket) ⅜ in.; baste.

4. Turn the skirt wrong side up, fold the bag in half vertically, with right sides together. Smooth the pocket bag toward the center front; pin and baste the top of the bag to the skirt.

5. Mark the waistline on the pocket bag, using the thread tracing at the skirt waistline as a guide. Mark the bottom of the zipper opening on the folded edge of the under pocket 7¼ in. below the thread-traced waistline.

### Join Skirt Back to Pocket Bag

1. Right sides up, align the seamlines of the skirt front and back at the pocket opening; top-baste them together so the right sides are together. Pin the pocket bag in place wrong side up. Align the thread-tracings at the waist and bottom of the zipper opening on the pocket bag and skirt back.

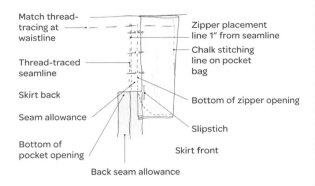

Match thread-tracing at waistline

Thread-traced seamline

Skirt back

Seam allowance

Bottom of pocket opening

Back seam allowance

Zipper placement line 1" from seamline

Chalk stitching line on pocket bag

Bottom of zipper opening

Slipstich

Skirt front

2. To complete the seam below the zipper opening, slipstitch the pocket to the skirt back seam allowance beginning at the mark at the bottom of the zipper to the clipped seam allowance (about ³⁄₄ in.). Remove the bastings and press the seam open. Knot the thread ends.

3. Spread the skirt wrong side up with the pocket on top. Smooth the pocket toward the front; pin the pocket bag together at the bottom.

4. Chalk-mark the pocket stitching line, beginning on the skirt front at the bottom of the opening, continuing to the front of the pocket. To chalk-mark the front edge, begin at the top about 1 in. from the fold and end on the fold about 5 in. from the bottom. Baste. When basting, hold the skirt seam allowances out of the way to avoid sewing through them.

5. Stitch, knot the thread ends, remove the bastings, and press flat.

6. Trim the pocket seams to ¼ in. Overcast the raw edges of the pocket together.

**Prepare Zipper Opening.** On the skirt back, stabilize the zipper opening, with a narrow strip of organza. Fold the seam allowances to the wrong side and baste ¼ in. from the edge; press. Baste and sew the zipper in by hand (see p. 101).

**Skirt Lining.** To finish the zipper, add the skirt lining and sew to the zipper by hand.

1. When lining the skirt, cut the lining seam allowances 1½ in. wide—at least on the left side, where the zipper will be located—since the placket is 1 in. from the side seam.

2. Right sides together, pin the lining seam; mark the bottom of the opening 7¼ in. below the waistline. Stitch and press the seam below the zipper, but not in the placket area.

3. Wrong sides together, pin the skirt and lining together with the seamlines aligned at the waist and sides.

4. Place the skirt, lining side up, on a large pressing stand. Adjust the back lining so the lining covers the skirt back and zipper tape; pin.

5. On the lining front, mark the end of the zipper; clip to the marked point. Using the point of the needle, tuck the seam allowances under at the bottom of the zipper; pin. Repeat at the sides; baste. Press the lining lightly and fell stitch it in place.

Always a smart touch for a tailored jacket, a double-welt pocket can be made with or without a flap. On this linen Yves Saint Laurent jacket from the 1970s, the pocket flap was inserted between the welts; it has been tucked inside the pocket to show the opening. Wider flaps are sometimes used and applied by hand to the fabric above the pocket.

(Photo by Susan Kahn. Author's collection.)

6. Remove the skirt from the pressing stand. Trim the lining seam allowances as needed in the zipper area. Trim the seam allowances below the zipper to 1 in., remove all bastings and overcast the edges.

## BOUND SLASH POCKET

Many styles of slashed pockets are found on couture garments. I've included directions for two, a bound or jetted pocket and an applied-welt pocket, because these styles are the most popular and the most difficult to sew.

The bound pocket is a type of double-welt pocket, which has two narrow welts visible on the garment right side and a pocket bag hidden between the lining and garment. A bound pocket can be plain, it can have a flap covering one or both of the welts, or it can have an applied welt covering both welts.

There are many couture methods for making bound pockets, but I particularly like one that uses two fabric strips to bind the edges of the pocket opening. This method can also be adapted for making a bound buttonhole (see p. 91) and is suitable for many fabrics, including those with an obvious grain or pattern to be matched. The finished pocket is flat, and the two welts are exactly the same depth. Each welt is interfaced with its own seam allowance and can be cut on the bias and shaped as needed for a curved opening.

The pocket size will vary with the style and pocket location. The pocket bag should not extend below the jacket's finished edge or overlap the hem allowance (although I have seen pockets that extended into the hem).

### BOUND POCKET

**STITCH WELTS**

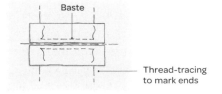

Baste

Thread-tracing
to mark ends

### Prepare the Opening and Welts

1. Thread-trace the pocket opening and the stitching lines on the garment for the first fitting so you can check the pocket placement and size of the opening.

   After the fitting, remove the bastings and lay the garment flat.
2. Stabilize the opening on the wrong side to support the weight of the pocket. Cut the stay 2 in. wide and several inches longer than the pocket opening. Baste it in place and thread-trace the pocket opening precisely.
3. From the shell or garment fabric, cut two welts 1½ in. wide and at least 1 in. longer than the pocket.

CLAIRE'S HINT *I cut the welts with the lengthwise grain parallel to the opening, but they can also be cut on the crosswise grain to match an obvious pattern, or on the bias.*

4. Interface the welts with a very lightweight interfacing if they are cut on the crossgrain or bias, or if sewn from stretchy or soft materials.

CLAIRE'S HINT *This is one of the few times I use a fusible interfacing.*

### Stitch Welts

1. Right sides together, align the edge of one welt to the thread traced pocket opening; pin. Repeat for the other welt, butting the edges together. Baste on the stitching lines. If this is one of a pair, baste the welts on the second pocket as well. When matching a fabric pattern, match the pattern at the stitching line, not the pocket opening. Also, double baste to be sure the welts won't slip when stitching.
2. Machine stitch on the basted lines. Examine the wrong side to be sure the distance between the stitched lines is even, the lines are straight and the proper length, and that paired pockets match. Remove the bastings. Pull the thread ends sharply to remove any slack in the thread; knot them securely.

### Slash Pocket

1. Slash the pocket opening, beginning and ending ½ in. from the ends and taking care not to cut

the welt strips. Clip diagonally to the ends of the stitched lines, being careful to avoid cutting the welt and pocket seam allowances.

2. Wrong side up, press the welt seams open, pressing the interfacing and garment seam allowances away from the opening. Press the triangles at the end away from the opening. If the fabric is very lightweight, press the seams flat instead of open.

### Finish Welts

1. Turn the garment right side up, push the welts through the slash and wrap them around the welt seam allowances. Straighten the welts so they're

## BOUND POCKET

**SLASH POCKET**

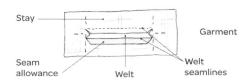

Stay

Seam allowance

Welt

Garment

Welt seamlines

**FINISH WELTS**

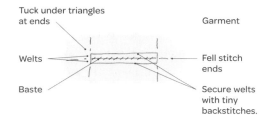

Tuck under triangles at ends

Welts

Baste

Garment

Fell stitch ends

Secure welts with tiny backstitches.

**JOIN UNDER POCKET TO UPPER WELT**

Baste on welt seamline

Under pocket

Pin under pocket to upper welt

Garment

even and fill the opening without overlapping. Tuck under the fabric triangles at each end of the opening so they are between the garment and welts. The welts should be flat and barely touch at the center. When the fabric is thick or bulky, trim the edges of the welt seams so the welts lie flat.

2. Right side up, pin each welt in the well of the seam. Check to be sure the widths between the seamlines are even, they fill the opening without overlapping, and that both welts on both pockets are identical. Using diagonal stitches, baste the welts together at the opening.

3. Using tiny backstitches, sew the welts permanently in the well of the seam.

4. Right side up, fold the garment back to expose the triangles at the ends. Give them a sharp tug to keep them from showing at the corners. Use felling stitches at the ends of the welts to sew permanently.

5. Place the garment section facedown on a softly padded surface and press lightly. Remove the bastings and press again.

### Set Pocket Bags

1. Turn under the top of the upper pocket (lining) about 1/2 in.

CLAIRE'S HINT *In couture, small sections like the under pocket and upper pocket are not cut out using a pattern; instead, a fabric scrap at least 1 in. wider than the pocket opening is used. If the fabric has a prominent pattern, align the under pocket with the fabric design on the garment section; then trim as needed.*

2. Wrong side up, pin the upper pocket to the lower welt so the folded edge just covers the stitching on the welt.

3. Use slipstitches to sew the upper pocket permanently.

4. Wrong side up, center the under pocket over the opening. Pin the under pocket to the upper welt seam allowance, and baste on the original seamline.

5. To stitch the under pocket permanently, turn the garment right side up and fold back the garment

This traditional man-tailored jacket from Yves Saint Laurent's 1978 Collection has an applied-welt breast pocket and two patch pockets at the hips (see the full view of the jacket on p. 172). The topstitching on the welt is decorative, and the ends are sewn together by hand, then sewn to the jacket with catchstitches. Both the pocket and the jacket are lined with silk charmeuse.

(Photo by Susan Kahn. Author's collection.)

section to expose the basted seam. Stitch on the basting.

CLAIRE'S HINT *When the pocket is decorative or will receive only light use, I use running stitches to sew it permanently.*

6. Wrong side up, smooth the under pocket over the upper pocket. Pin the sides of the pocket bag together, keeping the bag flat. Hold the under pocket taut to prevent the pocket from curling toward the outer shell, and baste the bag together. Stitch, rounding the corners to prevent them from

catching lint. Remove all bastings and press. Trim away any excess. Don't worry if the pocket edges do not match. It's more important for the pocket bag to lie smooth.

7. Before lining the garment, fasten the ends of the pocket stay to the interfacing, or when possible to a dart or seam allowance. Trim any excess fabric. If the bottom of the pocket overlaps the interfacing at the hem, sew them together with a running stitch.

## APPLIED-WELT POCKETS

The applied-welt, or stand, pocket is a slash pocket with a single welt attached at the lower edge of the opening. The welt is sewn from self-fabric, usually interfaced and always lined. The lining can be made from lining fabric and cut separately, or it can be self-fabric and cut in one with the welt itself.

The applied-welt pocket can be set straight or at an angle. Breast pockets in traditional tailored jackets are set at a slight angle, even though they may appear at first glance to be straight. Hip pockets on dresses and coats are often set at a flattering 45° angle.

**The Welt Pattern.** These directions are for a single-piece breast pocket set at a slight angle, with a folded edge at the top and self-fabric lining. When making a two-piece welt with a separate lining, you can adapt the directions for a patch pocket on p. 160.

1. When using a commercial pattern, begin by trimming the seam allowances from the welt pattern so you can mark the seamlines accurately on the fabric.

2. To make your own pattern for the welt, fold a rectangle of pattern paper horizontally; outline the finished shape of the welt on the paper, with the top of the welt positioned on the fold. Place the pattern on the jacket front on the location line. Mark the grainline on the pattern so it is the same as the front.

When the welt is set at an angle, the ends are parallel to the center front and the pattern will have angles at the ends. When the welt is placed

# APPLIED-WELT POCKET

### CUT WELT

Welt lining

Welt

1"

Grainline

³⁄₈"

Foldline

### JOIN WELT TO POCKET OPENING

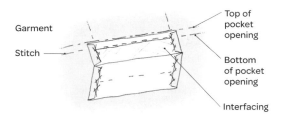

Garment

Stitch

Top of pocket opening

Bottom of pocket opening

Interfacing

### JOIN UNDER POCKET TO POCKET OPENING

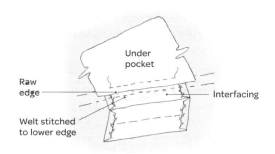

Under pocket

Raw edge

Interfacing

Welt stitched to lower edge

### FOLD WELT INTO PLACE

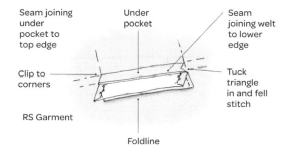

Seam joining under pocket to top edge

Under pocket

Seam joining welt to lower edge

Clip to corners

Tuck triangle in and fell stitch

RS Garment

Foldline

### FINISH WELT

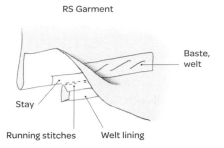

RS Garment

Baste, welt

Stay

Running stitches

Welt lining

### SEW UPPER POCKET TO LOWER EDGE OF OPENING

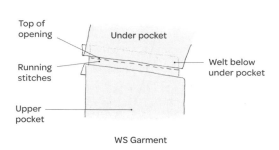

Top of opening

Under pocket

Running stitches

Welt below under pocket

Upper pocket

WS Garment

horizontally, the pattern will be a simple rectangle. Don't add seam allowances to the pattern. You will add them when you cut out the welt.

**Mark and Cut the Welt.** Use these directions to mark and cut the welt so it matches the fabric pattern of the jacket.

1. Right side up, pin the welt pattern to the garment section. Chalk-mark around it; then thread-trace.

CLAIRE'S HINT *To hide the pocket opening under the welt, I mark the stitching line at the top about ³⁄₈ in. shorter than the bottom. To determine whether I need to shorten the top line, I pin the paper pattern on the garment; if the top line extends beyond the pattern, I shorten it.*

2. When the fabric has a matchable design, such as a stripe or plaid, don't remove the pattern from the garment section until you mark the design on the pattern.

CLAIRE'S HINT *I place a small scrap of the fabric on the pattern and move it around until it matches the garment section; then I pin it in place securely.*

3. Right side up, place the welt pattern on a larger fabric scrap, matching the grain. Chalk-mark around welt; then thread-trace. If the fabric has a design, move the welt pattern around until the designs on the welt and garment match.

4. Chalk-mark ³⁄₈-in. seam allowances at the bottom of the welt and at each end. At the top, chalk-mark a 1-in. seam allowance; this is the edge that will join the pocket bag. Thread-trace the fold and seamlines on the welt.

5. Cut out the welt.

6. Cut the interfacing the size of the finished welt.

## MAKE THE WELT

These directions are quite different from home sewing methods; but the technique used here, wrapping the seam allowances around the interfacing and sewing the welt by hand, guarantees a successful outcome. This is a basic couture technique that can be used for many applications such as patch pockets, waistbands, even necklines.

1. Wrong side up, place the interfacing on the welt. Using catchstitches, secure the edges.

2. Fold and press the seam allowances at each end of the welt to the wrong side. Clip as needed so the seam allowances lie flat; baste about ¼ in. from the ends. Check the size of the welt against the pattern and rework the welt if it needs to be larger or smaller.

3. Wrong side up, press. Spank with a clapper, if needed, to flatten the seam allowances.

4. Trim close to the bastings; then use catchstitches to sew the seam allowances to the interfacing. Remove all bastings except at the foldline.

5. For a topstitched welt, topstitch the top of the welt and the ends ¼ in. from the edges. When the fabric is a pile or napped fabric, camel's hair, satin, brocade, or other special occasion fabrics, I skip this.

6. Fold the welt on the foldline; the top of the welt—the welt lining—should be slightly narrower than the welt itself. Press.

## ASSEMBLE THE POCKET

The pocket opening is just a slash in the fabric. The welt is stitched to the bottom and the under pocket is sewn to the top.

1. Stabilize the opening. I baste a 2-in. by 6-in. piece of organza to the wrong side of the garment.

2. Cut out the under pocket so it is at least 1 in. wider than the pocket opening and about 5 in. long. If the fabric has a design, match the design on the under pocket to the garment section above it.

3. Right sides together, align the lower seamline on the welt with the lower stitching line on the garment with the welt ends positioned precisely at the ends of the stitching line; pin. Baste on the seamline next to the welt interfacing.

CLAIRE'S HINT *Before stitching, I fold the welt into its finished position to be sure the fabric pattern on the welt matches the garment and the ends of the topstitching line are under the welt. Matching patterns and carefully positioning the ends of the stitching lines are particularly important when the pocket is on a slant.*

4. Right sides together, place the under pocket on the garment, aligning the raw edge with the stitching line at the top of the opening; pin. Baste. Machine stitch the basted lines, knotting the thread ends securely. For added control when stitching the welt, I begin and end the machine stitching one stitch short of the needed length, leave long thread tails, and hand-sew the final stitches.

5. Wrong side up, press the marked opening flat. Slash the opening, stopping ½ in. from the ends; then clip to the ends of the stitched lines without cutting into the welt, under pocket, or stitches. Push the under pocket through to the wrong side and press both seams open.

Before cutting, I always fold the welt in place to be sure it will cover the ends of the topstitching line. If you can see the top line, remove the stitching and restitch.

6. Right side up, fold the welt up into position. Wrong side up, press the welt seam open.

7. Fold the welt at the foldline with wrong sides together. Baste the ends together ¼ in. from the edge. Use blindstitches between the layers to sew the ends invisibly.

8. Right side up, push the unfinished edge of the welt and the triangles at the ends to the wrong side. Turn the section over and lightly press the seamline at the bottom of the welt.

9. Right side up, use diagonal stitches to baste the welt in its finished position, being careful not to catch the under pocket.

10. Fold back the garment to expose the seam allowances at the bottom of the opening. Using running stitches, sew the unfinished edge of the welt to the seam allowances at the bottom of the pocket.

## FINISH THE POCKET BAG

The last step is to finish the pocket bag. In couture, a pattern for the pocket sacks is rarely used. Instead, the two scraps of fabric are sewn to the back of the welt; and after the pocket is stitched, the excess is trimmed away.

1. Cut the upper pocket from lining fabric, making it 1 in. wider than the pocket opening.

2. Wrong side up, fold under and pin the top of the upper pocket to the bottom of the welt so it covers the raw edge about ¼ in. If the pocket has a slant, adjust the fold at the top so the pocket will hang perpendicular to the floor, not perpendicular to the opening.

3. Using fell stitches, sew the upper pocket to the bottom of the welt.

4. Smooth, pin, and baste the edges of the pocket sections together. Machine stitch around the pocket bag catching the triangular ends and being careful not to stitch into the welts or the garment. Remove all bastings and trim away the excess fabric. Press.

5. Wrong side up, use two rows of running stitches at each end, one near the edge and the other about ¼ in. away to sew the ends of the welt permanently. The welt should "float" on the jacket without any evidence of stitching. Place the stitches close enough to the welt ends to conceal the underside of the welt.

# 10

# Jackets & Coats

INITIALLY MADE JUST FOR GENTLEMEN, tailored jackets were first worn by women to ride or join the hunt in the 17th century. By the 1850s, several tailors in London and Paris had ladies' departments. Most credit English tailor John Redfern with creating the "tailor-made"—a lady's jacket and skirt. Located in Cowes, a seaport on the Isle of Wight, Redfern's shop specialized in

The body of this traditional man-tailored jacket from Yves Saint Laurent's 1978 collection is backed with bias-cut interfacing; and even though it was made several decades ago, it has maintained its shape. The jacket is lined with silk charmeuse.

(Photo by Ken Howie. Author's collection.)

mourning suits. When Cowes became the center of yachting in the 1870s, the enterprising Redfern adapted his designs for sailing outfits. After actress Lillie Langtry wore one of his trainless tailor-mades to the Cowes Regatta in 1879, his success was assured.

The tailor-made quickly became a staple for leisure-class women and continued for several decades. At couture houses today, most jackets are made in the tailoring workroom and require sometimes hundreds of hours of labor, which comes at a price. Haute couture suits begin at $5,000 in London and cost several times that in Paris. A suit from a well-known house can cost $50,000. The time invested in an average suit is from 100 to 130 hours for the jacket and an additional 25 to 50 hours for the skirt.

# Tailoring Basics

The jacket is the most common garment produced in couture tailoring workrooms. The techniques for jackets can also be applied to coats and tailored dresses. These techniques are intended to supplement, not replace, standard guides provided with commercial patterns.

A few patterns such as *Vogue Patterns'® Custom Couture Collection*, which features my designs, provide directions for couture construction. When buying your garment fabric, purchase an additional ½ yd. to allow for the wide seam allowances needed in couture construction; purchase more when matching a fabric pattern. Check to be sure the fabric is "needle-ready," or preshrunk.

Many couture jackets are interfaced and almost completely backed so they will be smooth and wrinkle-free. Interfacings and backings are, in fact, the skeletal framework of the jacket that controls its shape (see below).

## INTERFACINGS

When choosing an interfacing, consider the shell fabric's weight, fiber content, color, and hand (whether it is soft or crisp) in relation to the garment's design and the desired effect, such as an exaggerated silhouette or one that softly skims the body. Fabrics like hair canvas, Hymo, collar linen, Utica linen, French canvas, handkerchief, and dress linen; organdy, muslin, and fine cotton are all good choices for interfacing and backing a tailored jacket. (By contrast, fusible materials are rarely used because they're not as supple as sewn-in backings and interfacings.)

For the collar on a wool jacket to be crisp and have a sharp roll, collar linen is a good choice. For a collar with a soft roll, use hair canvas. For a linen or silk collar, Utica and handkerchief linens, cotton, and even self-fabric are good choices. For interfacing the body of the garment, hair canvas or Hymo, with a high wool and goat hair content, is always the tailor's first choice when sewing wool, because it is more malleable than other interfacings. When sewing linen or cotton, consider either self-fabric or plain-weave linen to interface the body.

Tailors often use a variety of interfacings cut on different grains within the same garment because each element—collar, pocket, lapel, and hem—has different requirements. For example, the interfacing for a collar is generally cut on the bias to produce a nice roll, while the interfacing for a patch pocket is cut on the same grain as the pocket itself (generally the straight grain) or the crosswise grain to create a firm pocket that holds its shape.

Backings and interfacings are applied to the wrong side of each garment section before assembly. Then the two layers are handled as one when most of the seamlines are stitched.

CLAIRE'S HINT *I preshrink all interfacing and support fabrics by soaking them in cold water for two hours, hanging them to air-dry, then pressing with a steam iron.*

## MAKE THE TOILE

Constructing a tailored jacket involves a number of fittings—one for the muslin toile (in couture this fitting is done on the dress form rather than on the figure); then two or three fittings for the garment itself. Begin by making a muslin toile, which can be ripped and rebasted until it fits well.

1. Purchase muslin that is on grain. If the fabric or the sections are not cut on grain, the jacket cannot be accurately fitted.

2. Cut all sections from muslin except the top collar, front facings, and pockets with 1-in. seam allowances.

3. Use a tracing wheel and tracing carbon, mark all stitching lines, garment centers, waistline, grainlines, and cross-chest and cross-back lines.

4. Draw the pockets and buttons on the muslin and baste the toile together. I prefer hand basting. If you are machine basting, use a long stitch and set the tension so the basting will be easy to pull out.

5. Baste the sleeve seams; don't baste the sleeves into the armscyes until the body of the jacket is fitted.

# Characteristics of a Couture Jacket

**CREATING A COUTURE JACKET** requires skill that comes with practice, but above all it requires attention to detail.

➤ All edges should be interfaced to maintain their shape. They should be thin and curl slightly toward the body. Even seamlines on edges, like those on the lapel, roll slightly inward so they do not show on the right side of the garment.

➤ The garment centers are perpendicular to the floor even when the jacket is unbuttoned.

➤ Seams and edges are straight and well pressed.

➤ All hand sewing is even and inconspicuous, and any topstitching is straight and even.

➤ Fullness at the back shoulder, back armscye, back neckline, sleeve cap, and elbow has been shrunk out so the garment conforms to the body.

➤ The armscye seams are reinforced, and the sleeves, which are usually two-piece, hang in vertical cylinders without diagonal ripples.

➤ Sleeve heads are inserted into sleeve caps to keep them from "breaking" (collapsing) or dimpling.

➤ Lapels and collars are interfaced and hand padded so the points don't curl up. Lapels lie against the chest, and the lapel roll lines hug the body.

➤ The collar fits the neck smoothly without standing away from it. The collar's outside edge covers the neckline seam and fits the shoulders without rippling. The gorge line is finished by hand.

➤ Darts are balanced with an extra layer of fabric or by slashing and pressing them open.

➤ Buttons are attached with hand-sewn stems and stitches that don't show on the facing.

➤ Buttonholes are handworked on tailored jackets with a keyhole opening, and bound on more feminine dressmaker jackets.

➤ Linings, usually silk, don't interfere with the drape of the jacket. Sewn in by hand, they are loose but fit smoothly with a pleat at center back. The lining often takes the place of a back neck facing for a softer, more comfortable garment.

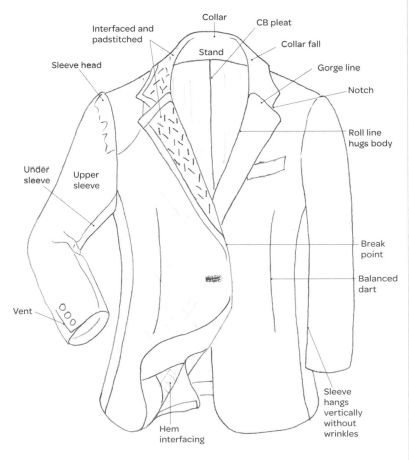

6. Turn under and baste all hems and seam allowances on the sleeves and jacket; press lightly.

7. Baste the undercollar in place.

8. Baste the shoulder pads in place. The shoulder pads are so important to the drape and fit of the jacket that the toile, and later the jacket, cannot be fitted accurately without them. Keep a variety of sizes and shapes on hand so you can experiment. Later, you will make shoulder pads specifically for the jacket.

## FIT THE TOILE

The toile will help you to fine tune the fit before cutting the fabric. If your fabric has a pattern or design, the toile can be used to position the fabric design attractively. It also provides an opportunity to perfect your sewing skills which help to preserve the pristine quality of the fabric; and it reduces the temptation to try on the jacket during the construction.

1. Try on the toile.

2. Pin the center fronts together as they would be when buttoned. Begin by analyzing the relationship of the design to your figure. It should look the same on the right and left sides, even though your body may be asymmetrical. Check the line and proportions of the silhouette. If it's not becoming, correct it or start again with a new design.

3. To check the fit, look for the following:

➤ The grain is parallel to the floor at the bustline, across the chest, and across the back.

➤ The grain is perpendicular to the floor at the garment centers.

➤ When unbuttoned, the front edges hang perpendicular to the floor.

➤ Seamlines are straight.

➤ There are no vertical or horizontal wrinkles.

➤ It fits smoothly with no draglines.

➤ It's neither too tight, nor too loose at the bust, waist, and hips.

➤ The shoulders are smooth in the front and back.

➤ Darts are appropriately placed and sized.

➤ The neckline fits smoothly.

➤ The armhole is neither too tight nor too loose.

➤ The armscye seam is appropriate for the design, shoulder width, and current fashion.

➤ The hem appears parallel to the floor.

4. You may need to fit the toile several times, and perhaps make additional toiles, before you're satisfied. This is not uncommon.

5. After the toile body has been fitted, pin the sleeves in; make any necessary adjustments (see p. 147).

6. After the fitting, mark all new seamlines and matchpoints carefully before removing any bastings and pins.

Here you can see the canvas used to shape this jacket by Yves Saint Laurent shown at left. Bias-cut hair cloth has been machine-quilted to the hair canvas to provide shaping. The dart is balanced to prevent a ridge on the outside of the jacket. The lapel and collar are hand-padded.

(Photo by Susan Kahn. Author's collection.)

This Valentino jacket is underlined with silk organza with bias-cut cotton interfacings at the upper back, below the waist, and at the hem. The wide interfacing on the jacket skirt helps to reduce wrinkling and preserves the shape. Only silk organza is used at the waist; this allows the jacket to move with the body when worn.

(Photo by Author.)

## PREPARING JACKET BODY INTERFACING

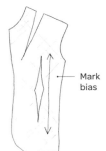

**FRONT INTERFACING**

Mark bias

**FRONT CHEST PIECE**

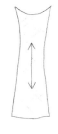

**SIDE PANEL INTERFACING**

**BACK INTERFACING**

**BACK SHOULDER PIECE**

7. Remove all bastings; press the sections flat with a dry iron to check the corrections. Remark the corrections if necessary, using a ruler or curve to true any uneven lines. If I've made a lot of corrections on the toile, I'll trace the corrected toile to make a clean muslin pattern.

8. Later you may want to convert small darts on the toile to ease (see p. 60).

### CUT AND MARK THE JACKET

Once the toile is fitted and the pattern corrected, you're ready to cut out the jacket.

1. Using the corrected toile as a pattern, cut the fronts, backs, any side sections, sleeves, and undercollar from the shell fabric. Cut the undercollar and its interfacing on the bias with a seam at center back. Don't cut the sleeves, lapel facings, top collar, pockets, or linings at this time. When the fabric has a pattern to be matched, wait until after the first fitting to cut the fabric for the sleeves, lapel facings, top collar, or pockets.

2. Thread-trace all stitching lines, garment centers, matchpoints, and grainlines as well as locations for buttons, buttonholes, roll lines, pockets, and decorative details.

### THE ENTOILAGE

The tailoring term canvas or entoilage refers to all the interfacings and backings after they've been cut. The backings and interfacings can be combined in numerous ways, but the methods used by

Valentino for dressmaker jackets and by Yves Saint Laurent for tailored jackets are good models for home sewers.

At Valentino, a silk organza or silk muslin backing is cut for the entire jacket, and hair canvas interfacings are cut to support the front edge, front and back shoulder areas, underarm, sleeve cap, and hemline, leaving the waist area without interfacing so it's very supple. The backing is applied to the garment fabric at the outset, and the two layers are handled as one throughout the garment's construction.

At Yves Saint Laurent, a hair-canvas backing, which also serves as the interfacing, is cut on the bias with seam and hem allowances for the fronts, backs (full or partial), underarm panels, and two-thirds of the sleeve cap. Then a second, smaller layer of hair canvas is cut on the bias for the front chest piece, which fills in the area above the bust but doesn't extend into the lapels. A back shoulder piece is also cut for the upper back. Since the hair canvas is very crisp and resilient, darts are cut out and lapped before the canvas is applied or simply cut out and hand sewn to the garment or backing dart or seam.

1. Cut out the hair canvas for the fronts, back, underarm panels, and sleeve cap. It can be cut on the lengthwise grain, or, for a more supple look, like those on the Yves Saint Laurent jackets (p. 173 and p. 181), cut on the bias, leaving ⅝-in. seam and hem allowances. At YSL, the true bias was marked

at the center of each section so it could be aligned with the lengthwise grain on the wrong side of the garment.

2. Cut a second layer of hair canvas for the front chest piece and the back shoulder. Place the chest piece on top of the front interfacing; pin. Then quilt the interfacing and chest piece together by stitching 1-in. squares parallel to the grainlines; press. As you press, stretch the shoulder seam slightly.

3. To shape the canvas and eliminate bulk, cut out the darts so they're slightly wider and longer than the darts on the jacket itself. Baste the darts for the fittings; after the fitting, remove the bastings so the interfacing darts can be slipped over the jacket darts.

## INTERFACE THE JACKET FRONT

In these directions, the jacket front is completely interfaced with a piece of bias-cut interfacing and a second, smaller piece is used above the bust to create a smooth line from the shoulder to the bust point.

1. Baste the darts on the jacket fronts and backs.

2. Baste a strip of interfacing or self-fabric to each dart to balance the dart (see p. 60). Stitch and press the darts. If you didn't make a toile, don't stitch the darts until the jacket has been fitted.

3. Wrong side up, place the front canvas on the jacket so the chest piece is uppermost. Arrange and pin the interfacing around the darts. Use loose catchstitches to sew the jacket and canvas together on the dartline. This allows the interfacing to serve as a buffer for darts in the garment fabric and reduces shadows and ridges on the right side of the garment.

4. Turn the front over and smooth the fabric over the canvas, checking to be sure the darts are aligned.

5. Baste on the roll line. Baste a vertical row beginning about 2 in. below the midpoint of the shoulder seam and ending at the hemline. Baste another row close to the roll line and down the front of the jacket about 1 in. from the edge. Baste a third row around the armscye about 1 in. from the armscye seam and continuing to the hem.

CLAIRE'S HINT *In some workrooms, they shape the lapels next; in others, they set the pockets. I prefer to shape the lapels first, before the fronts are joined to any side sections, only possible when I've fitted a toile.*

## SHAPE THE LAPEL

These directions assume you have fitted the toile. If you haven't and plan to fit as you sew, then baste the jacket together before you padstitch the lapels and tape the front edges.

1. Measure the roll line on the pattern, excluding the seam allowances. To make the bridle, measure and mark the roll line on a piece of stay tape this length. The bridle prevents the roll line or creaseline from stretching and shapes the roll line to the fit the body. It's made from a narrow cotton or linen tape, rayon seam binding, or a lightweight selvage that has been preshrunk. It can have a plain or twill weave. I prefer a ¼-in. plain-weave cotton tape, but you can use a ⅜-in. tape.

2. On the jacket roll line, mark a point 3 in. below the neck seamline and another point 4 in. above the breakpoint. Place the outer edge of the bridle on the roll line; pin one end to the seamline at the neck. Hold the bridle taut and pin the other end at the breakpoint, the beginning of the roll line.

CLAIRE'S HINT *I make the bridle ⅜ in. shorter than the roll line, but it can be ¼ in. to ½ in. shorter. For a softer roll at the breakpoint, end the bridle about 1 in. above the breakpoint. Distribute and pin the ease evenly under the bridle, setting the pins at right angles to the tape. Using short basting stitches, baste through the center of the bridle after the fitting, the bridle permanently with fell stitches.*

3. To padstitch the lapel, place the jacket face up; fold the lapel back on the roll line. Pin the sections together on the seamline. At the corner, use chalk to draw a triangle about 1¼ in. long on each side. When you fold the lapel into position, the jacket fabric will show at the lapel edge.

4. Hold the lapel over your hand; begin the padstitching next to the roll line. Make the stitches about ⅜ in. long. Work the rows parallel to the roll

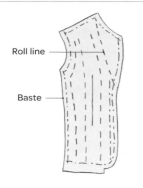

Roll line

Baste

## SHAPING THE LAPEL

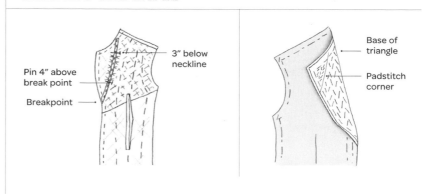

Pin 4" above
break point

3" below
neckline

Breakpoint

Base of
triangle

Padstitch
corner

line and about ⅜ in. apart, staggering the stitches to avoid creating ridges on the interfacing. Release the pins on the seamlines as needed to ease the interfacing to the fabric. Don't padstitch into the triangle or seam allowances at the neck or front edges. The length of the stitches and distance between the rows will affect the firmness of the lapel. For a softer lapel, make longer stitches and space them farther apart.

5. To padstitch the corner, reposition the lapel to hold the triangle base over your hand. Work the rows parallel to the marked line, making the stitches shorter (¼ in.) and closer together (¼ in.). The change of direction at the corner shapes the lapel corner, so it will curl toward the body attractively.

6. Padstitch the second lapel, checking periodically to be sure the two lapels look the same.

7. Interfacing side up, place the roll line over the edge of the pressing board, and press the lapel. Rearrange the section so you can press the front with the roll line rolled over the edge of the pressing board. Cover the pressing board with a large piece of wool when sewing a wool jacket. To press the lapel, first moisten it with a damp sponge; press until dry. Turn the front faceup, and cover with a wool press cloth. Then cover with a cotton press cloth, dampen, and press again. Don't move the section until it's completely dry.

## TAPE THE FRONT EDGES

Taping the edges is one of the secrets of couture. It reduces bulk in the seamline so you can stitch through two layers only, making the seam very flat and thin. When taping a jacket with a fold at the front edge, I frequently use a softer material such as silk organza or chiffon and center the stay over the foldline.

1. Mark the seamlines on the interfacing at the front edge, lapel, and gorge line clearly and accurately with a sharp pencil.

2. Carefully trim away the interfacing seam allowances plus an additional ³⁄₁₆ in., beginning at the notch or end of the collar.

3. Wrong side up, begin taping about 1 in. from the shoulder seam. Place the preshrunk tape on the

### TRIMMING INTERFACING AT FRONT EDGE

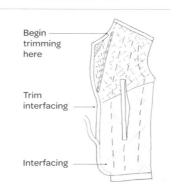

Begin
trimming
here

Trim
interfacing

Interfacing

jacket with the outer edge on the seamline. Ease the tape slightly over the ends of the roll line, and pin to the corner of the lapel. At the corner, clip the tape, leaving only a thread. Lap the cut edges, and reposition the tape. Pin it to

## TAPING THE FRONT EDGE

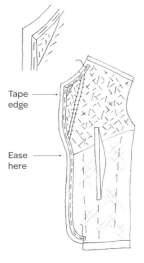

Tape edge →

Ease here →

the edge of the lapel so it's smooth, but not taut.

CLAIRE'S HINT
*The term "lay fair" is used when the tape is laid flat against the fabric without any easing or tautness. When the tape is held taut, it is called "hold short."*

4. Ease the tape slightly at the breakpoint—the bottom of the roll line. Below the breakpoint, pin the tape to the edge to the bottom button so the tape is smooth, but not taut. Below the bottom button, hold the tape taut as you pin to the hemline. Baste the tape in place, remove the pins, and press lightly. When pinning around a hemline curve, continue to hold the tape taut. The curved edge should curl very slightly toward the body. If necessary, clip the tape so the tape lies flat around the curve.

5. Compare the two front edges to be sure they've been taped identically and they hang straight without curling at curves and corners. Press lightly.

Press with the canvas uppermost; hold the edge of the front section and use the iron to stretch the fabric slightly around the bust point. Notice that the edges are taped and the dart is balanced.

(Photo by Susan Kahn.)

## FELL TAPE EDGES

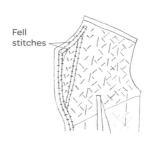

Fell stitches →

6. Fell stitch the inner edge of the tape to the interfacing, working carefully so the stitches don't show on the face side of the jacket. Fell stitch the outer edge to the seamline.

Interfacing side up, press the bust area, beginning at the roll line. At the bust point, shape the front to fit the bust by using just the point of the iron at the bust point (see photo at left, below). Fold the lapel in place and steam the roll line; finger-press firmly as you steam.

7. If the design has bound buttonholes, make the buttonholes before setting the facings.

This evening suit was designed by John Galliano for Dior. The buttonholes have been carefully applied to match the stripes on the jacket. To do this, double baste the buttonhole welts before machine stitching.
(Photo by Author.)

## THE FACING

Unlike in luxury ready-to-wear and home sewing, in haute couture and bespoke tailoring, the lengthwise grain of the lapel facing is usually parallel to the lapel edge, even though the jacket edge is shaped. This is particularly attractive for fabrics with stripes or plaids, and it reduces stretching and rippling on plain fabrics.

**Facing a Straight Edge.** When the edge is straight or almost straight, it's not difficult to change the grain and cut the facing with the grain parallel or perpendicular to the front edge. In the photograph below of a YSL ensemble from 1982–83, the lapel fabric has been cut with grainline parallel to the lapel edge so that checks are parallel to the edge.

1. Right sides together, begin at the end of the collar and pin the facing on the seamline next to the stay tape; baste. When pinning the facing, hold the front taut above the breakpoint so the facing is slightly eased. At the breakpoint, ease the facing so it won't restrict the roll line. Below the breakpoint, hold the facing taut so the edge will curl toward the body.

2. Stitch on the basted line. Before stitching, turn the section right side out to be sure you like the

This classic ensemble from Yves Saint Laurent's 1982–83 Fall/Winter Collection features a plaid jacket in the Prince of Wales pattern and a houndstooth-check skirt. The skirt fabric (used on the lapels of the jacket) employs the straight grain parallel to the edge of the surplice cut front even though the jacket edge is cut on the bias.

(Photo by Anthony Hall, courtesy of *Australian Stitches.* Author's collection.)

## FACING A JACKET WITH STRAIGHT LAPELS

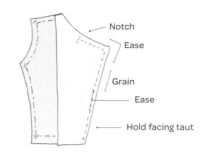

Notch
Ease
Grain
Ease
Hold facing taut

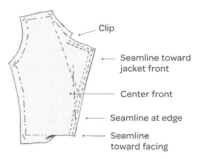

Clip
Seamline toward jacket front
Center front
Seamline at edge
Seamline toward facing

way it looks. Then press the basted line so it will be easier to stitch.

3. Knot the thread ends, and clip to the stitching. Press the seam open.

4. Grade the seam allowances so the front is a little wider than the facing below the breakpoint and the facing is a little wider above the breakpoint.

Turn the section right side out. Baste about ¼ in. from the edge so the seam is toward the jacket front above the breakpoint and toward the facing below the breakpoint. At the breakpoint, it should be right on the edge. Baste again ¾ in. from the edge.

5. Right side up, press to the roll line. Turn the front wrong side up, press the jacket and facing to the roll line. Don't press over the roll line. Use a press cloth.

**Facing a Shaped Edge.** In a couture workroom, a facing pattern is rarely used. Instead, a rectangle of fabric is pinned and shaped to fit the garment section

*Continued on p. 185*

# The Shaped Facing Pattern

The facings on this tailored jacket designed by Yves Saint Laurent have been cut so the dominant color bars frame the top of the lapels. When this is done, it doesn't matter that the color bars on the lapel and jacket front do not match at the seamline where they join.

(Photo by Author.)

## MAKE THE FACING PATTERN

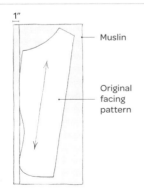

Mark the straight grain on a piece of muslin or nonwoven pattern paper 1 in. from the edge.

Position the facing pattern so the widest sections touch the marked grainline. Trace the facing pattern and mark the straight grain. Cut out the pattern. This can be a rectangle with the facing outlined on it or it can be cut out, leaving a seam allowance only at the front edge.

## CUTTING AND SHAPING THE FACINGS

In couture tailoring, the leading edge is straight regardless of the shape at the jacket edge.

**1.** Place the new facing pattern on the fabric to determine which section of the pattern or which color bar will be at the front edge before cutting out the facing. A dominant color will generally be the most attractive. When working with a plaid, don't overlook the neck edge of the lapel when planning the facing.

**2.** Pin-mark the seamline on the facing about 1/8 in. from the stripe you want at the edge. When working with a heavier fabric, place it 1/4 in. away.

When the facing is stitched and turned right side out, part of the color bar will be lost at the edge. I pin a fabric scrap to the jacket

and turn it right side out to check the stripe placement.

**3.** Thread-trace the seamlines, leaving 1-in. or more seam allowances.

**4.** Beginning about 1 in. above the breakpoint, put in a row of ease basting for 2 in. to 3 in. Pull up the ease basting, and shrink out 1/4 in. to 3/8 in. at the breakpoint.

CLAIRE'S HINT *I stack the two facings right sides together so they will be shaped the same. Then I put the ease basting in by hand-sewing through both layers. After shaping, I remove the ease basting and separate the facings.*

**5.** Align the thread-traced seamlines on the facings to the curved line on the muslin pattern you traced at the outset.

**6.** Press the lapel edge into a convex curve, continuing until you have shrunk away as much of the rippling as possible at the inside edge of the facing.

When working with some worsted wools, linens, and cottons, the fabric may not shrink enough to fit the shape of the edge. To resolve this, some designers shape the lapel and ignore the grain direction below the breakpoint, while others cut the facing into two sections and place the seam between the

In couture, folded edges are preferred to seams because they are flatter. On this Dior design, the front edge is finished with an extended facing while the collar is cut separately so the stripes attractively frame the face. The two facings are seamed at the first buttonhole. On similar designs, the seam was located between the first and second buttonholes.

(Photo by Ken Howie. Author's collection.)

## SHAPING THE FACING

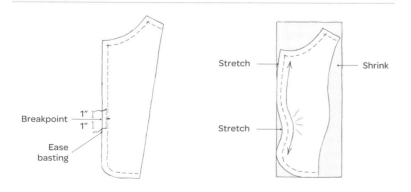

first and second buttonholes. If you make a seamline, position the top of the lower section on the crossgrain. On a jacket with bound buttonholes, locate the seam behind the top buttonhole, leaving an opening in the seam to finish the back of the buttonhole.

### Apply the Facing

If the jacket has a pronounced curve on the lapels, the lapels will require additional shaping when they are basted to the jacket.

**1.** Right sides together, begin at the breakpoint and work toward the neck edge. Hold the front lapel edge taut and ease the facing very slightly to the front, leaving a little additional ease just above the breakpoint and at the lapel corner.

**2.** Pin the facing to the lapel. This is called "fulling in" the facing. If you full in too much, the facing will bubble at the edge. If you don't full in enough, the seamline will show on the right side and the lapel point may curl up. I set the pins parallel to and on the seamline so I can turn the facing right side out after it's pinned to check the edge and corner, as well as how the patterns match.

**3.** Use short basting stitches to baste the layers together—the basting should be at the outer edge of the stay tape beginning at the notch and ending at the breakpoint.

Carefully turn the lapel right side out, but don't trim it. Before turning the lapel, fold the seams at the lapel point so they are flat; then, using a point turner, turn the facing right side out to be sure the corner looks sharp. There's a lot of bulk here, but you'll be surprised how flat the corner looks at this stage. The facing should be smooth with the basted seamline sitting just to the underside of the lapel so it's not visible on the jacket right side.

**4.** Reposition the sections right sides together; baste the facing to the jacket front from the breakpoint to the hem. Ease the facing for ½ in. just below the breakpoint.

If the design has bound buttonholes, ease the right facing slightly in the buttonhole area so there will be enough fabric to finish the facing side of the buttonholes smoothly. Below the buttonholes, hold the facing taut to the hemline. Turn the facing right side out again to be sure the edges do not curl.

**5.** After you've tailored a few jackets, you may prefer to baste the entire edge before turning it right side out to check it.

When you're satisfied the lapel is perfect, repeat for the other lapel, then check to be sure they look the same. Some prefer to begin basting at the breakpoint; if part of the facing needs to be repositioned, there's less stitching to be ripped.

## BASTING JACKET AND FACING

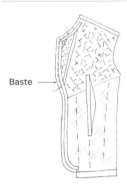

Baste

**6.** Beginning at the end of the collar, stitch on the seamline next to the tape. Continue to the end of the facing.

Before stitching, I double baste to prevent the layers from shifting and press the basted seam. The pressing will flatten the seam allowances and make them easier to stitch smoothly. Since the facings are basted securely, you can stitch both fronts from the collar to the hem.

**7.** Turn the sections right side out and check the stitching.

**8.** Reposition the sections right sides together. Secure the thread ends with a knot at the beginning of the stitching; then clip to the end of the stitching.

**9.** Remove the bastings, and press the seams first flat, then with a point presser, press them open. Below the breakpoint, trim the seam on the front to ⅜ in.; trim the facing seam to ¼ in. Above the breakpoint, trim the seam on

the facing to ⅜ in. Trim the front seam to ¼ in.

**10.** For added control and a flatter edge, tame the corners by sewing the front seam allowance to the stay tape; then sew the facing seam allowance to the front seam allowance. Steam-press the point, then spank it briskly with the clapper.

**11.** Turn the fronts right side out and gently straighten the corners with a point turner. For difficult corners, I use a small needle and unknotted thread to work the corner out without distorting it. Take a short stitch in the seamline and, holding the needle and the unknotted end, tug gently to pull the seamline to the edge. Repeat until the corner is turned.

**12.** Before pressing the front, baste through all layers ¼ in. from the edge, shaping the edge as you baste so that the seamline rolls to the underside when the jacket is worn and is therefore invisible. Above the breakpoint,

## STITCH JACKET AND FACING

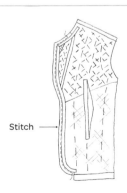

Stitch

the seamline should roll toward the jacket front, while below the breakpoint it should roll toward the facing so it doesn't show on the garment right side.

For about ½ in. both above and below the breakpoint, the seamline should be right on the edge. Baste a second row of stitches about ¾ in. from the edge. Next, fold the lapel into its finished position and smooth the facing over the lapel line. Baste on the roll line with long diagonal stitches. Then baste through all layers from the shoulder point to the hem, and chalk a line on the facing about 1 in. away. Trim on the chalked line, baste around the buttonhole markings, and press.

**13.** Right side up, press the edges of the lapel and the jacket front. I cover the edges with a wool press cloth and use a damp sponge. In the lapel area, I press from the underside of the lapel. Below the breakpoint, I press from the facing side.

## SEAM ALLOWANCES

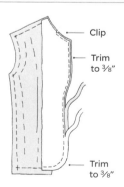

Clip

Trim to ⅜"

Trim to ⅜"

before it's cut. To shape the facings for a design with a pronounced curve at the edge (like the YSL herringbone jacket on p. 172), the facing will require easing and shrinking to fit the jacket edges. The "Shaped Facing Pattern" on p. 182 will help you learn the technique.

## BASTE THE JACKET

To prepare the jacket for fitting, interface the remaining sections; then baste the body of the garment.

1. Apply the interfacing to the remaining garment sections. Baste the canvas and garment sections together at the center on the aligned grainlines. Baste the backing and fabric together on the vertical seamlines. When using a crisp interfacing like hair canvas, hold the garment fabric and backing layers in the round with the backing on the inside to duplicate the way the layers will fit the body. When using a soft backing fabric, full it in (see p. 130) and baste the vertical seams like any other seam.

2. If the design has pockets, set the pockets (see chapter 9, p. 159) before basting the front sections to the back.

## BASTING JACKET SEAMS

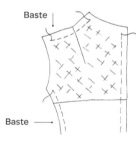

Baste

Baste

3. Right sides together, baste the center back seam, stopping at the neckline seam; baste the side seams, stopping at the armscye seam. Fold under and baste the hems. Baste the shoulder seams, easing the back to the front. On most figures, the shoulder seam will fit better if it is slightly scooped, rather than straight. When interfacing with hair canvas, lap the canvas over the shoulder seams instead of sewing it into the seams.

4. Assemble the sleeves (see p. 154)

# Extended Facings

**IN COUTURE, SEPARATE** facings at the opening are avoided whenever possible; instead, extended facings are used so there will be no seams at the edges. Obviously, this is much flatter than a seamed edge.

This is pretty straightforward when the design has no collar like the Ungaro jacket pictured at right. At the top of the opening, the facing was folded into a miter so it could be shaped to fit the front neck. The miter was sewn permanently with fell stitches.

The front neck and opening were stabilized with a 2-in.-wide bias silk organza strip, which had been wet and pressed to remove all the stretch. Then the stay was centered over the foldline and sewn permanently with long running stitches.

This attractive jacket and dress from the 1960s is attributed to Ungaro. The v-neck jacket frames the set-in details on the dress. Extended facings are used at the neck edge of the jacket as well as the front edges. A peek inside this jacket reveals a small hand-sewn miter on the facing where the neckline meets the front edge.

(Photo by Ken Howie. Author's collection.)

The folded edges are stabilized with a bias stay to prevent stretching.

(Photo by Ken Howie. Author's collection.)

## UNDERCOLLAR

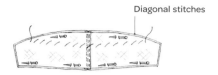

Diagonal stitches

### PREPARE THE UNDERCOLLAR

You can fit the jacket before the collar is applied; however, it's better to wait to avoid stretching the neckline.

1. To prepare the undercollar for fitting, thread trace the seamlines on the undercollar. Right sides together, stitch the undercollar at center back. Press the seam open and trim to ⅜ in. Lap the edges of the undercollar interfacing at center back; align the seamlines, and stitch. Stitch again on each side of the seamline; and trim away the excess.

2. Wrong side up, pin the interfacing to the undercollar. Use diagonal stitches to sew the layers together at the roll line.

CLAIRE'S HINT *I tighten the stitches to hold the roll line in slightly.*

3. Fold on the roll line right sides together. Press and shrink the roll line, shaping it into a concave curve and stretching the outer edge at the center back. The depth of the curve is determined by the slope of your shoulders. If you have square shoulders, make the arc deeper and stretch the edge more so the roll line will hug the neck and the outside edge will fit the shoulders smoothly.

4. Using the undercollar thread tracings as a guide, pin the interfacing and fabric together on the seamlines. Mark the seamlines on the interfacing with a sharp pencil and baste the seamlines together.

### PRESSING UNDERCOLLAR

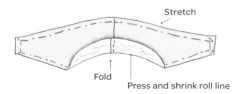

Stretch

Fold

Press and shrink roll line

For the first fitting, fold the seam allowances toward the interfacing and baste flat.

5. Before attaching the undercollar to the jacket body, measure the necklines on both—the undercollar should be about ½ in. larger. Pin the undercollar to the neckline at the center back and shoulder seams, and ease it slightly for 1 in. on each side of the shoulder seams. Beginning at center back, baste the undercollar to the jacket.

6. After basting the undercollar, baste the shoulder pads in place. They extend about ½ in. beyond the armscye seam.

### THE FIRST FITTING

1. Examine the roll lines. The ease on the lapel roll line should be distributed evenly and smoothly, and the collar roll line should hug the neck closely. The roll lines on the lapel and collar should be aligned.

2. The outer edge of the undercollar should cover the neckline seam and lie smoothly without rippling. If the neckline seam shows below the outer edge of the undercollar, the outer edge is too tight or the wearer's shoulders are very square, and you'll need to stretch the edge more so it will cover the neckline seam or cut a new collar. After stretching the undercollar to fit the body, mark it with matchpoints at the shoulder seams.

3. Check the front armscye. There should be enough room to insert your index finger between

### FIRST FITTING OF JACKET (WITHOUT SLEEVES)

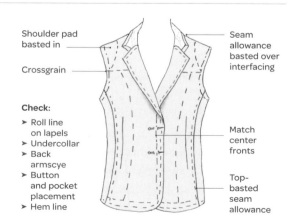

Shoulder pad basted in

Crossgrain

**Check:**
➤ Roll line on lapels
➤ Undercollar
➤ Back armscye
➤ Button and pocket placement
➤ Hem line

Seam allowance basted over interfacing

Match center fronts

Top-basted seam allowance

the fabric and body. If the armscye is just a little tight, it can be stretched by pressing. If it really binds, the shoulder seam needs to be let out.

4. Check the back armscye; it should hug the body without gaping. If it gapes, ease and shrink the excess before setting in the sleeve.

5. Check the shoulder pad size and placement, and the pocket and button locations.

6. Pin in the sleeves and adjust their hang.

7. Correct the hemline for the jacket and sleeves as needed.

## STITCH THE JACKET

Before stitching the jacket permanently, make all marked corrections and baste it together for stitching.

1. After the first fitting, remove the bastings, lay the sections flat to make corrections. Indicate the corrections on the toile for future reference.

2. On the jacket backs complete the darts. Mold the backs to fit the shoulder blades by shrinking away the excess fullness at the shoulder seams and armscye and stretching the fabric in the shoulder blade area (see p. 64 for instructions on shrinking and stretching).

   Stitch and press any seams and trim the interfacing to ⅛ in. At the waistline, stretch the side and back seam allowance edges so they will lie flat against the jacket when the seams are pressed open. Shrink away any excess on the jacket body.

3. On the jacket fronts, complete any seams. If the design has underarm panels, join the panels to the fronts.

4. Set the pockets permanently.

5. Stitch the side seams.

6. Baste the shoulder seams and hem.

7. Baste in the sleeves.

8. Hang the jacket for the second fitting.

## FINISH THE UNDERCOLLAR

1. Before padstitching the undercollar, remove the bastings on the seamlines that join the interfacing and undercollar at the edges. Made by sewing small diagonal stitches (see p. 30), padstitching is used to

## PADSTITCHING THE COLLAR STAND

Gorge liner

shape and add firmness to the undercollar so it will maintain its shape.

2. To padstitch the collar stand, hold the stand over one hand, interfacing side up. Start at the roll line, work the padded rows horizontally down to the penciled seamline at the neck edge. The stitches should be short and closely spaced, approximately ¼ in. long and ¼ in. apart for a crisp, sturdy stand.

3. To padstitch the collar fall, continue with the undercollar in the rolled position and the interfacing side up. Begin at center back. Use slightly longer stitches from ⅜ in. to ½ in. long and space the rows about ⅜ in. apart. To make the collar points firm and keep them from curling up, I mark them with a small triangle about 1 in. from each point and padstitch using stitches about ⅛ in. to ¼ in. long, spaced ⅛ in. to ¼ in. apart. This is done like the lapel corners, beginning at the penciled base of the triangle and working toward the collar points.

## PADSTITCHING THE UNDERCOLLAR FALL

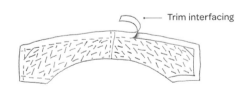

Trim interfacing

4. Examine the collar carefully to be sure both sides look the same.

5. Remark the penciled seamlines on the interfacing so they are aligned with the thread-tracing on the undercollar; trim away the interfacing seam allowances. Before trimming,

I examine the marked line carefully to be sure the line is smooth and accurate and both sides of the collar are identical. If I've padstitched too far, I unpick the extra stitches; if I haven't padstitched enough, I add a few more stitches.

6. At the neck edge, fold the seam allowance over the interfacing; baste and press the edge. Trim the seam allowance close to the basting; use catchstitches to sew the edges to the interfacing.

7. Interfacing side up, press the undercollar, using a moderately hot, dry iron. Moisten the fall of the

### FINISH THE NECK EDGE

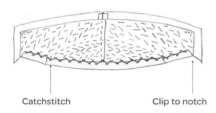

Catchstitch          Clip to notch

collar with a damp dauber or sponge and press the ends flat. Press up to the roll line but not over it. Continue pressing until the interfacing is dry and firm; repeat for the collar stand.

## THE TOP COLLAR

The top collar, like the front facings, is often shaped at the outer edge and will be more attractive if the edge follows a grainline.

1. To make the top collar, cut a rectangular piece of garment fabric 2 in. longer and wider than the undercollar. Since the grain of the top collar should match the grain of the jacket at the center back both vertically and horizontally, the top collar rarely matches the lapels at the gorgeline.

CLAIRE'S HINT *When sewing stripes or plaids, I plan the fabric placement so both ends of the collar are the same or look attractive as a pair. I also try to shape the collar at the outer edge so it's on grain, using the same technique I use for shaping the lapel facings. Sometimes this is very challenging.*

2. Use a steam iron to shape the top collar. Wrong side up, press the two long sides separately, using

### JOINING TOP COLLAR AND UNDERCOLLAR

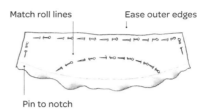

Match roll lines          Ease outer edges

Pin to notch

a circular motion to stretch the edges and shrink the center so the top collar will fit the undercollar smoothly and the crossgrain will follow the collar's edge. If you can't follow the grain at the edge easily, thread-trace the seamline. To see if the top collar is shaped enough, check occasionally as you're working by laying it on top of the undercollar.

3. To join the top collar and undercollar, begin with right sides together. Match and pin the roll lines. Then pin the seamlines together at the outer edge, beginning at center back, stopping at the notch and easing the top collar to the undercollar along the outer edges. To check the collar, set the pins parallel to the seamline, unpin the roll line, and turn the collar right sides out. The top collar should have enough ease so the seamline will roll under, but not so much ease that it ripples. The ends should appear identical.

4. Adjust the collar as needed, reset the pins, and baste the collar securely with short stitches. Check the collar again, and double-baste.

5. Press and stitch the edges permanently, stopping at the notch at each end of the collar without stitching into the seam allowance.

6. Remove the bastings, press and grade the seams. For sharp collar edges, press the seam flat, then open. Trim the seam allowance on the top collar to 3/8 in. Trim the seam allowances on the undercollar to 1/4 in.; sew them flat against the interfacing with catchstitches.

7. Turn the collar right side out. With the undercollar toward you, baste about 1/4 in. from the edge. Hold the collar in the finished position and smooth out the top collar; baste the roll line. At the gorge

line, trim the seam allowances to $3/8$ in.; turn them under and baste. Press. To avoid a pressing imprint when pressing over bastings, baste with soft cotton or silk thread or hand embroidery floss. When pressing the collar, don't press the roll line flat.

8. Before basting the collar to the jacket, trim the neckline seam on the jacket to $1/2$ in.

9. Baste the collar to the jacket for the second fitting; baste the gorge line.

10. Baste the sleeves into the jacket.

## THE SECOND FITTING

1. Check the hang and length of the jacket and the sleeves.

2. Check the fit of the collar. The roll line should hug the neck closely and the outer edge of the collar should cover the neckline seam and lie smooth without rippling. If the neckline seam shows, it's generally because the outer collar edge is too tight or the shoulders are square.

3. After the fitting, remove the collar. Pin it to a tailor's ham and set it aside.

4. Remove the sleeves.

CLAIRE'S HINT *I stuff the sleeve caps with tissue so they won't lose their shape.*

5. Release the bastings at the shoulder seams so you can spread the jacket on the table.

6. Stitch and press any remaining seamlines.

## THE LINING

Even though it lies inside the jacket, the lining should be slightly larger in length and width than the garment because the lining material is generally more firmly woven and less elastic than the shell fabric. As discussed in Chapter 8, the sleeves are lined before they're set, and the lining for the jacket body can be put in before or after the shoulder seams are finished. In these directions, the lining is put in before the shoulder seams are stitched.

1. Make the lining pattern using the toile or jacket sections as patterns. This works well when the lining sections more or less duplicate the garment

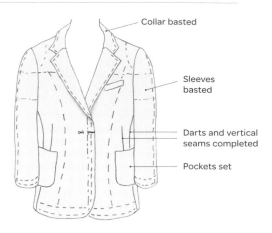

Collar basted

Sleeves basted

Darts and vertical seams completed

Pockets set

sections. If there are extensive alterations or design changes, however, the lining can be cut or torn into rectangles then fitted to the inside of the garment. Making a lining this way is not nearly as difficult as it seems, especially if the lining is fitted before the shoulder seams are machine-stitched so the garment can be spread flat.

2. Spread the jacket wrong side up. Interface the hem (see p. 72).

3. Chalk-mark the lining seam on the facing. Cut the lining with 1-in.-wide minimum seam and hem allowances.

Cut the front lining so the front edge is on the selvage and laps the front facing by about $1½$ in. Cut the back lining, allowing for a 1-in. center back pleat. Don't cut out the neckline on either the back or front lining.

4. Mark the vertical seamlines and matchpoints with chalk or tracing carbon, but don't mark the hem or any darts or seamlines on the front edges, back neckline, shoulders, or armscyes.

5. Before stitching the lining vertical seams, pin them as marked and baste a scant $1/8$ in. away from the seamline toward the raw edge so the lining will be slightly larger than the jacket. Stitch; remove the bastings, and press, clipping the seams as needed so they will like flat.

6. To control the hang of the garment at the opening, side vents, seamlines, and back, place weights inside the jacket hem. Lead drapery

## LINING THE JACKET

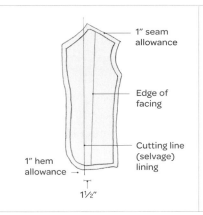

1" seam allowance

Edge of facing

Cutting line (selvage) lining

1" hem allowance →

1½"

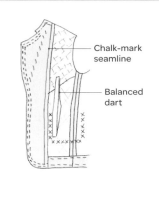

Chalk-mark seamline

Balanced dart

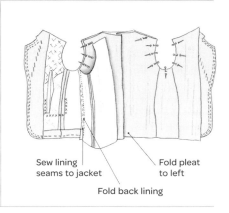

Sew lining seams to jacket

Fold pleat to left

Fold back lining

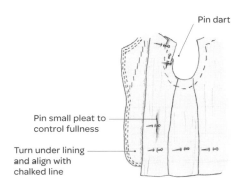

Pin dart

Pin small pleat to control fullness

Turn under lining and align with chalked line

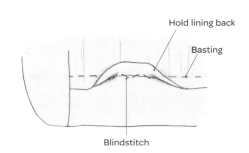

Hold lining back

Basting

Blindstitch

weights are suitable and readily available in most notions departments.

CLAIRE'S HINT *If the weight is too heavy or too large, use an old pair of scissors to cut it into smaller pieces and pound it flat with a hammer so it won't show when the garment is worn. To eliminate sharp edges, cover each weight with a square of organza. Place the weight in the center of the square and wrap first the sides, then the top and bottom around the weight. Secure the covered weights with a few stitches and sew them to the interfacing on the hem.*

7. Hem the jacket.

8. Spread the jacket wrong side up; chalk-mark the facing/lining seamline on the front facing so it begins 1 in. or less away from the neckpoint. If the facings have not been sewn to the interfacing, use loose catchstitches or blindstitches to sew them permanently.

9. Wrong sides together, place the lining on the jacket so the center backs and vertical seamlines are aligned; pin. Full in the lining so it's a little larger than the jacket itself and fits with some ease. If the lining is too tight, the jacket will be uncomfortable and the lining will pull at the seams. If it's too loose, the lining will wrinkle and may show when the jacket is worn.

10. Beginning at the side back seam, smooth and pin the lining toward the center back and pin the pleat in place so the underlay is toward the left. Smooth and pin the back around the armscyes.

11. If there are any darts, pin small pleats to control the fullness.

12. Fold the side panel linings out of the way so you can sew the side back seams of the lining and jacket together. Using loose running stitches, begin and end about 3 in. from the beginning and end of the seamline. Repeat to join the side front seams of the lining and jacket.

13. Smooth and pin the front lining around the armscye, then toward the facing.

14. At the front edge, fold the lining under on the lengthwise grain and align the folded edge with the chalked seamline on the facing.

As you pin toward the shoulder, you'll have excess lining. You can fold under more of the lining, put a pleat in at the shoulder, or do both. If there is still some excess fabric, pin out a small pleat at the armscye. Trim only as needed.

15. Baste the lining to the jacket beginning about 3 in. below the shoulder seams and armholes.

16. To tame the fullness at the waist, make vertical pleats on the front and back linings. To sew pleats permanently, make a small thread bar (see p. 36) across the folded edge. I pin the lining and jacket together about 5 in. above the jacket hem; this makes it easier to control the lower edge of the lining when it's trimmed and hemmed.

17. Trim the lining hem so it's even with the jacket. Turn under the lining hem so ¾ in. of the jacket hem shows; baste about ½ in. above the folded edge of the lining.

18. Hold the folded edge of the hem back with your thumb. Using blindstitches, hem a single layer of lining to the jacket hem; press lightly. When you remove the basting, the lining will have a soft fold at the bottom to provide ease in the length.

19. Hold the lining sections out of the way to baste and sew the shoulder seams. Press.

20. At this stage, the lining is only partially finished and you're ready to set the sleeves.

## SET THE SLEEVES

1. Before permanently setting the sleeves, tighten the back armscye between ¼ in. and ½ in. by shrinking out the excess. Beginning with a doubled thread, place a row of backstitches on the back armscye just inside the seamline, beginning about 1½ in. below the shoulder seam and ending about 2 in. from the underarm. Pull the stitches taut to hold in the excess fabric.

2. Wrong side up, place the garment on a flat pressing surface; use the point of the iron to shrink out the ease on the back itself near the armscye for 1 in. to 1½ in.

CLAIRE'S HINT *If the fabric is tightly woven or you have pulled the stitches too tight and can't shrink away all of the ripples, remove the stitches and try again. Otherwise, the ripples will be permanent and will look unattractive on the finished garment.*

3. Hold the lining out of the way. Baste in the sleeves, which have already been lined; stitch. The sleeves can be sewn permanently by machine or with hand backstitches.

4. Sew in the sleeve heads and shoulder pads (see p. 156).

## SET THE SHOULDER PADS

When you turn the jacket wrong side out to set the pads, the shoulder curve is reversed.

1. Fold back the lining to insert the pads. Adjust as needed to fit the shoulders; pin.

2. To sew permanently, use long running stitches at the armscye and shoulder.

## SET THE COLLAR

1. On the jacket, smooth and pin the front facing toward the neckline; trim the seam allowance at the neck edge to ⅜ in. Turn the edge under, align the folded edge with the seamline; and baste about ⅛ in. from the seamline. Ease the facing slightly at the roll line to avoid flattening the roll.

2. Pin the undercollar to the neckline, beginning at center back; match the notches; baste.

3. Beginning at center back, smooth the neck edge of the top collar over the jacket seam allowance. Use short running stitches to secure it at the neckline. When the lining is applied, the raw edge will be covered by the back lining.

4. Fell stitch the undercollar in place.

5. Smooth the top collar toward the gorge line and front neckline. Trim the seam allowance to ¼ in. Turn under the edge and align the folded edge with the seamline; baste.

6. To finish the gorge line, use a draw stitch to join the top collar and lapel facing.

CLAIRE'S HINT *The draw stitch is a variation of a fell stitch. Make the stitches short and perpendicular*

## PINNING FRONT FACING

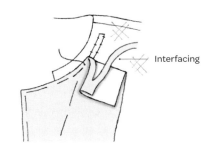

Interfacing

## PINNING UNDERCOLLAR

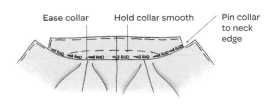

Ease collar    Hold collar smooth    Pin collar to neck edge

## FELLING COLLAR

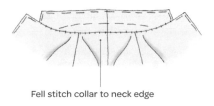

Fell stitch collar to neck edge

## GORGE LINE

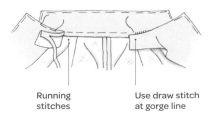

Running stitches    Use draw stitch at gorge line

---

*to the seamline like a ladder so they'll be invisible and look like a machine-stitched seam. If the stitches slant, they will show and the gorge line will be unattractive.*

7. Remove the bastings; press the gorge line and collar lightly. Press all edges firmly.

## FINISH THE LINING

The lining is shaped to fit the jacket; in home sewing and ready-to-wear, it is cut to fit. The advantage is it's easy to adjust the lining size if the garment was been altered during construction. It provides more ease in the lining since tucks replace darts. The disadvantage is that it requires more time.

1. To finish the lining, smooth the front lining over the shoulder seam, baste to the back seam allowance; trim away the excess lining.

2. Smooth the back lining to the neckline, clipping as needed so you can turn it under and pin the edge. Continue pinning the back lining over the shoulders, easing it slightly at the shoulder seam. Trim the seam allowance at the shoulder to 1 in., turn it under, and baste.

3. At the top of the armscye, trim the lining so it's even with the garment seam allowances; baste the lining around the armscye.

4. Pin the sleeve linings at the armscye. Trim as needed, turn the raw edge under; baste (see p. 149). The seam at the underarm should stand up; and the lining should come up and over it without flattening the seam. Otherwise, the sleeve won't hang properly.

## THE FINAL FITTING

At this fitting, check to be sure your jacket exhibits all the points listed in "Characteristics of a Couture Jacket" on p. 175. Check the lining to be sure it's not too tight.

## FINISH THE JACKET

To finish the jacket, fell stitch the basted seams, complete the buttonholes, and attach the buttons.

1. To finish the lining, fell stitch the lining in place at the shoulders, neck, front edges, and armscyes.

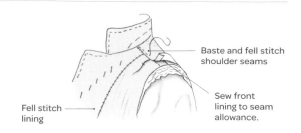

Fell stitch lining

Baste and fell stitch shoulder seams

Sew front lining to seam allowance.

2. Complete the buttonholes. If the design has bound buttonholes, finish the facings. If it has handworked thread buttonholes, make them now.
3. Sew on the buttons.

## Lining Stays

The technique described here was used on a Dior jacket made in the 1950s. The lining stay consists of a narrow silk strap sewn to the right front lining which hooks to an eye at the edge of the underlap. Less bulky than traditional ties, it can be used on jackets, coats, and coat dresses, and it can be added to a finished garment. The length of the stay and its placement will depend on the garment design, but on many jackets it's located the same distance from the hemline of the garment as the top button.

1. Make a stay ¼ in. wide and 8 in. to 10 in. long from the lining fabric (see "Belt and Hanger Loops," p. 123).
2. Place the jacket on a dress form or try it on. Pin the center fronts together. On the right front, mark the edge of the underlap with a pin even with the top button. You can feel the pin through the overlap.
3. Remove the jacket. Measure the distance on the right front between the pin and the side seam. Mark that length plus ¼ in. on the stay.
4. Beginning at the side seam, baste the stay to the lining, leaving an extra ½ in. at the side seam for finishing and stopping 2 in. to 3 in. from the pin mark.
5. Try on the jacket and pin the stay to the underlap. Check the stay position when moving and sitting; correct as needed.

6. Remove the stay to finish the ends. Turn under one end ¼ in. and catchstitch neatly. Place the hook over the raw edges of the end; sew it permanently.
7. Trim the other end of the stay, leaving ¼ in. for finishing. Fold this end up instead of under and catchstitch it. Fell stitch the end to the lining side seam with the raw edge enclosed.
8. With several backstitches, fasten the stay to the lining 2 in. to 3 in. from the hook end.
9. Make a permanent thread eye in a corresponding position on the edge of the underlap.

### MAKING A LINING STAY

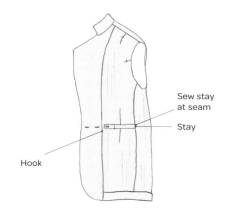

Sew stay at seam

Stay

Hook

## "Chanelisms"

The details and construction techniques on Chanel's legendary suits were described by *Vogue* magazine editors in the 1960s as "Chanelisms" (at *Elle*, they were called "Chaneleries"). Most of these techniques are traditional couture details but Chanel used them so extensively and consistently that she is often credited with having invented them.

The classic Chanel suit appears to be a loosely fitted cardigan and skirt with a well-coordinated blouse or a cardigan jacket with a matching dress. Casual in appearance, the ensemble is assembled with meticulous attention to detail. Linings for jackets and skirts are cut from the same fragile fabric as the blouse—a technique used earlier by the designer Mainbocher. This makes it almost impossible to wear the suit with a different blouse.

This beautiful Chanel suit from 1967 appears to be made from a single piece of fabric on the front. Instead, it has a princess seam to the shoulder. The front sections were cut as rectangles and shaped into a princess seam design.

(Photo by Taylor Sherrill. Author's collection.)

Lightweight and comfortable to wear, the suits have just two fabric layers—the shell fabric and the lining. Many of the shell fabrics are textured Scottish wools or Linton tweeds and bouclé materials—fabrics that most designers would consider too loosely woven and too fragile for skirts and jackets. Others are made from guipure lace, chenille, brocade, and cotton or sequin embroideries.

The linings are often delicate materials such as silk gauze, plain-weave silks, and silk charmeuse that feel wonderful next to the skin but aren't suitable for heavy wear.

On many suits, the shell fabric and lining are machine-quilted together so the loosely structured shell fabric will not sag and the garment will maintain its shape. On traditional suits, this support is provided by backings and interfacings. The quilting on Chanel's suits is often invisible, since the stitching thread often matches one of the colors in the shell fabric. When the thread

shows, it is a status symbol, and an element of the construction that easily sets any real Chanel apart from the innumerable copies.

Other finishing touches on Chanel suits include signature buttons and buttonholes, functional sleeve vents, and chains, which act as weights on the inside of jacket hems. Many of the jackets are also trimmed imaginatively at the edges, pockets and sleeve vents with self- or contrast fabric, braids, ribbons, yarns, bias bindings, topstitching, decorative selvages, or pipings.

## THE QUILTED LINING

In the directions below, the individual sections are quilted to the corresponding lining sections before the seams are stitched. Since quilting, like embroidery, tends to reduce the size of the garment section, I do the quilting on a fabric rectangle before cutting out the sections.

1. Cut a rectangular piece of shell fabric and lining for each section that is 3 in. to 4 in. larger all around than the finished section.

2. Thread-trace the seamlines on the shell fabric rectangle. This is a temporary guide, and it doesn't have to be exact.

3. Plan the quilting pattern. The quilting can be vertical, horizontal or rectangular, depending on the shell fabric. Generally, the quilting rows should be inconspicuous and parallel to grainlines and stripes. Quilt tweeds and fabrics without prominent fabric patterns vertically. If the design has princess seams, horizontally quilted rows placed perpendicular to the seamline may be less conspicuous than vertical quilting. On plaid fabrics, quilted rectangles are sometimes most unobtrusive; and when quilting lace or large prints, hand quilting is sometimes best.

4. Wrong sides together, pin the shell and lining fabrics together, easing the lining some so it will give with the shell fabric. Using large diagonal stitches, baste.

CLAIRE'S HINT *I place the basting where I plan to stitch and use soft, cotton basting thread so the threads will break and be easy to remove without disturbing the stitches after quilting.*

## MAKING A QUILTED LINING

**SEAMING JACKET AND LINING**

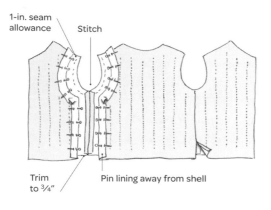

1-in. seam allowance

Stitch

Trim to ¾"

Pin lining away from shell

**FINISHING SEAMS WHEN JACKET IS BACKED**

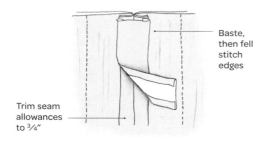

Baste, then fell stitch edges

Trim seam allowances to ¾"

5. Right side up, machine quilt; beginning and ending 2 in. to 3 in. from the seamlines and hem so you can complete the seams and hem without ripping the quilting. Leave long thread ends. Silk machine thread, fine cotton machine-embroidery thread, and mercerized cotton are all suitable for machine quilting.

6. Pull the thread tails between the shell and lining—a calyx-eyed needle works well for this; knot and trim. Remove the bastings, and press lightly.

7. Right side up, place the pattern on the quilted section. Mark the seamlines and hems with pins. Remove the pattern. Thread-trace the shell fabric without catching the lining. I use a different thread color for the second thread tracing.

8. Trim away the excess fabric, leaving 1-in. seam allowances and a 2-in. hem.

9. For the first fitting, baste all the seams and darts, then top-baste the seams. Fold and baste the hems.

10. After the fitting, remove the bastings, and make any corrections.

11. Fold and pin the lining out of the way; baste and stitch the vertical seams. Press the seams open and trim evenly to ¾ in. or less.

12. To finish the lining seams, trim the seam allowances so they are slightly narrower than those on the jacket. Fold under one raw edge, aligning the folded edge with the seamline; baste about ⅛ in. from the edge. Repeat for the corresponding garment section. Slipstitch the lining. Remove the bastings; press lightly.

13. On some Chanel suits, particularly on the skirts, the lining and shell fabric are seamed together like a backing; then the seams are covered with a strip of lining fabric. If you prefer this method of attaching the linings, turn under the long edges of the lining strip; baste, fell stitch the strips in place.

## WEIGHTS

On Chanel jackets and sometimes blouses and coats, chain weights are used on the inside at the hemline to make them hang smoothly and remain level without "catching" at the top of the skirt. On jackets, the chain is usually sewn around the entire hem, starting and ending at the center front or at the facing edges. On jackets with heavy buttons or multiple pockets, which provide extra weight for the front, the chain is only used on the back.

The chain is located just above the hemline when the jacket is lined to the edge. When lined to the top of the hem allowance, the chain is located just below the lining. On one Chanel jacket I examined, the chain was positioned at the top of the hem allowance under a silk chiffon lining. On blouses, the chain is usually a lighter weight.

### HAND-SEW THE CHAIN LINKS

Sew next to adjacent link

Sew the chain weight after the jacket has had its final press. Hand-sew both sides of the chain links very close to the next link so the stitches don't show. To prevent unsightly press marks when the suit is dry-cleaned, remove the chain for cleaning.

## TRIMS

Chanel fashioned striking, imaginative trims from unusual materials; this custom continues today at the House of Chanel. Many trims incorporate yarns braided, crocheted, or embroidered onto the fabric. Some are made from decorative selvages enhanced with matching yarn or transformed into pipings. Others feature grosgrain ribbons, bias strips, or ordinary topstitching. Most trims are applied after the jacket is quilted but before the lining is sewn to the jacket edge and the buttonholes are made. Some trims are sewn on the right side of the jacket while others are joined to the edge itself.

**Ribbon.** Grosgrain ribbon is used frequently as a base for custom-made or purchased braid. On some Chanel suits there's a single piece of grosgrain under the braid, while others have two narrow pieces on either side of the trim because they are easier to shape at corners and curves. The braid can be ready-made, or you can make it yourself from purchased yarns.

1. Shape the grosgrain with a steam iron so it will fit around any curved edges. Small hand-sewn darts work well on sharp curves.

2. Starting at a side seam, sew the grosgrain to the garment by hand with small running stitches placed in the center of the ribbon. Miter the ribbon with a fold at each corner. When making a miter at a corner, fold the miter with the fold down.

3. Center a braid such as gimp or plaited yarns on the ribbon; use running stitches to sew it on permanently.

4. To make a plaited braid, cut six to twelve strands of yarn at least three times the finished length of the trim. Knot the strands together at one end; pin the end to the pressing stand. Hold the strands taut while you plait them. To finish the ends, secure the yarns with machine stitching.

**Selvages.** Another favorite, selvages can be used alone or embellished with topstitching, embroidery or another trim. Sometimes at the front edges, the selvages are used as woven at the fabric edges; but in most instances the selvages are first cut from the fabric, then joined to the edge or used as pipings.

1. Cut the selvages at least ½ in. wider than the finished width. Thread-trace the finished width on the selvage.

2. Turn under the seam allowance at the jacket edge; baste. Use catchstitches to secure it permanently.

3. Right sides up, tuck the raw edge of the selvage under the finished edge. Align the thread tracing with the edge; baste.

4. Use running stitches to sew the selvage permanently.

This collection of Chanel cuffs from the 1960s shows the diversity of the trims used to enhance the Chanel suits. From the top, a piping using the wrong side of the blouse fabric; wool yarn wrapped around the edge; two rows of corded piping made from self-fabric with a flat piping made from silk blouse fabric; and silver crochet trim with self-fabric insertion. (Photo by Author.)

**Topstitching.** Another simple but elegant and versatile trim, topstitching can be sewn with regular cotton thread or silk buttonhole twist, with a single row, double row, or multiple rows, or with a regular stitch length or a longer stitch. Don't worry if the topstitching is not perfectly regular; Chanel's is not always perfect either.

# Designing
## *with* Fabric

# 11

MANY HAUTE COUTURE DESIGNS utilize fabrics in unusual, but not necessarily difficult, ways. Some are labor intensive and require time and patience, while others are simple ideas easily implemented. Most utilize techniques you already know. In this chapter, we'll focus on a variety of design ideas and specific techniques to inspire you to use fabrics more creatively.

Lace, for example, is one of the most fascinating and versatile fabrics. It can be used for complete garments, trims, or small details. Other books, including my own, have included only the most basic lace sewing techniques. Even though space does not allow a truly in-depth study of lace, it's an opportunity to add a variety of design ideas and a few construction techniques.

Most machine made laces are manufactured with a scallop design on one edge. Some laces, called galloons, have scallops on both sides, while a few allover laces have two straight edges. Both scalloped and straight edges can be used to finish garment edges.

Lace fabrics can be cut lengthwise or crosswise, and it's not uncommon to find both on the same garment. Technically, lace does not have grain since it is not woven;

Designed in the 1950s, this beautiful lace blouse is just as wearable today as it was then. The blouse front is cut on the lengthwise grain with the back on the crossgrain. The blouse is assembled with appliqué seams and appliqués are used on the shoulders and edges to fill any voids.

(Photo by Ken Howie. Author's collection.)

however, it generally has more stretch in the width, as well as finished edges that can be called selvages. A variety of different laces are frequently used together and edges from one or more can be used for finishing on the same garment.

The design and use of lace on the blouse shown on p. 198 is extraordinary. The only label in the bodice identifies it as a garment from Rizik Brothers, a very high-end retailer in Washington, D.C. The construction and quality of the lace are more consistent with couture than ready-to-wear so it's quite possible that it was a required purchase when the buyer attended the couture collection presentation; this mandatory purchase is then called the *caution*.

Fabricated in a guipure lace, the bodice front is cut lengthwise and the sleeves and back are cut crosswise. The finished edges of the lace are used at the neckline, center front, sleeve, and lower edges. This is possible only when you cut the lace apart and sew it back together because, even though this particular lace was 12 in. wide and had scallops on both sides, it had no finished shapes at the cut edges.

Lace appliqué seams were used extensively on the blouse. You can see a small amount of overlapping in the bust area to transition from the lengthwise to the crosswise direction and provide shaping. The scallops at the lower opening are only 1 in. wide and at the sides, the same scallops are 4¼ in. wide. The shoulders are trimmed with lace "leaves" cut and applied to the taffeta backing.

## SEAMING LACE TO LACE

Most lace garments are sewn by hand with appliqué seams or narrow plain seams overcast or bound. The appliqué seam is a good choice when you want to conceal the seamlines; the plain lace seam is a good choice for seams in areas with stress, like armscye seams. These seams are described in Chapter 3. Other lace seam choices include lapped, buttressed, and ribbon seams.

**Lapped Seam.** A lapped seam is normally used for joining interfacing sections, and underlayers to avoid bulk, but this seam can be used on the garment face side because it's inconspicuous as well as flat.

On a Jean Louis lace skirt in my collection, the lace was not wide enough to accommodate the height of the client so a 5½-in.-wide yoke of matching lace was inserted between the waistband and the skirt. The skirt has three layers: the lace overskirt, an organza underskirt with a lace ruffle at the hem, and a silk crepe slip. The overlap—the wider piece of lace—has a scalloped edge sewn with running stitches which are not especially strong. On seams where strength is important, catchstitches can be added to cover the lace edges.

To make a lapped lace seam like the one shown:
1. Thread-trace the seamline on the lace with the cut edge. Thread-trace a seamline on the lace skirt on the baseline—a line at the base of the scallops. Mark the matchpoints.
2. Right sides up with the skirt on top, align and pin the seamlines together.
3. Using short running stitches, join the yoke and skirt on the baseline. Sew a second row of running stitches ⅛ in. below the first.
4. If the scallops extend more than ½ in. above the baseline, use running stitches to outline the edges of the scallops.
5. Remove all bastings.

On this sample, the seamlines were first thread-traced, then basted together. To sew permanently, use two rows of short running stitches. (Photo by Author.)

6. Wrong side up, press the seam lightly on a padded pressing pad.

**Buttressed Seam.** The buttressed seam takes advantage of the seam allowance bulk by using it to support the top of a ruffle so it will stand away from the garment body. The lace buttressed seam is slightly different from a regular buttressed seam (see p. 221). It rarely has an extra-wide seam allowance; it's usually gathered and often applied as a trim to a skirt or bodice base.

To make a lace buttressed seam:
1. Thread-trace the seam location on the skirt or garment section.
2. Mark matchpoints on the seam and ruffle tiers.
3. Use matching thread to gather the ruffle on the seamline. Place a second row of gathering stitches in the seam allowance $1/8$ in. away.
4. Pull up the gathering stitches and distribute the gathers evenly.
5. Right sides together, match the seamlines and matchpoints; pin the ruffles to the skirt. Baste. Machine stitch. You may find that hand sewing the ruffles in place at this point makes the fabric bulk easier to handle.
6. Remove the bastings and steam the ruffles.

**Ribbon Seam.** The ribbon seam is stitched wrong sides together and then ribbon covers the seam allowances. The seam is often used to join a ruffle or even two ruffles one on top of the other to a skirt. To make a ribbon seam:
1. Thread-trace the seamlines and matchpoints.
2. Wrong sides together, match and pin the seamlines together; baste. Stitch.
3. Fold the seam away from the gathered edge.
4. Right sides up, cover the seam with the ribbon and pin. Baste.
5. Sew the ribbon at the top and bottom with short running stitches or by machine.
6. Remove the bastings and press lightly. Steam the ribbon to avoid making an impression of the lace on the ribbon.

## SEAMING LACE TO FABRIC

Lace can be joined to fabric in myriad ways, ranging from narrow plain seams and French seams to appliqué seams. Frequently used in haute couture, the lace-on-fabric appliqué seam is suitable for fabrics that don't ravel easily and for curved seamlines. In couture, this seam is usually hand stitched or machine sewn with a straight stitch. On ready-to-wear of any quality, lace is generally applied with a zigzag stitch.

**Lace-on-fabric Appliqué Seam.** These lace seams can be planned on the muslin toile or directly on the garment sections. The latter allows more flexibility when positioning the lace and more control when sewing the seam. This is more important on some designs than others. It's more economical to plan the lace sections on the muslin toile.

These directions can be adapted for appliqués and other designs as well.
1. Plan the lace design and placement before cutting out the fabric to determine where it will be seamed to the fabric and if it requires seaming within the lace portion(s). For a simple design like the dress on p. 202, plan the design on muslin first.
2. Thread-trace the seamlines, neckline, and armscyes on the lace. Thread-trace the seamlines and hems on the skirt. To mark a seamline on a scalloped edge, I thread-trace the baseline.
3. Finish the shoulder and side seams on the lace yoke, and finish the neckline and armscyes with narrow bindings. The seams can be narrow plain seams with overcasting a flesh-colored binding, or French seams.
4. Finish the side seams on the dress.
5. Right sides up, align the thread traced seamlines on the yoke and dress. Baste the lace to the fabric $1/8$ in. from the appliqué seamline.
CLAIRE'S HINT *I baste with matching thread and short stitches so it doesn't have to be removed.*

6. Right side up, use very small running stitches, backstitches, or whipstitches, and fine silk or

The yoke seam here is relatively simple to duplicate when working with the muslin toile. Thread-trace the seamlines on the lace and fabric and baste them together. Sew the seam permanently with running stitches or whipstitches, depending on the seam's location and the amount of stress it will have.

(Photo by Taylor Sherrill. Author's collection.)

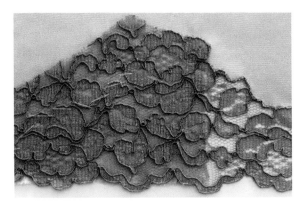

This sample shows a lace motif applied to fabric. Place the lace on the silk and baste it in place. On the right side, the lace edges were sewn permanently with whipstitches, then the fabric under the lace was trimmed away.

(Photo by Author.)

cotton thread in a color that matches the lace to appliqué the seam permanently.

7. Wrong side up, press the seam on a softly padded surface.

8. Remove the bastings, if needed.

9. Trim away the fabric under the lace, leaving a ⅛-in. to ¼-in. seam allowance. If the fabric ravels, hand overcast the edges.

**Applied Appliqué.** Frequently used on many designs and especially lingerie, the irregular edge of the lace on the appliqué seamline is opposite the finished edge of the lace. On this design, the finished edge of the lace is used at the hem.

Unlike the previous application, the lace is applied directly to the garment instead of working with a muslin toile. This allows more flexibility to place the lace attractively and more control when sewing the seam, but it requires more fabric.

1. Examine the lace to select the appliqué motifs; thread-trace around the motifs.

2. Plan the design and placement of the lace before cutting the fabric to determine where the lace will be seamed to the fabric and whether it will require any internal seaming.

3. Thread-trace the seamlines on the lace and on the fabric.

4. Wrong side up, baste any backing in place.

5. Baste the lace to the fabric on the appliqué seamline.

6. After the fitting, reposition the lace as needed if it's not smooth on the fabric.

7. Trim away the excess lace below the appliqué seamline.

CLAIRE'S HINT *Before trimming, I examine the lace one last time to be sure I like the overall effect. When in doubt, I leave more lace than I think I want because it's easier to trim again than to sew it back.*

8. Baste the lace to the fabric following the outline of the appliqué motifs.

9. Right side up, use very small running stitches, backstitches, or whipstitches and fine silk or cotton

thread in a color that matches the lace to appliqué the seam permanently.

10. Wrong side up, press the seam on a softly padded surface.

11. Remove the bastings.

12. Trim away the fabric under the lace, leaving a ⅛-in. to ¼-in. seam allowance. Trim the lace close to the appliqué seam.

## FINISHING EDGES

Although lace garments can be finished with traditional hems, facings, and narrow bias facings, many are finished with lace edgings, bias and ribbon bindings, and horsehair braid. The focus in this section is on lace edgings; directions for bias bindings, bias facings, and hems are included in Chapter 4.

Lace edgings can be used on garments in several ways. One is to cut the garment section so the lace scallops are positioned along a horizontal or vertical edge such as the hem, zipper placket, or front opening. This limits the design options to straight edges; and since this technique utilizes the shaped edge of the lace, scallops cannot be used on adjacent edges such as at a front opening and a hem or the ends and visible edge of a collar.

Most frequent, a scalloped trim is applied. The scalloped edges are cut from lace yardage, then sewn to the garment to trick the eye into thinking the edge originally had a shaped configuration.

The cut trim piece can be a scalloped or straight edge, from the same or a different lace, or it can be a separate narrow lace edging applied to the garment edge. Both can be applied to any shaped edge as well as to adjacent edges. For example, on the Givenchy dress on p. 204, a scalloped edge is applied to the shaped neckline and sleeves.

**Neckline Edges.** These directions are for finishing neckline and armscye edges with the scalloped edge cut from lace fabric. They can also be adapted to use with a narrow lace trim.

1. Assemble the garment.

A master with lace, Antonio Canovas del Castillo designed this evening gown in the mid 1960s. The dress is cut on the straight grain with a faux opening and appliqué seams on the left side. Notice that the lace pattern is off center. At the hem of the long overdress, a scalloped edging has been applied to cover the cut edge. (Photo by Taylor Sherrill. Author's collection.)

The front zipper facilitates dressing on this lace blouse and it is completely concealed under the lace appliqués. Notice the fabric-covered snaps.

(Photo by Ken Howie. Author's collection.)

This sample shows a lace edging applied to the lace fabric at the hem. Both the edging and fabric are thread-traced, then basted together on the traced lines and again at the top of the edging. The edging is sewn permanently at the top with whipstitches; then the excess lace under the edging is trimmed away.

(Photo by Author.)

2. At the fitting, check the thread traced neckline, and correct as needed.

3. Thread-trace the scallop baseline on the trim lace.

4. Examine the trim and the neckline to determine how the scallops will be placed. Will the baseline of the trim be aligned with the thread tracing at the neckline, with the top of the scallops on the thread tracing, or somewhere in between? On a neck edge, I generally align the scallop baseline with the neckline unless it's a jewel neck and fits the neck closely.

5. Thread-trace a new seamline on the lace if you're not using the baseline.

6. Right sides up with the trim uppermost, align and pin the thread traced seamlines on the lace trim and the garment; baste.

7. Use short running stitches or whipstitches and matching thread to sew the trim to the garment. CLAIRE'S HINT *Even though I match the thread traced seamlines, I frequently follow the design of the trim when sewing it at the bottom of the scallops; and, on some, I sew both the seamline and edge. On some hems, the edging is machine-stitched with a straight stitch or narrow zigzag.*

8. Trim away excess lace.

9. Wrong side up, press on a soft pressing pad.

**Hems.** Lace hems can be finished with the scalloped edge of the fabric, scallops purchased or cut from other lace fabric; bands, bias and ribbon bindings; applied motifs to simulate the look of scallops, and of course, with narrow machine stitched hems.

On the Castillo design (on the facing page), the ruffled tiers are cut crosswise so the finished edge can be used at the hems. To provide some additional crispness, 1/2-in.-wide strips of horsehair braid were sewn to the wrong side of the ruffles about 1/4 in. above the baseline. Two additional strips of horsehair braid spaced about 5 in. apart were sewn to the wrong side of the two lower ruffles.

Another finishing technique that I saw recently is most unusual. The garment was finished first

Designed by Hubert de Givenchy in the 1960s, this beautiful dress is finished at the neckline and sleeves with a lace trim, which was cut from the dress fabric. The trim has been stretched to create a shallow scalloped edging. The skirt tiers are cut on the crossgrain so the lace scallops at the edge are used at the hem. The dress is worn over a black silk slip.

(Photo by Taylor Sherrill. Author's collection.)

On this Castillo dress, horsehair braid was used like a facing to cover the raw edges of the lace that were turned to the underside. The hem allowance was turned to the wrong side and catchstitched to the back of the lace fabric. When the horsehair braid was applied over it, the outer edge was basted, then the thread on the remaining edge was pulled up to shape the horsehair to the edge. After it was basted in place, both edges were secured with short running stitches.

(Photo by Ken Howie. Author's collection.)

with a narrow hem. Then motifs cut from the lace fabric were applied at regular intervals to the hem edge. To select a lace for this technique, look for one which has design motifs which are simple, repeating, and no larger than 4 in. in diameter—the larger they are, the more difficult they are to work with. In this way, you are creating a unique scalloped-edge finish.

## DESIGNING WITH ALLOVER LACE PATTERNS

Allover laces and point d'esprit are frequently overlooked when purchasing lace because they have no scalloped edges. I've selected several dresses

This trapeze design by Castillo is fabricated in an allover lace pattern; appliqué seams are used at the front and sides. The underdress is satin-back crepe. This dress was imported through the Custom Salon at Bergdorf Goodman in New York; it is dated and was allegedly worn to the inaugural events for John F. Kennedy.

(Photo by Taylor Sherrill. Author's collection.)

fabricated in allover lace to show a variety of interesting techniques.

The Castillo dress shown on p. 205 features an A-line lace cage over a slim satin-back crepe underdress. All edges of the lace—neckline, sleeves, front opening, and hem—are finished with a hand-sewn ¼-in. ribbon binding.

The lace yoke is backed with flesh-colored cotton net. There are no seams at the shoulders; lace appliqué seams are used to join the lace yoke at the front and on the lace overdress at the side seams. The silk underdress has a wide hem to encase a 4-in.-wide strip of horsehair braid. At the hemline, rectangular drapery weights were encased in plain-weave cotton tape. Unlike most dresses, this one has a zipper at center front; it's concealed by the lace overdress, which fastens with hooks and eyes under the decorative bow. The dress has bust pads to enhance the figure.

When I purchased this dress at a thrift shop, I did not know that it would fit almost perfectly. The horsehair braid had deteriorated and the lace was badly damaged at the shoulders, which was probably the result of hanging on a wire hanger. The horsehair braid was easy to replace, but the lace repair took some time.

# Designing with Stripes

Many striped fabrics can be reconfigured to improve the aesthetics of the design. This can be done in a variety of ways: cutting them apart and sewing them back together to change the repeat or stripe arrangement, by tucking and pleating, or shrinking and stretching.

Often couturiers will cut the fabric apart and rearrange it to create more interesting designs or to simply trick the eye. These techniques are just a few for you to consider.

### REARRANGING STRIPES

I have seen several garments with stripes that have been rearranged. On some, the new seams are so inconspicuous that I didn't realize the stripe pattern had been changed until I found the seams on the wrong sides.

The dress shown on the facing page is cut on the straight grain so the original stripes were woven horizontally on the fabric. There is a seam on a cream-colored stripe midway between the narrow green stripes. I can only guess how the original striped pattern looked since the stripes have been rearranged on the entire garment. When I examined the wrong side, I found a 2-in.-wide cream stripe on the hem and adjacent to the narrow green stripes. My guess is the fabric had a wide cream-colored stripe between the narrow green stripes.

On the blouse shown on p. 208, you can see the original repeat of the stripes: white, aqua, gray. If this pattern had continued, the white stripe at the hem would have been aqua. To create a more pleasing design, a seam was added between the two gray stripes.

## SHRINKING AND STRETCHING

Wools and loosely woven fabrics aren't difficult to shape by shrinking and stretching. This technique for shaping a collar is just an extension of the technique you've used in the past to shrink out the fullness at the top of a sleeve.

### INTERFACE THE SHAPED COLLAR

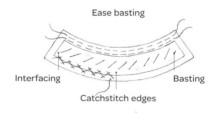

Ease basting

Interfacing

Basting

Catchstitch edges

### APPLY THE COLLAR LINING

WS lining

RS collar

Attributed to Chanel, this silk taffeta–striped dress is made of seven strips that have been seamed together horizontally to change the sequence of the stripes on the fabric. With the exception of a seam at the bottom, all seams are located in the center of the cream/green stripes. The bottom seam is in the middle of the pink stripes.

(Photo by Taylor Sherrill. Author's collection.)

On the jacket shown on p. 64, the collar was cut as a rectangle so the color bars would be parallel to the neckline and end attractively at center front. To create a shaped collar:

1. Mark the seamlines on the collar pattern.
2. Trace the seamlines onto a full muslin pattern. (I sometimes trace the pattern onto the collar interfacing.)
3. Thread-trace the finished width of the collar on the fabric. The collar can be cut on the straight or crossgrain depending on the fabric design.

4. Place two rows of ease basting on the upper edge—one on the seamline and the other about 1/8 in. into the seam allowance.
5. Pull up the ease basting; steam the basted edge. Repeat several times until the rectangle has a nice curve.

CLAIRE'S HINT *When steaming, I use my hand to pat and flatten the fabric; then I pull up the ease basting and shrink out the fullness. On many fabrics, you have to shrink a small amount, then shrink again until you get the shape you want. The most important consideration is to avoid pressing an unwanted crease.*

Made of a wool and mohair knit this striped blouse was worn with the Chanel suit shown on p. 195. There are several seams to rearrange the stripes. The most obvious is the seam between the two gray stripes. Without this seam, the hem of the blouse would have been in the midst of a turquoise stripe, which would not have been as pleasing aesthetically.

(Photo by Taylor Sherrill. Author's collection.)

Very subtle and easy to overlook, a band has been added to the wrist of this Chanel jacket from the 1970s.
Without the band, the plaid would be uneven at the wrist. The band joins the wrist with a plain seam; there is no mitered seam at the corner.

(Photo by Author.)

6. Cover the collar with a press cloth and gently stretch the lower edge.

7. Pin the upper edge of the collar to the muslin pattern and continue shrinking until the collar fits the muslin pattern smoothly.

8. Thread-trace the collar ends, using the pattern as a guide.

9. Wrong side up, place the interfacing on the collar. Baste with large diagonal stitches. Use catchstitches to secure the edges.

10. Turn under the collar seam allowances on all edges. Baste ¼ in. from the edges.

11. Wrong side up, press lightly. Trim the seam allowances to ¼ in. and catchstitch the edges to the interfacing.

12. Wrong sides together, using diagonal stitches, baste a rectangle of lining fabric to the collar.

13. Trim the lining so it extends ¼ in. to ⅜ in. beyond the finished collar edges. Baste and press.

14. Turn under the edges of the lining and fell stitch permanently.

15. Set the collar to the garment.

## PLEATS AND TUCKS

With the use of pleats and tucks, a striped fabric can be transformed into a solid or a smaller scaled motif. If the garment section has no darts or shaping, the easiest procedure is to pleat or tuck the fabric, then cut out the garment section. When it has shaping, it's easy to hide the darts in the tucks or pleats.

Any garment section can be tucked to change the appearance of a striped fabric. The specific amount will depend on the garment size and the stripe patterning.

1. Note the finished garment pattern piece size needed (including ease). To determine the number of stripes used, divide that measurement by the width of each stripe, and round up to a whole number.

2. If you're creating a shaped piece, i.e., a skirt with a smaller waist than hip measurement, taper the stripe tucks to accommodate the difference.

3. Thread-trace the stitching lines for the tucks, tapering as needed to accommodate the garment shaping. Not all stripes need to be stitched exactly the same width—adjust them slightly as needed to fit. No one will be the wiser visually.

4. Rights sides together, baste the tucks.

5. After the fitting, stitch and remove the bastings.

6. Wrong sides up, press all tucks in one direction.

## CUTTING AND SEAMING

One of the most fascinating elements in couture is the many designs which are created by cutting the fabric apart and sewing it back together. Generally, even though you can see the seam and the differences in the grain on the sections, you don't notice it.

**Straight Bands.** Many Chanel trims feature self-fabric that has been cut off and sewn back together. On most sleeves, the wrist edge is off-grain and when the fabric is a plaid or stripe, this may not be aesthetically pleasing. This disturbing line is easily corrected by adding a band at the bottom of the sleeve.

On the cuff shown on the facing page, your mind and eye assume that the stripe at the edge is simply a continuation of the fabric pattern. Creating a similar trim is not difficult. The stripe at the vent opening extends to the shoulder point ends at the top of the stripe that encircles the wrist.

**Points.** Like the band trim described previously, you might not notice that the fabric stripes have been cut off and rearranged on the ends of the pocket flap (see p. 158). You might think it's a binding or an applied trim.

More challenging than applying a band to a straight edge, these directions are for applying a band to a pointed pocket flap. These same bands can be adapted for collars or belts, and for squared ends.

Choose a flat, firmly woven fabric. For each point, cut a square of china silk or silk organza to use for a facing.

### APPLYING THE FACING

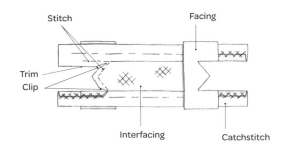

### FINISHING THE ENDS

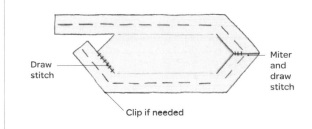

### FINISHING ALL EDGES

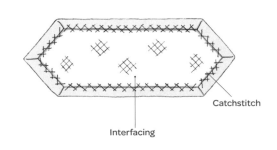

The House of Worth used the selvage edge of the fabric turned wrongside up to create the neckline of this 19th century dress.

(Photo by David Arky, courtesy of the Museum of the City of New York, gift of Mrs. Winthrop W. Aldrich.)

1. Thread-trace the seamlines on the pocket at the outside edges and also the inside corners and point. The accuracy of the thread tracing will determine the success of the pocket.

2. Wrong side up, baste the interfacing in place if there is one; use catchstitches to sew it permanently.

3. Right sides together, baste the silk square to the end of the flap on the thread traced lines.

4. Begin stitching on one long edge ½ in. from the corner. Stitch to the corner; break the threads, and begin again to stitch to the point.

5. Pivot at the point, and continue to stitch the other side. Tie the threads at the corners. At the corners, give the thread ends a sharp tug before tying them to be sure there is no slack in the last few stitches.

6. Clip to the faced corners. Trim the seams in the faced section to ¼ in.

7. Press the seams open. Turn the end right side out. At the point, trim the seam close and sew the seam allowances flat.

8. On the unfaced sections, use catchstitches to sew the seam allowances flat.

9. Right side up, abut the finished edges at the end; sew permanently with a draw stitch, stopping about ¼ in. from the point.

10. At the point, fold one end into a miter, baste. Place it on top of the other end. Slipstitch the ends together. Remove the bastings. Press the seam open and trim.

11. To finish the pocket, turn under the edges on the thread tracings; baste. Trim the seam allowances as needed and catchstitch the edges flat. Remove the bastings, and press.

12. Wrong sides together, baste the lining to the flap using diagonal stitches. Trim the lining so it extends ¼ in. beyond the flap edges. Turn under the edges; and baste. Fell stitch the lining in place.

13. Wrong side up, press lightly.

# Designing with Other Fabrics

When designing, don't overlook fabrics that have an attractive wrong side or selvage. The House of Worth used both of these to create interesting design elements even with plain selvages.

## WRONG SIDES AND SELVAGES

One of the most obvious design ideas is to use either the fabric wrong side or the selvage. Both are used extensively on Chanel suits, and on the designs by Charles Frederick Worth, the selvage is rarely cut off. Although this isn't unusual for seams, it's initially surprising to see it retained on the edges of chiffon ruffles. At first glance, the chiffon appears to be hemmed because the selvage is darker than the rest of the fabric.

## DESIGNING WITH PRINTS AND PATTERNS

**Matching Fabric Patterns.** Patterned fabrics provide many opportunities for creating interesting designs. One of the simplest is to match them attractively. These directions focus on matching a print at center front so the fabric design is not interrupted even though there is an opening. These directions can also be used for stripes and plaids.

This base fabric has two patterns to be matched: the weave—alternating chiffon and satin weave stripe—and the floral pattern. The colors are brighter on the satin than on the chiffon; the satin stripe also has a little more body. Although the fabric has even repeats in both the vertical and horizontal directions, the crossgrain has different flowers on the satin stripes. On a single width of the fabric, the flowers can be matched only by disregarding the stripe design.

1. Examine the fabric to identify the stripe you want to use for center front. On the vertical stripes, the flowers are always exactly the same.

2. Mark the center front with thread-tracing so it's at least twice as long as the cut garment front. On this design the center front is in the middle of a satin stripe.

CLAIRE'S HINT *Before marking, I measure the width of the front section. The thread-tracing must be at least this distance from the fabric edge.*

3. Cut two front patterns. Mark the center front on each.

4. Align each center front with the marked line, being sure to cut a left and right half.

5. Thread-trace the seamlines and matchpoints on the fabric.

6. Add seam and hem allowances, cut out the sections, and assemble the garment.

The sample shows the layout for the coat fronts. The two fronts were arranged in a vertical layout since both the print pattern and the fabric weave could not be matched horizontally. (Our photo is not to scale, for emphasis).

(Photo by Author.)

This little silk coat has two patterns to be matched— the print and the fabric weave with alternating satin and chiffon stripes. At the armscye seams, the floral pattern is matched so there is no abrupt change at the seamline. Since the pattern was different on the right and left sides, the cap of a muslin sleeve was marked with a fabric scrap for each sleeve.

(Photo by Taylor Sherrill. Author's collection.)

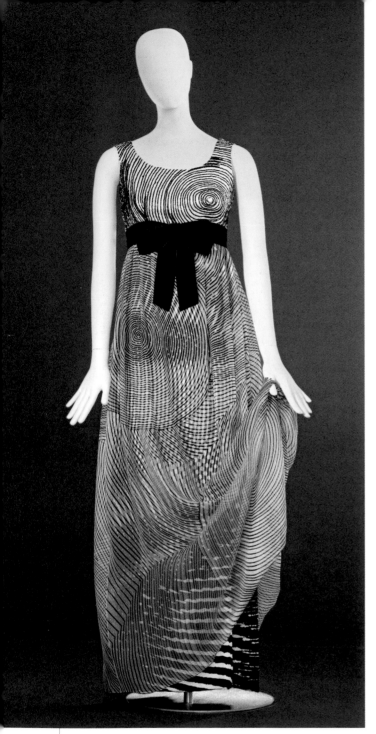

This stunning Hanae Mori evening gown from the 1970s is fabricated with two prints—one chiffon, one silk satin. The dress has an empire waist; the pop-art motif on the bodice is beaded in a concentric circle on the left breast, ending with a large ½-in. rhinestone. For the modest wearer a 10-ft. chiffon stole was provided.

(Photo by Taylor Sherrill. Author's collection.)

## DESIGNING WITH APPLIQUÉS

Woven fabrics can be appliquéd in several different ways. An extravagant ballgown I particularly like was designed by Pierre Balmain. The original fabric was cream silk taffeta with a scattered design of large pink flowers—some light, some dark. The dark pink flowers were cut out and appliquéd to the bodice to change the color of the entire section between the pleated bust and full skirt. It didn't matter that several meters of fabric were left with big holes when the flowers were removed; the dress was stunning.

On the Balenciaga dress shown at left, appliqué seams (see p. 47) were used on seams and darts to avoid cutting through the embroidered bows. On the same dress, several of the bow motifs were faced and sewn on one side of the back. After the zipper was closed, the bows were snapped to the other back.

Generally used as a decorative element, appliqués are also a good tool for redesigning the fabric. The fabric for the ensemble shown below was a border print. The large amount of black was aesthetically unattractive for the blouse design. To eliminate this problem, several floral motifs were cut from the fabric; then appliquéd to the blouse fabric. Although you can see them in the photo, they are not noticeable when the blouse is worn.

The I. Magnin dress was fabricated in a border print on a black background. To hide the background color on the back of the bodice, several floral motifs were appliquéd to the garment. These motifs are not noticeable when the blouse is worn.

(Photo by Ken Howie. Author's collection.)

The Victor Edelstein design, below at right, began with an embroidered cotton fabric. Like the Balmain, the flowers were cut from the original fabric, but since they were embroidered at the edges, they didn't have to be turned under when they were appliquéd. The first layer was appliquéd flat on the bodice, then additional flowers' were applied over it with only a few stitches so they were three-dimensional.

## SHEER FABRICS

I'm fascinated with sheers and how they can be combined creatively with other materials.

The evening gown shown on p. 214 is made of three-dimensional Mylar. Even though the fabric has been air-brushed to dull the glitziness, it's still a bit gaudy if worn without the organza cape.

On other designs, Mori used two different prints: one on the underdress and another on the overdress to create a third design when the two prints were combined.

Fabricated in silk gazar with embroidered bows, this Balenciaga evening gown from the 1960s skims the body attractively. Fabric appliqué seams are used at seams and darts to avoid cutting through the motifs. At the back zipper, a bow motif has been lined with chiffon and sewn to right side. When the dress is fastened the bow is snapped to the left side.

(Photo courtesy of The Ohio State University, Historic Costume and Textiles Collection.)

Designed by English couturier Victor Edelstein in the 1970s, the bodice on this dress is white pique with embroidered flowers and the skirt is navy four-ply silk. To make the bodice, approximated 50 flowers were cut from the embroidered fabric and appliquéd to the bodice base and on top of each other. There is a small amount of cotton padded between some of the flowers. The zipper in the back is hidden under a wide flower overlap.

(Photo by Taylor Sherrill. Author's collection.) ·

# 12

# Special
# Occasions

Special occasion designs run the gamut from unadorned, body-clinging dresses of bias-cut silk charmeuse to richly ornamented ball gowns, and wedding dresses with multiple skirts and extravagantly shaped garments that are almost impossible to sit down in. When planning a special occasion design, there are numerous details to

consider and questions to ask. Perhaps the most crucial questions concern the garment's construction: What kind of shape or silhouette will the garment have? What special support is needed inside the garment to maintain this shape? What kind of support will the body itself need to look attractive in the garment and minimize stress on the fabric and construction? And if the garment is to be embellished, how and when will that embellishment be applied?

Many answers to these complex questions are found in this chapter. Although sometimes used on daytime clothing, most of these techniques are characteristic of eveningwear, and many are used on bridal gowns.

The structural support for the silhouette of a special occasion design can simply be the lining, interfacing,

Fabricated with strips of Mylar on an organza base, this stunning Chanel design is finished at the hem with a ruffle cut that utilizes the selvage edge. The silk organza cape and dress have been air-brushed to create a more subtle design. The dress opens on the left with snaps at the shoulder and around the armscye to the zipper at the underarm.

(Photo by Ken Howie. Author's collection.)

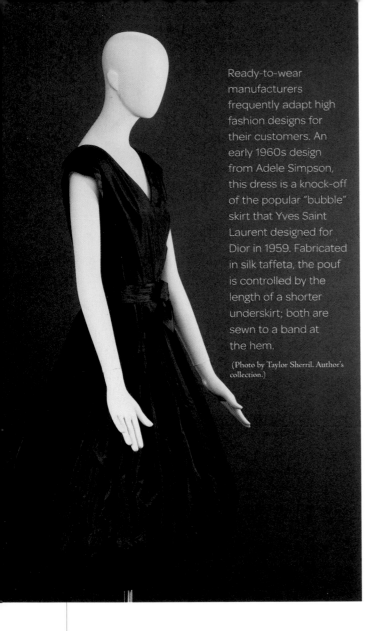

Ready-to-wear manufacturers frequently adapt high fashion designs for their customers. An early 1960s design from Adele Simpson, this dress is a knock-off of the popular "bubble" skirt that Yves Saint Laurent designed for Dior in 1959. Fabricated in silk taffeta, the pouf is controlled by the length of a shorter underskirt; both are sewn to a band at the hem.

(Photo by Taylor Sherril. Author's collection.)

and backing that lend body to the fashion fabric. Various materials are used for backing and interfacing special occasion designs. Some, including organza, silk muslin, chiffon, China silk, and hair canvas, are also used on day dresses and suits. Others, such as horsehair braid, nylon crinoline, and tulle, are generally reserved for eveningwear and wedding gowns because they are stiffer and produce more dramatic silhouettes.

Deciding which backing material to use, whether to combine it with an interfacing and whether additional underskirts or underpinnings are needed involves some trial and error. For

information on choosing and working with backing and interfacing materials, see p. 62.

## CREATE SHAPE WITH THE LINING

Backings and interfacings are generally used to give a garment shape. Rarely do linings serve to shape a garment, but there are notable exceptions. Dresses with balloon, pouf, or bubble skirts—also dubbed "harem dresses"—rely on a shorter lining to help give them shape. The fullness of these skirts can be controlled from the right or wrong side of the garment.

When a skirt's fullness is controlled on the right side, the skirt is generally narrow at the bottom and full above it, with the fullness gathered into a band at the hem. The lining, which supports the skirt, is a simple tube that fits the body smoothly, and the fuller outer skirt is at least several inches longer than the lining. When the skirt and lining are joined at the upper and lower edges, the outer skirt is forced to pouf out.

1. To create a dress or gown with a pouf skirt controlled from the right side, begin by assembling the skirt and lining. You may want to leave one of the lining seams open 9 in. to 12 in. so you can insert puffs of tulle or netting to support the outer skirt.

2. If the skirt has more fullness than the lining, add gathering stitches as needed at the top and bottom of the skirt.

3. Baste the skirt and lining together at the waist and put them on a dress form. You can use a hanger if you don't have a dress form, but it's a little more difficult.

4. Make a separate band of garment fabric; pin the bottom of the skirt to the lining. Adjust the fullness to create the desired pouf and baste the band to the skirt lower edge.

5. Baste the skirt to the bodice for the fitting.

6. After the fitting and any corrections, baste and stitch the skirt and band together right sides together. When working with some fabrics, this seam may be too bulky to machine stitch. If so, use backstitches to join the sections instead.

"Scherazade" was designed by Yves Saint Laurent for Christian Dior's Fall 1959 collection. The pouffed hemline of the silk shantung coat-dress was created by gathering the fullness at the hem into a shorter lining. The skirt was sewn to knickers so it would move attractively when worn.

(Photo by Susan Kahn, courtesy of the Metropolitan Museum of Art, gift of Baron Philippe de Rothschild, 1983.)

This detail of this gown shows one leg of the pantaloons, which were sewn into the dress and attached to the hem of the dress so the dress moved with the wearer when she walked. Notice the self-fabric lining on the back above the gathered hem.

(Photo by Susan Kahn, courtesy of the Metropolitan Museum of Art, gift of Baron Philippe de Rothschild, 1983.)

7. Press the seamline, wrap the band to the wrong side, and pin the band flat. Secure it permanently with a running stitch.

8. Cover the band with the lining, turn under the edge, and slipstitch it permanently. If the skirt needs to be shortened after the band is sewn permanently, you can hand-sew a horizontal tuck in the lining; this will both shorten the lining and increase the size of the pouf.

9. If desired, insert poufs of net or tulle between the layers to support the outer skirt. Close the lining seam with slipstitches. According to legend, Valentino once stuffed a dress with beautiful organza flowers. It was to be a secret between him and the client.

The fullness of a pouf skirt can also be created and controlled entirely on the wrong side of the

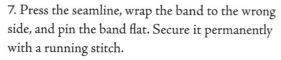

garment. In this case, the skirt hem wraps to the under side and is gathered to the lining, as in this design by Yves Saint Laurent for Dior, shown above. On this dress, the skirt is much longer than the lining—from 4 in. in the front to 22 in. in the back. The skirt is folded under at the hemline, then gathered at the edge to join the self-fabric lining. This is particularly attractive on skirts like this which are shorter in front, exposing the inside of the skirt back when the dress is worn.

This unusually deep hem can be extended to the waist to self-line the skirt. The extravagant use of self-fabric as a lining has several advantages. It adds volume without adding excess weight to the skirt, provides a soft roll at the hemline, and eliminates the shadow of a hem or any stitching that might show.

# Special Hem Finishes

**EVENINGWEAR DESIGNS** sometimes need special hems. Weighted hems make the skirt on a long gown hang close to the feet or they prevent the back hem on evening pants or a long skirt from catching on the wearer's shoes. A small arc built into the center-front hem of a floor-length ball gown will prevent the wearer from tripping.

## WEIGHTED HEMS

Weights can be enclosed between the garment and hem allowance before a garment is hemmed or sewn to the outside of the completed hem.

There are several different types of weights: lightweight self-fabric and twill tape, separate round or square lead weights, chains, or cotton weighted tapes with small lead rectangles or pellets.

Self-fabric or twill tape is a good choice for the back hems of pants or long skirts. When the weights can be concealed inside the hem, use individual lead weights. Chains are an attractive means of keeping blouses and jackets from riding up, and weighted tapes are generally used when large sections of the hemline are to be weighted.

When the weights are applied to a finished hem, chains or decorative weights are most attractive. Since decorative weights are almost impossible to find, heavy, flat buttons can be substituted or lead weights can be sprayed with gilt paint or covered with fabric.

To add weights before hemming a design, first interface the hem with cotton flannel, hair canvas, or muslin (see p. 72). Then, if you're adding a chain, baste it loosely to the interfacing at the hemline before completing the hem. If you are fastening individual weights, baste them just above the hemline at the garment openings, the ends of the seamlines, and between seams as needed.

## ARCED HEMLINES

Most women look beautiful in floor-length ball gowns—until they start walking. An arc at the center-front hem easily eliminates clumsy entanglements with billowing skirts and allows the wearer to move, and even dance, gracefully. The arc can be created by making the hemline shorter in front or by doubling the hem at center front. Doubling the hem is frequently preferable to making the hem shorter in front because it's easier to control and shape the curved edge.

When doubling the hem, you can raise it half the hemline depth. That is, if you start with a 4-in. hem allowance, you can raise the hem 2 in. A hem can be raised in front by as much as 5 in. without distortion, but that, of course, requires a 10-in. hem allowance. A more practical solution to raise a hem by 5 in. is to begin with a hemline that's already 2 in. to 3 in. shorter in front than in the back and double it.

To create an arc by doubling the hem, first finish the hem in the usual manner (see p. 69). Then fold the hem under at center front and pin it, tapering each end to the finished hemline. Baste the hem and put the garment on a dress form or hanger to make sure the effect of the arc is pleasing. Then secure the hem permanently, remove the bastings, and press the hem lightly.

### DOUBLE HEM

Hem

# Underskirts

One method of supporting a skirt's fullness is with one or more attached underskirts or separate petticoats. These undergarments range in shape from simple tubes that might be found below a slim or knife-pleated skirt to billowing, multi-layered and multitiered skirts beneath yards of satin on a wedding dress or ball gown. The design of the underskirt and the fabric it's sewn from are determined both by the garment's silhouette and by the drape, hand, and weight of the fashion fabric.

Often sewn into the garment, underskirts can also be mounted on a separate corselette, slip base, or waist cincher, and can be made from various fabrics such as cotton or nylon tulle, silk taffeta, nylon crinoline, and soft plain-weave silks. To reduce bulk at the hip on a multi-tiered underskirt, each of its several layers is longer and sewn to the base foundation a little higher than the layer immediately beneath it. The shortest, bottom layer is sewn by hand to the foundation or slip base first; and the longest, uppermost layer, the one closest to the waist, is sewn last. The seam allowances joining these tiers to the foundation slip can be a narrow $\frac{1}{2}$ in. and turned toward the bodice, with the raw edges flattened against the foundation with catchstitches. Or the allowances can be wide, turned under, and sewn with buttressed seams.

The underskirt on the Dior dress (shown at right) is a relatively simple design with six tulle skirts applied to a corselette base. Only the top skirt is cut in the usual manner with the straight grain perpendicular to the floor, all of the underskirts are cut on the crosswise grain so there is only one seam on each. The corselette was extended 11 in. below the waist to accommodate the underskirts. Here are the directions for the underskirt:

1. Make the corselette long enough to extend 11 in. below the waist, or you can use a long-line bra.
2. Cut out 6 to 8 top skirt sections on the lengthwise grain 36 in. wide and 4 in. longer than the desired length. Reduce the bulk at the waist on the top skirt by tapering the sides 3 in. to 5 in. at the waist.

3. Cut out the tulle underskirts on the crossgrain so they measure 6 to 8 yd. at the hem. It's easier to cut them all the same length at the outset; then trim as needed after they are attached.
4. Assemble the underskirts and gather them at the waist.
5. Place the corselette on a dress form. Adjust the gathers; and pin the first underskirt 1 in. from the

The slip or, more correctly, the understructure for the dress above was built on a corselette with six tulle skirts. Only the top skirt was cut on the straight grain in the usual manner. The others were cut on the crossgrain with a single seam. Each skirt was sewn to the corselette by hand with catchstitches.

(Photo courtesy of the Chicago History Museum, 1969.)

bottom of the corselette. Use running stitches to sew it permanently. Catchstitch the upper edge to the foundation.

6. Mark the location of the second skirt 3½ in. above the first skirt.

7. Apply it to the foundation as you did for the first underskirt.

8. Apply the third underskirt 1 in. away; the fourth 1½ in. away; the fifth 1 in. away; and the top skirt at the waist 3 in. above the last underskirt.

9. Measure and mark the length on all skirts; trim away the excess. Do not be surprised if the skirts stand away from the form and there is less to trim than you expected.

By comparison, "Mexico," also by Dior (shown at right) is quite different. "Mexico" is made of a lightweight, silk muslin similar to silk organza, but more opaque and softer. Its top skirt, cut on the crossgrain with the selvage at the hem, measures 7⅔ yd., not including the front drape. Its second circular skirt is pleated to a yoke and measures 5¼ yd. at the hem.

The horsehair braid on the underskirts is flexible and lightweight. Since the fashion fabric is lightweight, the underskirts have been designed to accentuate the gossamer quality of this two-piece dress. The skirt consists of two overskirts cut from the design fabric, supported by two underskirts attached to a slim, silk crepe slip. Made of silk muslin, the first underskirt has six tiers, each one about twice the fullness of the one above it. To give the underskirt some body, a strip of narrow, soft horse-hair braid was applied to the hem edge and to the seamlines at the tops of the three lowest tiers. The second underskirt is made of cotton tulle. It's gathered into the seam at the top of the third tier. Two bands of horsehair braid are enclosed inside the hem.

The underskirt for the I. Magnin® dress on p. 5 provides another method for supporting a diaphanous design. The dress is made of a lightweight, silk muslin. The skirt is circular, and measures 11⅛ yd. at the hem.

To accentuate the filmy quality of this two-piece dress, the skirt consists of two overskirts—one

Made from delicate silk muslin printed with scallops, Christian Dior's "Mexico" was created for his Spring/ Summer 1953 collection. The dress has two overskirts, one with the selvage at the hemline, and one a complete circle, finished with a hand-rolled hem. The underskirts are shown on the right on p. 217.

(Courtesy of Christian Dior.)

from the design fabric and one from flesh-colored silk chiffon. It's supported by an underskirt made of silk crepe. The skirt is gathered to a yoke below the waist. Both the chiffon overskirt and the underskirt are semi-circles and measure 2¾ yd. at the hem.

The silk crepe underskirt is underlined first with cotton net. The net backing begins 4½ in. below the waist and is sewn into the seams. The net is attached at the top to the underskirt with catchstitches. The bias-cut silk-organza hem interfacing is 14 in. wide. It's attached at the top to the net with catchstitches; but it is not sewn into the seams. Hidden inside the hem is 2-in.-wide horsehair braid.

To support a heavier garment fabricated in heavy silk, faille, taffeta, embroidered fabric, and cotton pique, build an underskirt with two or more layers sewn to a corselette. Stiffen each underskirt with several horizontal rows of horsehair braid in various widths. At the bottom of the top skirt, cover the horsehair braid with a binding. If the underskirt is straight, the binding can be cut on grain. It should be about 12 in. wide on the right side and about 6 in. wide on the underside.

Horsehair braid can be sewn to the underskirts by hand or machine, or with several rows on each skirt, one above the next. It is available in widths up to 6 in. and in soft and heavy weights. The heavyweight horsehair braid is available in wider widths than the softer braid. The wider horsehair has a thread on one edge that can be gathered to shape it to fit a curve. Since it's stiffer than the lightweight version, it can support heavier garments, but it will, in turn, make the garment heavier.

### BUTTRESSED SEAM

A variation of the gathered seam, the buttressed seam can be used to support the silhouette. The gathered section is cut with an extra-wide seam allowance, which forms a foundation under gathered ruffles, flounces, and skirts and forces the fullness to stand away from the seamline. These directions for a skirt can be adapted for ruffles and flounces.

1. Cut out the skirt with a wide seam allowance. The width will vary with the design, but it's generally from 1 in. to 5 in.; and it's rarely the same width as the seam on the section it joins.

2. Thread-trace the seamline and matchpoints. If the seam allowance is 3 in. wide, mark the seamline 3 in. from the raw edge.

To increase the buttressed effect when the design fabric is unusually heavy, or when you wish to create an exaggerated effect, add a piece of crisp, lightweight interfacing at the top of the gathered skirt edge. Cut the interfacing on the bias at least twice as wide as the gathered seam allowance. Baste the interfacing to the wrong side.

3. Place two rows of gathering stitches on the seamline and ⅛ in. into the seam allowance. In couture, the gathering stitches are put in by hand. I usually put them in by machine.

4. Pull up the gathers so they fit the corresponding section.

5. Right sides up, turn under the gathered seam allowance. Align the seamlines and matchpoints; pin. Slipstitch or fell stitch the sections together. If you prefer a smoother line, reposition the sections right sides together, and stitch.

6. Remove the bastings and press. Don't press over the seamline, but instead press each section separately, stopping at the seamline.

7. Fold the seam toward the skirt.

## Skewed Ruffles

Skewed ruffles can also be use to provide support. The ruffles can be any width from 1 in. to 12 in. When used to provide support, however, they are generally 3 to 6 in. wide. Experiment with various widths and placements on underskirts. Wider ruffles can be skewed more than narrow ones; and the skewing causes all to narrow. On underskirts, skewed ruffles are generally placed near the hem; and can be located on the top side or underside of the petticoat. The skewed ruffle can also be used as a decorative trim on the outside of the garment.

1. Cut the ruffle 2½ times the desired finished width, plus two seam allowances. It can be cut on the straight grain or crossgrain. There's no reason to cut it on bias. This is only an estimated width.

2. Thread-trace the seamlines.

3. Wrong sides together, fold the fabric lengthwise; shift the top layer in one direction and the bottom layer in the opposite direction. Match the thread-traced seamlines at the top; pin. Experiment by shifting one layer more or less. The wider the ruffle the more you can shift the top and the narrower the ruffle will become.

4. Before removing the pins, mark both layers with matchpoints about 3 in. from the ends. Remove the pins.

5. Right sides together, stitch the ends together to make a circle; press. If the ends are not joined, stitch each end separately with right sides together.

6. Reposition the ruffle with wrong sides together; shift the layers to align the thread-traced seamlines and matchpoints. Baste, then gather the ruffle. The skewed ruffle appears to be cut on the bias, even though it may actually be cut on the straight grain or crossgrain.

7. Baste the ruffle to the garment with a buttressed seam (see p. 221); use short running stitches to sew it permanently.

8. For a firmer ruffle, tack the folded edge of the ruffle to the seamline every 5 or 6 in. so it's scalloped at the folded edge.

# Body-shaping Underpinnings

Some eveningwear designs are sewn with one or more custom-made underpinnings to support the garment's silhouette and hold the body in a smooth line underneath. Such underpinnings include a shaped waist stay, which hugs the waist and reduces stress on the fabric and fasteners at the waist; a corselette, or long-lined, boned brassiere that extends to the waist or below and gives the body a firm, smooth line; and bust enhancers, which add fullness to a small bust or roundness to a sagging bust.

## SHAPED WAIST STAY

Most eveningwear fits more closely than daywear so the waist stays on evening gowns are generally wider and stiffer and control the body more than on day dresses. Usually made of stiffer support fabrics such as Petersham, faille, taffeta, girdle elastic, or cotton coutil, waist stays on eveningwear are darted or seamed to fit the body and generally boned so they don't roll. You can add a waist stay to most gowns with little difficulty. (See p. 133 and p. 223 for more information on stays.)

1. To make a waist stay for eveningwear, cut the stay fabric 2 in. to 6 in. wide and 12 in. longer than the actual waist measurement. If the fabric isn't crisp enough to hold the body firmly, use two layers and machine-quilt them together.

2. Pin the stay around the waistline of the dress form. Pin out as many small darts in the stay as needed to make it fit the waist smoothly. Mark the waistline, garment centers, side seams, and opening.

3. Remove the stay from the dress form; repin the darts so they're on the inside of the stay, next to the body. Double-baste the darts and baste the stay to the vertical seamlines on the inside of the garment for the fitting.

4. Fit the garment, pinning the stay together at the opening so it fits snugly. Carefully mark the ends of the stay.

5. After the fitting, remove the stay from the garment; stitch, press, and trim the darts. If the stay needs boning to keep it from wrinkling and rolling, sew boning pockets over the darts (see the facing page).

## FINISHING WAIST STAY ENDS

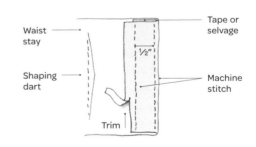

Waist stay

Shaping dart

Tape or selvage

1/2"

Machine stitch

Trim

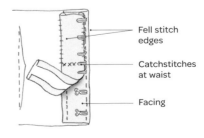

Fell stitch edges

Catchstitches at waist

Facing

# Boning

**THE BONING SEWN INTO** corselettes and shaped waist stays prevents horizontal wrinkles and supports the garment. Boning can also be used on skirts and underskirts to create unusual effects, like that in the Charles James's design shown on p. 10.

The whalebone and feather-bone quills once used as boning in couture corselettes have been replaced by spiral steel boning, while Rigilene® and poly boning are used for petticoats and hoop skirts.

Spiral steel boning is best for corselettes and waist stays because it bends sideways as well as back and forth. Generally used in the ¼-in. width, it's available in finished lengths from 2 in. to 17 in., and the ends are finished with metal tips (see Resources on p. 247). When the pre-cut lengths are not practical, use heavy-duty wire cutters to cut the boning to the length you desire. Then use a metal file to smooth away any roughness. Finish the ends with metal tips which can be purchased separately or a rubberized dipping liquid like Plasti Dip®.

Rigilene is a thin, flexible boning that provides good support for hoop skirts and petticoats.

Woven with fine polyester rods in the warp, it's pliable enough to sew through or it can be inserted into a casing. It can be cut easily with shears and is available by the yard in two widths and two colors—¼ in. and ½ in., black or white. It resembles the old feather boning which was made with feather-bone quills.

Poly-boning is best for hoop skirts and petticoats. It is made of a firm, but flexible, polyester, which bends forwards and backwards, but not sideways. When used in corselettes, it warms up from the body heat, bends more and often sticks into the body. It can be cut easily with shears, is ¼ in. wide, and available by the yard.

The amount of boning used in a corselette or waist stay varies with the weight of the dress or gown. Most corselettes have 14 to 18 bones.

When positioning the boning on a corselette or waist stay, begin with a piece of boning on every seam or dart line. On corselettes, place another midway between the bust and underarm and at center front. Add additional boning to create and maintain the desired shape and fit of the garment. Many couture workrooms extend the boning over the bust, and some never do because the support is more rigid.

Spiral boning can be sewn directly to the corselette with

## BONING A WAIST STAY

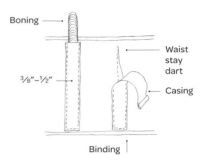

a catchstitch casing, but it is usually inserted into a casing ¼ in. to ½ in. longer than the boning, and made of narrow plain-weave tape or, less frequently, ribbon, rayon seam binding, or lightweight silk.

**1.** Center and pin a strip of plain-weave tape, ⅜ in. to ½ in. wide, over the seam or dart.

**2.** Stitch the sides and bottom so the boning will fit snugly inside the casing.

**3.** Slip the boning into the casing and close the end securely with hand stitches.

**4.** If the ends of the boning irritate the body, sew 1-in. squares of velvet or cotton flannel to the corselette over the casing ends.

Add additional boning if needed between the darts and the opening.

6. To finish the ends of the stay, mark the ends.

7. Wrong side up, place a piece of plain-weave tape or selvage over each marked line. Use running stitches to sew it in place.

8. Fold the raw edge to the wrong side. Edgestitch each end close to the fold; stitch again ½ in. away. For additional firmness, stitch several rows between the two rows of stitches you just sewed or insert a piece of boning.

9. Trim close to the stitching.

10. Wrong side up, sew the hooks to the end of the right back if the garment has a back opening. For a side opening, sew them to the front section. Sew the eyes to the other end of the stay.

11. To cover the hooks and eyes, cut a 1-in. facing for each end from lightweight silk or cotton tulle. Fold under the facing sides and edges so the hooks and eyes barely show. Baste and fell stitch the edges in place.

CLAIRE'S HINT *Charles Frederick Worth used silk seam binding for the facings. Sometimes I substitute rayon seam binding or ribbon.*

12. Bind the long edges at the top and bottom of the stay with a lightweight bias or narrow cotton tape.

13. Mark the stay waistline with catchstitches to use as a guide. When you sew the stay into the dress, match the waistline markings on the stay and dress. I generally add an underlap extension so the hooks won't be uncomfortable (see the facing page).

14. With the garment wrong side out, pin the stay at the waistline, matching the catchstitches on the stay and waistline markings. Beginning and ending about 1 in. from the ends, use running stitches to sew the stay to the waistline seam. On a design with no waistline seam, secure the stay with short French tacks (see p. 37) at the seamlines and darts instead.

## CONSTRUCTING A CORSELETTE

The corselette can extend to the waist or continue for several inches below it, depending on the gown's design and the figure of the woman wearing it. Traditionally a corselette was made of two layers of cotton tulle; in more recent years, fabrics such as silk, linen, and power net (a girdle fabric with spandex) are used more frequently. The cotton tulle, sometimes called English net or bobbinet, is lightweight, soft, cool to wear, and does not ravel; it is also expensive and difficult to find (see Resources on p. 247).

Many corselettes are simple, strapless designs, suitable for a variety of garments, but for backless designs and those with a décolleté or plunging V-neckline, the corselette will follow the lines of the bodice more closely. When made for such designs, the corselette is sometimes wired or stiffened with boning at the edges, and the bodice fabric is generally applied directly to the top of the corselette so it's difficult to determine

The corselette in this Dior dress is made of cotton net and boned with spiral boning. The bodice is backed with hair canvas. The casings for the boning are made of plain-weave cotton tape. The boning extends to the waist on the back and over the bust on the front. Hanger loops are located at the side seams. The top is bound with a strip of bias-cut silk faille to match the dress bodice.

(Photo by Taylor Sherrill. Author's collection.)

where the corselette ends and the bodice begins. Hand sewing the corselette into the garment and finishing the edges are a time-consuming tasks, but not particularly difficult.

The length of the corselette is determined by the design's silhouette. Although the corselette sometimes ends at the waist, it usually extends several inches below. For bouffant skirts, the corselette often extends 10 in. to 12 in. below the waist and serves as a base for attaching underskirts, which reduces waistline bulk. For close-fitting silhouettes and dropped waistlines, the corselette should be long enough to control the figure and maintain a smooth silhouette. Before the invention of pantyhose, the corselette was long enough to provide a base for the garters to fasten to hose.

These directions for a tulle corselette can be adapted for other fabrics and foundation designs. In couture sewing, the corselette pattern is draped on the client's dress form. If you don't have a dress form, you'll need someone to fit the corselette on you.

**The Corselette Toile.** Usually it is easier to begin with a pattern that is too large and take it in as needed until it fits like a second skin.

1. Begin with a dress pattern for a simple princess-line sheath or shift. On the front and back sections, measure and mark the bottom of the corselette about 7 in. below the waist and use the full pattern up to the shoulder. Once you have fitted a corselette toile, you will shape the top for the design.

2. Cut and baste the muslin corselette. I add seams at the center front and back and cut with 1-in. seam allowances at all edges.

3. Fit the muslin corselette and mark the upper edge so it will be hidden under the dress. If you are fitting yourself, put a zipper in so you don't have to pin it together.

4. Carefully mark the seamlines. Remove the bastings; press.

5. Using a stiletto tracing wheel, transfer the seamlines to a paper pattern.

CLAIRE'S HINT *When making a single garment, use this shortcut I saw in the atelier at Christian*

# Underlap Extension

ON A COUTURE GARMENT, AN UNDERLAP extension is often attached to prevent hook closures from rubbing against the body. Fabrics such as velvet, faille, grosgrain ribbon, cotton flannel, or cotton tulle are generally used for the underlap extension.

**1.** Cut the underlap fabric 2 in. to 4 in. wide and the length of the placket opening.

**2.** Wrong sides together, fold the extension in half lengthwise, machine stitch ¼ in. from the raw edges, then overcast the edges together.

**3.** Place the underlap under the eyes so it covers the facing; pin. Wrong side up, use two row of running stitches—one near the edge of the underlap and another at the edge of the stay to secure it permanently.

## UNDERLAP EXTENSION

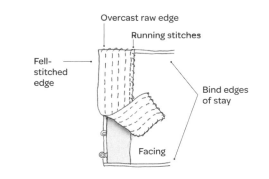

*Lacroix: Cut out the muslin on the stitching lines and use the muslin as a pattern.*

**Cut and Assemble the Corselette.** Cotton coutil, plain-weave silk, and silk taffeta can be used for the corselette, but my favorite is cotton net. It is flexible, lightweight, and cool to wear.

1. Cut the corselette from cotton net. It can be cut with one layer on the straight grain and one on the crossgrain for strength and flexibility. For more control, cut the corselette with the straight grain going around the body and a fold at the bottom. CLAIRE'S HINT *If the muslin was fitted accurately, I cut the corselette with ¹/₂-in. seam allowances so it will be easy to assemble. If I'm concerned that it won't be large enough, I cut with 1-in. seam allowances.*

2. Assemble the corselette, using short basting stitches.

**Fitting on a Dress Form.** Sometimes when it isn't possible to fit the corselette on the body, use a dress form and fine-tune the fit later.

1. Put the corselette on the dress form. Pin it together at the opening.

2. Pin out any excess fullness at the seams. At center front, pin small darts from the center front seam to the bust points so the corselette will fit like a second skin. This is easier if you rip the center front seam several inches from the top so you can pin the each dart separately.

3. Examine the fit; the corselette should be very smooth without any wrinkles or excess. Pin out additional darts at the waist, under the bust, or between the seams if needed. It's better to have several small darts instead of one large one.

4. Before removing the corselette, use the garment or the pattern as a guide to mark the style line at the top of the corselette; mark the hemline at the bottom. Pin a narrow plain-weave stay tape to the style line at the top to keep the edge from stretching; do not trim away the excess tulle above the style line until after it's fitted on the body.

5. Chalk-mark any seams you may have ripped while fitting.

6. Remove the corselette from the dress form; double-baste all seams and darts as well as the taped stay at the style line.

7. Finish the opening (see "Corselette Opening" on the facing page). Since a corselette fits the body so closely, the placket should be finished before it's fitted on the body. Or baste a 20-in. zipper in temporarily so any excess zipper hangs below the corselette hem.

8. If bust enhancers are needed, baste them in place for the fitting (see p. 228).

**Fitting the Figure.** Fitting a strapless corselette is easier when you add ribbon straps for the fitting process. Also, I try to avoid ripping seams when the corselette is on the body because it is difficult to repin them.

1. Fit the corselette on the figure without a bra. If you used a dress form to build the corselette, the corselette may be too loose since the body is softer than a dress form. Pin out any excess until the corselette fits snugly.

2. Remove the corselette, make any necessary adjustments. Check the fit and establish the locations for the boning as well (see "Boning" on p. 223).

3. When you've perfected the fit, machine stitch the seams permanently and press them open.

**Boning the Corselette.** Seam binding, narrow ribbon, plain-weave tape, and silk tubes can be used to make the casings for the boning. Today the casings for boning are machine-sewn, but the House of Worth continued to sew them by hand until the 20th century.

1. Make the casings for the boning (see p. 223), and insert the boning. If necessary, trim the boning so it's ¹/₈ in. to ¹/₄ in. shorter than the casing and doesn't extend into the upper seam allowance.

2. Sew the top of the stay permanently; trim away the excess net above it.

3. Finish the top of the corselette. This can be a binding made from the garment fabric or a narrow silk facing.

4. Secure the stay with short French tacks, thread guides, or a casing made from catchstitches.

5. If the corselette does not have a fold at the bottom, machine stitch ¹/₈ in. above the marked hemline; use hand overcasting to finish the edge. If the corselette ends at the waist, finish the edge with a grosgrain stay or a silk binding.

# Corselette Opening

**IN MOST INSTANCES, THE** corselette placket, or opening, is directly beneath the dress placket. For a hook-and-eye closure at a side opening, the ends lap front over back. For a center-back opening, the ends usually lap right over left. The corselette placket is sometimes offset about 1 in. to reduce bulk.

The placket for a corselette differs slightly from the placket on a shaped waist stay. The facings are generally made of cotton tulle, seam binding, or ribbon; and they're slightly wider so the facing can be machine stitched into the placket to reinforce the edge and be used as an underlap. The facings can vary in width, but the underlap facing is a little wider than for the overlap.

These directions are for finishing the ends with hooks and eyes. They can be adapted for a zipper placket.

**1.** Begin by cutting two stays from plain-weave tape or selvage the same length as the corselette opening.

**2.** Cut the overlap facing 4 in. wide and the underlap facing 5 in. wide.

**3.** Pin the stay to one long edge of the overlap facing. Fold the facing in half lengthwise with the stay tape in between. Align the raw edges, and baste the three layers together. Repeat for the underlap facing.

**4.** Mark both sides of the opening with thread tracing. Wrong side up, align the raw edges of the overlap facing with the thread tracing on the overlap side of the opening. Baste.

**5.** Fold and baste the seam allowance of the corselette over the raw edges of the facing. Stitch six to eight rows through all of the layers, spacing the rows $\frac{1}{16}$ to $\frac{1}{8}$ in. apart. Since the stitching both stiffens and reinforces the edge, the closer the rows are, the stiffer the edge will be. Repeat for the underlapping side of the opening.

**6.** Sew the hooks and eyes to the wrong side of the overlap, spacing them approximately $\frac{1}{16}$ in. from the edge.

**7.** Fold the facing over the eyelets so that only the hooks are exposed; fell stitch the folded edge flat against the tulle.

**8.** Sew the eyes to the underlap edge so they extend almost $\frac{1}{4}$ in. beyond it. Refold the facing strip so it extends $\frac{1}{2}$ in. beyond the eyes.

**9.** Fell stitch the layers together securely between the eyes and finish the top of the extension with overcasting stitches.

## FINISHING ENDS OF A CORSELETTE

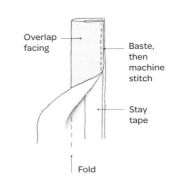

Overlap facing · Baste, then machine stitch · Stay tape · Fold

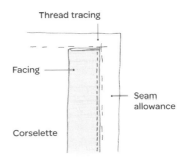

Thread tracing · Facing · Corselette · Seam allowance

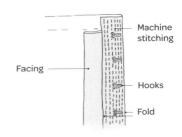

Facing · Machine stitching · Hooks · Fold

**Finish the Style Line.** The style line at the top of the corselette can be finished with a binding or a facing. The type of edge finish depends upon the fabric and style of both the corselette and the garment. For example, the corselette on the Dior dress on p. 224 is finished separately with bias binding. Since it's cut from the dress fabric, it's less noticeable if the top of the corselette shows when the wearer moves. Applied by hand, the binding is 1 in. wide on both the outside and inside of the corselette.

On garments where the top edge of the corselette won't show, the edge is generally finished with a silk bias facing or tulle strip ½ in. to 1 in. wide and sometimes a piece of seam binding. In these directions, the style line is finished with a bias facing.

1. Wrong side up, turn under the seam allowance at the style line. Baste, and trim it to ½ in. or less; use catchstitches to secure the edge.

2. Cover the raw edge with the bias strip; fell stitch the strip in place (p. 33).

3. To anchor the corselette and better define the bustline (see p. 141), add a stay under the bust made from grosgrain or elastic.

4. Add a second stay at the waist, if needed.

5. Finish the corselette placket with hooks and eyes or a zipper.

### BUST ENHANCERS

Used for both large-busted and small-busted figures to create a smoother, more attractive bustline, bust enhancers can be sewn into the garment or the corselette. These bust pads are made either as full or partial circles. Full-circle pads are placed at the crest of the bust to create a smooth look. Partial-circle pads are placed under the bust to lift it into a more flattering position, above the bust to fill in a hollow, or near the side seams to add width.

Sewn from lambswool or cotton batting, bust enhancers are constructed like shoulder pads. The following directions for circular bust enhancers can be adapted for partial circles or other shapes as needed.

1. Begin with five or six circles of padding in graduated sizes from 1 in. to 3 in. in diameter. Slash each circle to the center on one side and cut out a small triangle.

To make larger pads, cut more circles; the bottom layers can be larger than 3 in. or the pads can be more graduated. When working with cotton batting, use your fingers to feather the edges to prevent ridges. If you are working with lambswool, cut the edges.

2. Begin with the smallest circle; close the edges of the triangle and sew them together to make a small cone. Place the next size circle on top and shape it over the first one. Use loose stabstitches to sew them together. Repeat until all circles are sewn together. When stacking the circles, I offset the next slash about ¼ in. from the one below it.

3. When making crescent-shape pads, experiment with the arrangement of the stack until you get the shape you want. Center the smaller sections as you would for a full pad or align one or more edges.

4. After you've made the pads, cover both sides with cotton tulle or lightweight silk before sewing them into the garment. Or sew them in uncovered and cover them with a single layer of cotton tulle or silk.

## Embellishments

Many types of embellishments used on couture garments, like embroidery, beading, and appliqué, are sent outside to small firms specializing in a particular ornamentation instead of executed in the couture house workrooms. The most important of these firms today is the Parisian firm of Lesage, Master Embroiderer, which specializes in beading and embroidery.

Founded circa 1870 by the well-known embroiderer Michonet, who did work for both the House of Worth and Vionnet, the firm has a reputation for its creative use of materials and creative designs.

All garments are precisely fitted before any embellishment begins. The corrected muslin toile is used to make a paper pattern for designing the embellishment, which, like the garment itself, is proportioned for a particular garment and figure. For the home sewer, the easiest approach to embellishment is to use the corrected toile as a pattern, thread-trace each garment section on a rectangle of garment fabric, and embellish the sections before cutting them out.

## PREPARING FOR EMBELLISHMENT

The ultimate success of the embellishment depends in part on the care with which you approach initial preparations like dressing the frame and transferring the embellishment design to the fabric.

A frame is recommended for appliqué, beading, embroidery, quilting, and some passementerie because it holds the work taut and prevents the fabric from shifting and puckering.

1. Use the corrected toile to cut out the fabric for each section to be embellished. For each section, cut a fabric rectangle several in. wider and longer than the section itself.

If you're fitting the garment itself instead of a toile, trace the sections with at least 1½-in.-wide seam and hem allowances.

2. Using the toile, cut a duplicate paper pattern for each section. Use a crisp paper such as brown wrapping paper. If you fitted the garment, take it apart after the fitting to make the paper patterns.

3. Use the corrected toile to transfer all stitching and grainlines to the paper pattern.

Place the pattern paper on a resilient surface like a cork table, felt table pad, or piece of cardboard. Place the toile on top of the paper, smoothing it and pinning it to the pattern with pushpins, working from the center out to the edges. Use a stiletto tracing wheel or a fine needle to transfer the lines to the paper pattern. Then draw or trace the embellishment design on the paper pattern, modifying the design as needed so that it fills the space attractively and doesn't extend into the seam allowances, hem, or darts.

4. Thread-trace all stitching lines and grainlines on each fabric section.

5. The design for the embellishment is usually transferred onto the fabric before the fabric is mounted on the frame, but large designs may be easier to transfer with the fabric in place on a frame.

6. Once you've transferred your design to the fabric, the next step is to mount the fabric on the frame. If you're working with the fitted garment rather than the corrected toile, baste the center of each garment fabric section being embellished to a large rectangle of muslin, anchoring the section with long stitches and a four-pointed to eight-pointed star.

7. Using a short stitch, baste the seam allowances to the muslin. Turn the section over, remove the basted star at the center and carefully trim away the muslin in the area to be embellished.

8. To check the alignment of the framed section, compare the grainlines and stitching lines to the toile or pattern and make any necessary corrections before beginning the embellishment.

9. After you've finished the embellishment, check the garment section again against the toile or pattern. Embellishments usually cause the design area to shrink, and you will probably have to relocate and thread-trace new seamlines.

10. Once the embellishment is finished, remove the garment section from the frame.

11. Remove any bastings on the design, leaving thread-tracings on the grainlines and stitching lines, and press the garment section. To avoid flattening the design, cover the pressing table with a thick towel and press lightly from the wrong side.

## APPLIQUÉ

One of the simplest and most versatile embellishments, appliqué is created by applying one layer of fabric—the appliqué—to the surface of another—the background, or ground, which is usually the garment section. Both the appliqué and ground can be made from a variety of fabrics. The appliqués on couture garments are usually bold and decorative, but they can also enhance the design more subtly, especially on printed fabrics.

There are several ways to sew an appliqué, but the hemmed and embroidered methods are used most often in haute couture. For hemmed appliqués like that on the Adrian design shown at right, narrow seam allowances are left at all edges and turned under, then secured by tiny fell stitches. Some embroidered appliqués are finished by covering the raw edges with a decorative cord secured with couching threads on the right side or running stitches from the wrong side.

Embroidered appliqués and large hemmed appliqués are always worked on a frame. Smaller hemmed appliqués, however, are sometimes worked in the hand on a flat surface.

1. Transfer the design to the right side of the ground fabric.

2. Transfer the design motifs to the appliqué material. The traced line should be the finished edge of the motif, not the cutting line. Generally, the garment will drape better if the appliqués are cut on the same grain as the ground, particularly if they're large.

3. Cut out the motifs with ¼-in. to ½-in. seam allowances. It's usually easier to handle and less likely to distort the appliqué if you baste it to the garment section before cutting around the motifs. I usually cut with the ½-in. seam allowance and trim just before turning the edges under.

4. Working from the center toward the side seams, use fine needles to pin the appliqué to the ground, aligning the grainlines. Evaluate the design, and when necessary, rearrange the motifs.

5. Baste the motif centers to the background with a four-pointed to eight-pointed star, depending on how large and complex the appliqué is.

6. Beginning with a small section, turn under the edge of the appliqué so both the markings on the ground and appliqué are invisible, cutting the basting threads if necessary.

7. Trim the seam allowances to ⅛ in. as needed around curves and points; finger-press the edge. Turn under the edges and pin. Secure the thread with a waste knot or backstitch and trim away the tail to avoid an unwanted shadow in the appliqué. Use short appliqué pins at the edges of the appliqué.

8. Using fine cotton or silk thread in a color that matches the appliqué, use fell stitches to sew the

Made of wool gabardine, this attractive Adrian suit from 1947 is embellished with large appliqués and silk-thread embroidery. The front is finished with a fly placket, and the lapel is turned back to create a soft collar effect.

(Photo courtesy of the Chicago History Museum.)

appliqué permanently. On straight edges, make eight stitches per inch.

On curves and angles, clip or notch as needed so the edges can be turned under neatly and space the stitches more closely. The sharper the curve, the closer the stitches and clips should be.

CLAIRE'S HINT *I use the needle point to coax the seam allowances in place. When the edge of the appliqué comes to a point, I taper the seam allowance to the point and use the needle to work any stray threads neatly under the point.*

**Bias Appliqué.** Decorative bias strips can be used to create elaborate appliqués or simple trims on suits and day dresses as well as special occasion designs.

## MAKING A HEMMED APPLIQUÉ

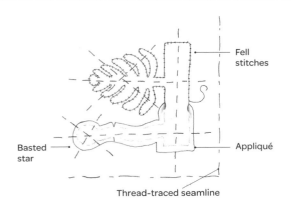

1. Cut the bias strip ½ in. wider than the finished appliqué and add ¼-in. seam allowances to the long edges. Cut a cardboard template the finished width of the trim.

2. Press the strip, stretching it slightly. Don't remove all the stretch or it will be difficult to shape curves.

3. Wrong side up, place a strip of cardboard on the bias strip. Press the seam allowances over it.

4. To apply the bias to the garment, begin with an outside edge; shape and pin a few inches of the bias strip to fit the traced design. Baste.

5. To sew permanently to the garment, work with two needles, one on each side of the strip. First fell stitch 2 in. to 4 in. on the outside edge of the strip with one needle, then fell stitch the same distance on the inside edge with the second needle. Continue the length of the strip. When you sew both sides of the strip at once, it prevents the inevitable rippling that often occurs when sewing bias.

6. When the bias strip design has a corner, anchor the tip of the corner on the outside edge first; then sew the inside edge, using the needle point on both sides to shape the corner neatly.

7. On unlined designs, space the stitches evenly so that the wrong side will be attractive.

## PASSEMENTERIE

Passementerie is a form of embroidery using various trims and edgings such as braid, cord, fringe, and ribbon to produce decorative patterns on a ground fabric. The trims can be sewn directly to the ground fabric, or they can be applied to a fabric band that is in turn appliquéd to the garment. Passementerie is worked with some of the basic techniques used in appliqué and can be applied to the garment with a variety of stitches (hand or machine), depending on the trim and desired finish. For inconspicuous applications, use fine cotton or silk thread in a color to match the trim.

1. Transfer the design to the ground fabric right side.

2. On ribbons and wide trims, fold the end under, lay it flat against the fabric, and fell stitch it inconspicuously. For narrow trims, use an awl to make a small hole in the fabric; push the end of the trim through to the wrong side. Cut the trim end, leaving a tail about ½ in. long. Flatten the tail against the fabric so it's aligned with the stitching along the trim; trim the tail to ¼ in. Use several

This simple bias appliqué on a Chanel day dress would be equally appropriate for a special occasion design. The trim is corded, then handsewn with slipstitches. When working with bias trim, press the strip to remove a little stretch so it will be easier to handle; if you press too much, the bias will be difficult to shape.

(Photo by Ken Howie. Author's collection.)

whipstitches to fasten the end. When couching, sew through the trim inconspicuously.

CLAIRE'S HINT *When the end is frayed or soft, I insert a thread loop from the wrong side, thread the end of the trim into the loop, and pull the loop and trim to the wrong side.*

3. Pin the trim to the garment, working carefully to avoid twisting it. Corners should be sharp and curves smooth.

4. To sew flexible braids or cords, use running stitches with an occasional backstitch. For stiff braids and cords, use slipstitches, fell stitches or couching stitches (see the drawing below). For a decorative finish, use couching stitches with one or more contrasting threads. For wide trims, keep them flat, miter the corners, and secure both sides with fell stitches. For narrow trims, sew them flat with running stitches at the center or with fell stitches on both sides; or sew them on one edge with whipstitches so they stand up.

5. When sewing by machine, use a cording or braiding foot and a straight or zigzag stitch.

6. To avoid flattening the trim when pressing, cover the pressing surface with a thick, soft pad, or towel; place the garment section on it wrong side up. Press first with a damp cloth; then press with a dry iron until the fabric is smooth and dry.

## BEADING

Beading is a form of embroidery that can sumptuously cover every thread of a garment or be limited to just a few motifs. Apart from the expense of the beads themselves, the process is time-consuming and adds appreciably to the cost of a design.

## COUCHING STITCH

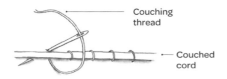

Couching thread

Couched cord

The detail of this walking suit from 1913 is decorated with elaborate passementerie. The corded design is sewn with couching stitches.

(Photo by David Arky, courtesy of the Museum of the City of New York. Gift of Miss Matilda Frelinghuysen.))

In the beading workrooms in Paris and London, beading is worked on a frame with a needle or tambour hook. Both methods have advantages and drawbacks. Beading with a needle attaches the individual beads securely but it cannot be as fine as beading with a tambour hook because the beads must be large enough for a fine needle and thread to pass through the holes.

For tambour beading, the hook does not pass through the beads; instead, it's used to make chainstitches with the thread holding the beads and allows the use of very small beads. However, if the thread holding the beads breaks, the chainstitches may unravel quickly and the beads will fall off. For both methods, a large frame is used to hold the fabric taut.

Beading can be applied directly to the garment section or to a tulle or silk organza backing for an appliqué. There are at least two advantages to beading separate appliqués. First, the garment or toile doesn't have to be fitted before it's beaded, and, second, the appliqué can be worked on a fabric that is better suited for beading—for example, tulle, organza, or the crisp tricot sew-in interfacing.

Almost any sewing thread in cotton, silk, polyester, or nylon can be used. For most designs, the thread color should match the beads or the fabric, but for a special effect, you can use a contrasting color.

**Beading with a Needle.** To bead with a needle you'll need beading or embroidery needles in a size appropriate for the beads or sequins.
1. Transfer the design to the right side of the fabric.
2. Mount the fabric on the frame right side up so it's taut.
3. Begin with a medium-short length of thread and sew a waste knot and then two backstitches at the location for the first bead.
4. Use running stitches to sew the beads quickly; but for more security, use a backstitch to go through each bead a second time before sewing the next one.
CLAIRE'S HINT *If the bead is too small for the needle to accommodate a second stitch, I sew a backstitch in the fabric beneath the bead.*

5. To sew several beads at a time use a lazy stitch or couch the strand of beads.
6. At the end, make a figure-8 knot after the last sequin and pull the knot through to the wrong side.

**Attaching Sequins**
1. To sew sequins flat, use matching or contrast thread. Insert the needle from the back into the center hole, then into the fabric at the edge. Repeat to make a stitch on the other side. If desired make a total of 4 stitches or 5 to make a star design on the sequin.
2. To sew a row of sequins, use backstitches and lap the last sequin over the previous one, hiding the thread on the last sequin.

Attributed to Oscar de la Renta, this simple jacket design is elaborately embroidered with chenille and silk threads; the beads include sequins, bugle beads, and pearls.

(Photo by Taylor Sherrill. Author's collection.)

3. For a sequin and a bead, insert the needle from the wrong side of the sequin into the center hole; pick up a bead, then insert the needle into the sequin hole again.
4. Use stabstitches to sew sequins that stand on an edge. Bring the needle to the right side of the fabric. Insert the needle into the back of the sequin, back into the fabric at the edge of the sequin.
5. At the end, make a figure-8 knot after the last sequin and pull the knot through to the wrong side.

**Tambour.** For tambour work, you'll need a frame and tambour hook. Similar to a crochet hook, the tambour hook has a sharp point with a latch above it (see Resources on p. 247). The beading is worked with the wrong side of the fabric uppermost on the frame with beads held in your hand underneath. Beads can be purchased prestrung on lengths of thread or loose.
1. Transfer the design to the wrong side of the fabric.
2. Mount the fabric wrong side up on the frame. Check to be sure the fabric is taut on the frame.
3. Restring the beads when working with prestrung beads. The original string is too weak and probably too short. Since you don't know how much thread you'll need, restring the beads onto a spool of thread rather than a cut length.

To restring, pierce the end of the spooled thread with the tambour hook or a needle. Pull the thread

## VARIOUS WAYS OF BEADING WITH A NEEDLE

**RUNNING STITCH**

**BACKSTITCH**

**SEQUIN WITH BEAD**

**COUCHING BEADS**

**SEQUINS IN A ROW**

**LAZY STITCH**

on which the beads are strung through this slit for several inches then slide the beads from the old string to the new one. Pull out and discard the original string.

1. Begin with one hand holding the tambour hook above the fabric and the other holding the restrung beads below the fabric.

2. At the beginning, pierce the fabric with the tambour hook, catch the spooled thread about 2 in. from the end and pull a thread loop through the fabric to the wrong side, without disturbing any of the beads.

3. With the hook still in the loop, secure the thread end by re-inserting the hook into the fabric behind where it first exited and pick up another loop.

4. Pull the new loop through the fabric and through the first loop, and then pull the first loop flat against the fabric.

## BEADING WITH A TAMBOUR HOOK

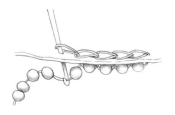

CLAIRE'S HINT *Always keeping the hook in the last loop, insert it into the fabric again ahead of or to the side of where you just exited, as called for by your pattern.*

5. Pick up the thread between the first two beads, turn the hook 180°. Pull it through the fabric and the previous stitch so the first bead is held tightly against the fabric right side. After you turn the needle so the thread wraps around it; push the unnotched side of the needle to make the hole in the fabric slightly larger. Some embroiderers call this "opening the door."

6. Continue in this fashion, making the stitches the same length as the beads, until all the beads are applied to the fabric.

CLAIRE'S HINT *When you're beading sequins with a tambour hook, the sequins will stand on edge.*

7. At the end, insert the hook behind the last stitch, pick up the thread before the next bead, and pull it through the fabric and the loop on the hook. Break the thread, leaving a short tail.

## TUCKS

Used singly, clustered or sewn over an entire garment, tucks can range in size from tiny pintucks to wide, flat tucks. They can all be the same size or graduated, and they can be flat or stand up. They're

# Transferring the Design

**THERE ARE SEVERAL WAYS TO** transfer a decorative design to the fabric: dressmaker's carbon, thread-tracing, and prick and pounce.

The prick and pounce method is the most versatile and used most often by couture houses. It's also the most time-consuming. Thread-tracing is a good choice for net or lace, or for transferring the design to both sides of the fabric when you're incorporating different types of embellishment on the same piece. Using a tracing wheel and white dressmaker's tracing carbon on the fabric wrong side is the easiest method and a good choice for medium or dark fabrics.

## PRICK AND POUNCE METHOD

Used by most professional embroiderers, the prick and pounce method begins with a perforated pattern. The pattern is laid on the fabric and a pouncer is used to force the dusting powder into the holes of the design.

**1.** You'll need a needle to prick the design into the paper; a pouncer, which you can either buy or make; and white or gray pouncing powder or cornstarch to mark the design through the pricked holes in the paper. Embroiderers use a special machine to prick out the outline of the design, but you can do this with a sewing machine set for 12 stitches per in. with a large sewing needle or with a stiletto tracing wheel.

**2.** To make a pouncer, place the powder or cornstarch in the center of a 6-in. muslin square. Gather the muslin tightly around the powder and fasten it with a rubber band.

**3.** Perforate the paper pattern along the design lines as well as the stitching and grainlines. If the design is symmetrical and is to be applied to two garment sections, stack and pin two paper patterns together and perforate them as one.

**4.** Remove the pins and separate the embellishment patterns without tearing them.

**5.** Smooth the holes by rubbing them lightly with fine-grade sandpaper, or place the patterns on the fabric with the rough side up.

**6.** Transfer the design to the fabric. When working with a needle, transfer the design to the right side; when beading with a tambour hook, transfer it to the wrong side (see page 234).

**7.** To transfer the design, place the perforated pattern on the garment section, aligning the grainlines and any marked stitching lines; pin the edges together.

**8.** Dip the pouncer in pouncing powder or cornstarch. Pat the holes with the pouncer. Work carefully to avoid shifting the pattern, checking as you go to be sure the design is completely transferred, because, once you have removed the pattern, it's almost impossible to reposition it precisely.

**9.** After you've transferred the design, remove the pattern and connect the dots with white dressmaker's pencil or a sharp lead pencil. The embellishment will cover your marks.

**10.** Shake the fabric to remove the excess powder.

**11.** Spray lightly with a fixative.

## THREAD-TRACING

Thread-tracing is a good choice when embellishing nets and laces. It also has the advantage of marking both sides when you're working with other fabrics.

**1.** Right sides up, place the design pattern on the fabric, and smooth and baste the layers together.

**2.** Working from the center out, use short basting stitches to trace the motifs, sewing through the paper pattern.

CLAIRE'S HINT *When making the stitches, I leave a small amount of thread on the pattern so it will be easy to tear away afterwards.*

**3.** Carefully tear away the pattern.

usually sewn on the lengthwise grain, but they can be sewn on the crosswise grain or bias, as well as on curves. When sewn on the crossgrain or bias, they won't lie as flat or press as well as when sewn on the lengthwise grain. Usually made by hand, tucks can be stitched completely from top to bottom or stitched partially and released.

Some designs require considerable planning. Simple parallel rows of tucks are less complicated in design and planning.

Tucks require extra fabric; the minimum amount needed is twice the width of each tuck. As with most embellishments, there will also be additional shrinkage in the tucked section. The amount of shrinkage depends on the number of tucks and the fabric. As a general guideline, add about $\frac{1}{16}$-in. to $\frac{1}{8}$-in. extra for every tuck.

1. For $\frac{1}{16}$-in. to $\frac{1}{8}$-in. pintucks, mark the foldline with thread tracing. For larger tucks, thread-trace the two stitching lines for each tuck.

2. Wrong sides together, fold narrow tucks on the thread tracing and baste. For wider tucks, pin the tucks so the thread tracings match; baste.

3. With a long, fine needle and very fine thread matching the fabric, use a short running stitch to sew the tuck permanently. Keep the stitches short and even, beginning and ending with two backstitches.

4. On curved tucks, pull up the thread tracing on the longer side before basting so the fullness will be distributed evenly. Baste from the right side up so you can adjust the fullness.

## The Bridal Gown

Traditionally, the finale of a couture collection is the bridal gown. From breathtakingly beautiful designs with yards of satin and lace to outlandish creations, bridal gowns are important to most couture houses and custom clothiers because they are often the first, and sometimes the only, design a client will order. Bridal gowns are also very important to home sewers, who may want to lavish more time and money than usual on labor-intensive couture techniques for this special garment.

Bridal gowns are an excellent source for inspiration when it comes to construction as well as design techniques. Many elements can be adapted for evening wear and sometimes day dresses.

A wedding is one of the most significant events in a woman's life. For hundreds of years and in many societies, brides have worn elaborate ceremonial robes that range from richly colored and brightly embroidered native costumes to royal robes woven with threads of gold and silver embellished with precious metals and jewels.

Many of today's most popular wedding customs began during the reign of Queen Victoria. For her marriage to Prince Albert of Saxe-Coburg in 1840, the young monarch chose a simple white dress. Fabricated from heavy silk satin woven in Spitalfields, England, and trimmed with handmade Honitan lace, it was austere when compared to the elaborate, ostentatious gowns of silver tissue worn by her predecessors.

The young monarch deliberately selected English fabrics and laces that would promote the country's textile industries, which had suffered as a result of the industrial revolution. The Queen's choices were an enormous success. Stylish and elegant, the dress created a demand, which continues even today, for beautiful white wedding gowns with an abundance of lace trims.

Another significant development around this time was the invention of the sewing machine in 1846. It had a profound and unexpected effect on dressmaking. Instead of shortening and simplifying the dressmaking process, the arrival of the sewing machine encouraged the use of more elaborate trims. By the end of the century when the passion for decoration reached its peak, wedding gowns were elaborately trimmed with a variety of ornate embellishments such as fringe, braid, pleating, shirring, and laces.

Among notable bridal gowns of the past century was that of Princess Elizabeth for her 1947 wedding. The gown took 350 workers at the House

Embroidered with pearls, glass beads, and silver thread, this dress was made by Lanvin in 1925. On the skirt, godets are outlined with beading; on the bodice, the double-oval motif leads to a larger design just below the waist. This large motif would have been covered by the bride's bouquet during the ceremony.

(Photo courtesy of the Chicago History Museum.)

diaphanous silk, its 12-gore skirt flared into an attractive bell shape supported by numerous layers of silk tulle and stiff nylon net. An inverted pleat at center back allowed the skirt to open for sitting and fall back into place when the princess stood, covering the wrinkles—another interesting design idea for home sewers.

Princess Diana's 1981 bridal gown was unforgettable and, like Queen Victoria's dress, designed to bolster English textiles. The dress featured two ruffles—one silk and one lace—around a gently curved neckline, very full sleeves trimmed with embroidered ruffles and lace, and sequin- and pearl-studded lace panels on the front and back. It was fabricated in ivory silk taffeta, which was woven especially for the occasion and trimmed with Carrickmacross lace. The bouffant skirt was supported by a petticoat with numerous layers of tulle over very crisp nylon net. The gown created an immediate demand for the look, described as "dressed-up peasant."

In the weeks before the wedding, the princess lost weight, so several toiles and partial toiles were made during this period. The actual cutting and making of the dress was delayed until a couple weeks before the wedding to ensure the most accurate fit, since there was a limited amount of the specially woven silk available.

## WEDDING DRESS DESIGNS
Wedding dresses have several elements which differ from traditional special occasion dresses. The two most outstanding are the train and how it is attached and the design of the back as well as the front of the dress. Secondary considerations include trims, the design—classic or avant garde, the image the bride wants to have, the incorporation of fabrics, laces, or beading from an older dress, and lastly, whether the dress will be incorporated into the bride's wardrobe or preserved for a daughter or granddaughter.

**The Train.** The train can be cut as part of the skirt or as a separate section which can be removed easily for dancing. When it is cut on the skirt,

of Hartnell in London seven weeks to make. Even though Great Britain was still experiencing major shortages and rationing because of the war, the dress was a show of extravagance. The satin dress and 15-yd. tulle train were richly embroidered with 10,000 imported pearls and crystals (the princess and her bridesmaids were allowed extra rationing coupons). The train was attached at the shoulders with buttons and loops—a nice detail for modern brides.

By contrast, Princess Margaret's 1960 bridal gown, also designed by Hartnell, was a simple, V-neck princess-line design trimmed only with a narrow bias binding. Made of 30 yds. of

Designed to showcase two beautifully beaded motifs, this elegant wedding gown is fabricated in silk velvet; it has a softly shirred panel at the hips with the decorative beading at each side. Beaded with pearl and crystals, the embellishment was done on a light backing, then applied to the dress.

(Photo courtesy of the Chicago History Museum.)

various methods such as buttons and loops, hooks and eyes, and internal ties can be used to raise the train to create a bustle effect. Many cut-on trains will wrinkle less and drape better when a dust ruffle is sewn to the underside. The skewed ruffle makes a nice firm ruffle.

A practical solution is to design a detachable train which can extend from the shoulders, the waist, or anywhere in between. The dress at left has a detachable train, which provides interesting contrast. The train is a simple rectangle that attaches inconspicuously at the waist. Once the train is removed, the dress can be added to the bride's wardrobe and worn for other special occasions.

**Back Designs.** During the wedding ceremony, the back of the dress is much more visible than the front. Many dresses are embellished with elaborate trains, as on the Lanvin dress on p. 237; and even simple designs might have a vertical row of buttons and loops at the back.

**Trims.** Trims for wedding dresses can run the gamut from small lace inserts or beaded trims to lavishly embellished dresses. The richly embellished dress from the 1920s shown at left, facing page, provides an interesting contrast in styles. The turquoise silk crepe features Egyptian-inspired embroideries, which were very popular in the mid-1920s after the discovery of King Tut's tomb in 1922. The simple silhouette, also typical of the twenties, would have allowed the bride to include the dress in her wardrobe for special occasions.

For professionals and home-sewers, the success of the bridal gown depends as much on advance planning as on the amount of money spent. The design can be traditional or high-tech, but whatever its style, it should fit and flatter the figure, hang perfectly without wrinkling and make the bride look as special as she feels. Making a toile for a wedding gown is crucial for a perfect fit and a flattering design. It also provides an opportunity to practice

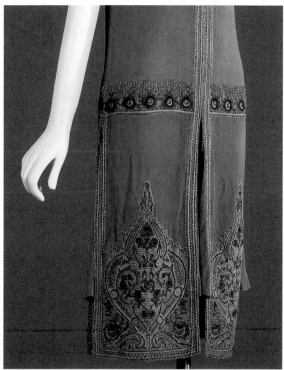

Made of lightweight silk crepe, this exquisite dress from 1927 is designed with four panels separated by shorter pleats. The panels are embellished with heavy bead and thread embroidery, which is not only decorative but also serves as a weight.

(Photo courtesy of the Chicago History Museum.)

This 1900 evening gown by Charles Frederick Worth, is one of my favorite dresses. With exquisite fabric and impeccable craftsmanship, this dress is the essence of haute couture and an inspiration for all who enjoy the art and craft of sewing.

(Photo by David Arky, courtesy of the Museum of the City of New York, gift of Mrs. Donald P. Spence.)

new techniques and prevents overhandling the gown during its construction. Choosing the right backing and interfacing materials as well as making a corselette or appropriate underpinning are also important for the gown's success (see pp. 62, 126, and 222 for information on backings and interfacings, and p. 229 for information on making a corselette).

I could never afford to purchase a couture garment; but I can create my own, and so can you. A beautiful, tailored jacket, blouse, or designer wedding gown is a series of basic couture techniques. Yes, couture requires time and patience, but very few of the techniques in this book are difficult and many utilize skills that you already have. If you can sew, you can sew couture.

# Selected Glossary of Terms

**Applied-welt pocket:** See Set-in pocket.

**Armscye:** Armhole.

*Atelier flou:* Dressmaking workroom.

*Atelier tailleur:* Tailoring workroom

**Backing:** Layer of support fabric applied to the wrong side of a garment section before the seam is sewn; called the underlining in home sewing.

**Balance lines:** Horizontal and vertical lines marked on the garment or muslin pattern to aid in fitting the garment.

**Basting(s):** Sewing temporary stitches into the garment for marking or holding fabric layers together until they're permanently stitched; also, the threads that are basted and generally removed before pressing.

**Bespoke:** English term describing a garment cut from a pattern custom-made for an individual client.

**Bias:** True bias refers to a hypothetical line at a 45° angle to the lengthwise grain of the fabric. Generally the term bias refers to any line that's off-grain but, in this book, it is used to mean true bias.

**Blind buttonhole:** Decorative, nonfunctional buttonhole that can be either handworked (in which case the opening is not cut) or bound (in which case, the facing is not cut).

**Bobbinet:** Cotton tulle used for corselettes and sometimes called English net.

**Bound buttonhole:** Buttonhole made with fabric strips.

**Bound pocket:** See Set-in pocket.

**Breakpoint:** Beginning of the roll line on the front edge of the jacket.

**Bridle:** Roll line on a tailored jacket or coat; also the tape applied to roll line.

**Canvas:** Hair canvas interfacing; also, the inner structure of interfacings and backing of a tailored garment.

**Catchstitch:** Hand-sewn stitch that looks like an "X" and is used for sewing one edge or layer flat against another.

**CB:** Center back.

**CF:** Center front.

*Chambre syndicale de la couture parisienne:* Parisian High Fashion Syndicate, the organization governing the French haute couture industry.

**Collar fall:** Section of collar between the roll line and outer edge.

**Collar linen:** Crisp interfacing used in tailoring, sometimes called collar or French canvas.

**Collar stand:** Section of collar between the roll line and neckline.

**Cording a buttonhole:** Supporting and enhancing the appearance of a bound or handworked buttonhole with cord or several strands of thread inserted into the welts of a bound buttonhole or laid around the opening of a handworked buttonhole and covered with buttonhole stitches.

**Couching:** Embroidery technique for securing cords, threads or braids laid in decorative patterns on a fabric's surface by sewing over them with fine, inconspicuous, or decorative thread.

**Couturier:** French term for a male or female designer at a couture house.

**Couturière:** A French seamstress or dressmaker, occasionally used to describe a female couturier.

**Creaseline:** Synonym for roll line.

**Crossgrain:** The weft yarns in fabric, which cross the vertical warp yarns and are at a right angle to the selvage.

**Dart take-up:** The fabric between the stitching lines of a dart, which is stitched out on finished garment.

**Dauber:** Small roll of muslin or wool, dipped in water and used to apply moisture to sections of a garment for pressing.

**Domette:** Synonym for lambswool.

**Ease:** To join two garment sections unequal in length, smoothly without gathers or pleats; also, a small amount of fabric fullness on one garment section, making it longer than the section it joins. Ease is used to provide shaping on the sleeve cap, back shoulder, bust, and skirt waist.

**Edgestitch:** Row of stitching positioned about $\frac{1}{16}$ in. from an edge or seamline.

**Embroidered buttonhole:** Same as Handworked buttonhole.

**Face:** Right side of the fabric or outside of the garment.

**Fell:** Inconspicuous stitch used for hemming, seaming, and basting; also, to sew with a fell stitch, generally from the right side of the fabric.

**Finger-press:** Light pressing of the fabric with the fingertips after it has been steamed.

**Fitting:** In couture, the term refers to the several sessions in which the client tries on the garment, whose fit is checked and adjusted as needed.

**Flange:** Pleat extending from the shoulder at the armscye.

**Fulling:** Adding fullness to the garment lining or backing so that the firmly woven lining or backing fabrics will not pull at the seams or restrict movement; also, the process of easing lapel facings to the jacket fronts or the collar to the undercollar to build shape into the garment.

**Garment body:** Garment front and back, excluding the sleeves.

**Gorge line:** Seamline that joins the collar and lapel.

**Grainline:** Direction of the yarns in the fabric's weave; the lengthwise, straight, or vertical grain is that of the lengthwise warp threads; the crossgrain, crosswise grain, or horizontal grain is that of the crossing weft threads. Unless otherwise specified, grainline in this book refers to the lengthwise grain.

**Grosgrain:** A firmly woven ribbon with crossgrain ribs.

**Ground:** Background material for appliqué, embroidery, and beading.

**Handworked or hand buttonhole:** Buttonhole worked with thread and a buttonhole stitch.

**Holding short:** Shaping the garment to fit the contours of the body by holding one edge taut while basting.

**Hong Kong finish:** Home-sewing term to describe a bias-binding seam finish.

**Hymo:** Type of hair canvas, available in several weights.

**Inseam pocket:** See Set-in pocket.

**Interfacing:** Layer of support fabric between the garment and facing, generally applied at the garment to add body and stabilize the edge.

**Lambswool:** Soft, knitted fabric with fleece on one or both sides, used for interfacing and backing.

**Matchpoints:** Marked points on seamlines that are aligned when the garment is assembled. In home sewing, matchpoints are marked by notches on cutting edges and with circles or squares on seamlines.

**Miter:** Diagonal seamline at a corner; also, to join two edges at an angle.

**Muslin:** Inexpensive, plain-weave cotton fabric available in several weights and used for making toiles; also, the muslin toile itself.

**Neckpoint:** Point on the body at the base of the neck where the shoulder begins.

**Notch:** Angle formed where the collar joins the lapel.

**Padstitch:** Small diagonal stitches used in tailoring to sew two layers together to shape or add body to a garment section.

**Petersham:** Belting material similar to grosgrain but slightly heavier and crisper, used for interfacing, facings, and stays.

**Plain-weave silk:** Silk such as China silk, silk muslin, and silk organza with a plain weave, which is generally used for linings, backings, underpinnings, blouses, and some dresses.

***Première d'atelier*:** Head of a couture workroom, usually a woman (premier refers to a male head of a workroom, usually a tailoring atelier).

**Press:** To apply heat and sometimes moisture to flatten or permanently set a seam, hem, or other part of a garment or garment section. In this book, the instruction "press the seam" generally means first to press it flat as sewn then to press it open.

**Rever:** Lapel.

**Roll line:** Creaseline that separates a jacket front from the lapel.

**Round corners:** To trim and transform a square corner into one with a gentle curve.

**RS:** Right side of the fabric, garment, or garment section.

**Rucks:** Valleys between ridges of gathers.

**Running stitch:** Permanent stitch used for seams, tucks, gathers, and quilting, which can be even or uneven and long or short; sometimes called a forward stitch.

**Seam slippage:** Undesirable separation of fabric yarns at seamlines when stressed.

**Set:** Term used in fitting to describe how a garment sits on the body; *also*, a pressing a pressing term meaning to establish the permanent position of an edge or other part of a garment; *also*, to sew or apply one section to another.

**Set-in pocket:** Bound, inseam, or applied-welt pocket, which is set into a seam or slash in the garment body.

**Shape:** To shrink or stretch a garment section with heat and moisture.

**Shell:** Outside part of garment, not the lining.

**Shell fabric:** Garment fabric.

**Shoulder point:** Point on the body at the end of the shoulder seam.

**Sleeve cap:** Section of the sleeve above the under-arm seam.

**Sleeve head:** Strip of wadding or interfacing used to support the sleeve cap; sometimes called a leadder.

**Slipstitch:** Stitch made from the right side of the fabric and used both for basting (and then called "slipbasting") and for permanently sewing seams that are intricately shaped or need to have patterns matched or be eased.

**Sloper:** Very fitted, basic muslin garment, used as a guide for adjusting the fit of other garments, for developing other designs and for padding a dress form; in French, referred to as a *toile de corps*.

**Stay:** Tape sewn to an edge or seam to prevent it from stretching; *also*, a small piece of interfacing used to reinforce an area like a pocket opening; *also*, a device like lingerie straps used to anchor a garment and prevent it from shifting unattractively when the body moves.

**Styleline:** The outside edge of a collar, cuff or lapel; the upper edge of a strapless garment; also, an unusual pocket opening, hemline, or sleeve edge.

**Tailor's tacks:** Small thread tacks used in tailoring for marking seamlines and construction matchpoints on the fabric.

**Thread-tracing:** A basting stitch used for marking seamlines and construction matchpoints on the fabric.

**Toile:** A fitting garment made of muslin for an individual client or a new design; also, the pattern this fitting garment produces.

*Toile de corps*: See Sloper.

**Top-baste:** To baste on the right side of the garment through all layers in order to hold a seam, dart, or edge flat for sewing, pressing, or fitting.

**Topstitch:** Row of stitching that show on outside of garment.

**Underlining:** See Backing.

**Underpinnings:** Undergarments such as foundations, petticoats, and corselettes that are necessary to support a design.

**Utica linen:** Closely woven linen used for interfacing.

**Vent:** Finished opening at one end of seam, used at the wrist edge of sleeves and at the hemline of some jackets and skirts.

**Wadding:** Cotton batting with a slick finish on one or both sides, used for making padding, shoulder pads, and sleeve heads.

**Wheel:** To trace markings on cut or uncut fabric, the muslin toile or paper patterns with a dressmaker's tracing wheel.

**Wigan:** Cotton interfacing used in tailoring.

**WS:** Wrong side of the fabric, garment, or garment section.

# Metric Equivalency Chart

One inch equals approximately 2.54 centimeters. To convert inches to centimeters, multiply the figure in inches by 2.54 and round off to the nearest half centimeter, or use the chart below, whose figures are rounded off (one centimeter equals ten millimeters).

| | |
|---|---|
| ⅛ in. = 3 mm | 9 in. = 23 cm |
| ¼ in. = 6 mm | 10 in. = 25.5 cm |
| ⅜ in. = 1 cm | 12 in. = 30.5 cm |
| ½ in. = 1.3 cm | 14 in. = 35.5 cm |
| ⅝ in. = 1.5 cm | 15 in. = 38 cm |
| ¾ in. = 2 cm | 16 in. = 40.5 cm |
| ⅞ in. = 2.2 cm | 18 in. = 45.5 cm |
| 1 in. = 2.5 cm | 20 in. = 51 cm |
| 2 in. = 5 cm | 21 in. = 53.5 cm |
| 3 in. = 7.5 cm | 22 in. = 56 cm |
| 4 in. = 10 cm | 24 in. = 61 cm |
| 5 in. = 12.5 cm | 25 in. = 63.5 cm |
| 6 in. = 15 cm | 36 in. = 92 cm |
| 7 in. = 18 cm | 45 in. = 114.5 cm |
| 8 in. = 20.5 cm | 60 in. = 152 cm |

# Bibliography

## EMBELLISHMENTS

Bryant, Jan. "Tambour Beading." *Threads* 44 (December 1992): 50–53.

Caulfeild, S.F.A. and Blanche C. Saward. *Encyclopedia of Victorian Needlework*. New York: Dover Publications, 1972. (Good section on embroidery.)

de Dillmont, Thérèse. *The Complete Encyclopedia of Needlework*. Philadelphia: Running Press, 1978. (Good embroidery information; available from Lacis—see Sources of Supply.)

Jarratt, Maisie. *How to Bead: French Embroidery Beading*. Kenthurst, Australia: Kangaroo Press, 1991. (Available from Lacis—see Sources of Supply.)

Leffingwell, Jeanne. "A Thousand Points of Light." *Threads* 30 (August 1990): 38–41.

Morgan, Mary, and Dee Mosteller. *Trapunto and Other Forms of Raised Quilting*. New York: Charles Scribner's Sons, 1977.

Thompson, Angela. *Embroidery with Beads*. London: B.T. Batsford Ltd., 1987.

## FASHION HISTORY AND HAUTE COUTURE

Arch, Nigel, and Joanna Marschner. *The Royal Wedding Dresses*. London: Sidgwick & Jackson, 1990.

Batterberry, Michael and Ariane. *Mirror, Mirror*. New York: Holt, Rinehart and Winston, 1977.

Bertin, Célia. *Paris à la Mode*. London: Victor Gollancz Ltd., 1956.

Boucher, François. *20,000 Years of Fashion*. New York: Harry N. Abrams, nd.

Charles, Regan. "La Creme de la Hem." *Avenue* 13, 6 (January 1989): 94–107.

Coleman, Elizabeth Ann. *The Genius of Charles James*. Brooklyn: The Brooklyn Museum, 1982.

Contini, Mila. *Fashion from Ancient Egypt to the Present Day*. New York: Odyssey Press, 1965.

Cumming, Valerie. *Royal Dress*. New York: Holmes & Meier, 1989.

de Marly, Diana. The *History of Haute Couture 1850–1950*. London: B.T. Batsford Ltd., 1980.

de Pietri, Stephen, and Melissa Leventon. *New Look to Now: French Haute Couture 1947–87*. San Francisco: Fine Arts Museum of San Francisco, 1989.

Deslandres, Yvonne, and Florence Müller. *Histoire de la mode au XXe siècle*. Paris: Somogy, 1986.

Dior, Christian. *Christian Dior and I*. New York: E. P. Dutton & Co., 1954.

Garfinkel, Stanley. *Completely Dior*. Cleveland: Telos Video Communications, 1987. Videotape.

——. Unpublished interview with Henriette Moon and Mrs. William Randolph Hearst.

*Givenchy: 30 Years*. New York: Fashion Institute of Technology, 1982.

Jones, Kevin and Christina Johnson. *High Style Catalogue*. Los Angeles: Fashion Institute of Design and Merchandising, 2009.

Lambert, Eleanor. *World of Fashion: People, Places, Resources*. New York: R. R. Bowker, 1976.

Laver, James. *Costume*. New York: Hawthorn Books, 1963. Reprint. New York: Dover Publications.

Long, Timothy. *Dior: The New Look*. Chicago, IL: Chicago History Museum, 2006.

——. *I Do: Chicago Ties the Knot*. Chicago, IL: Chicago History Museum, 2010.

——. *Chic Chicago*. Chicago, IL: Chicago History Museum, 2008

Lynam, Ruth, ed. *Couture*. New York: Doubleday and Company, 1972.

*Man and the Horse*. New York: Metropolitan Museum of Art, 1984.

Martin, Richard, and Harold Koda. *Flair: Fashion Collected by Tina Chow*. New York: Rizzoli International Publications, 1992.

Milbank, Caroline R. *Couture: The Great Designers*. New York: Stewart, Tabori & Chang, 1985.

Mulvagh, Jane. *The Vogue History of 20th-Century Fashion*. London: Viking, 1988.

O'Hara, Georgina. *The Encyclopaedia of Fashion*. London: Thames and Hudson, 1986.

Penn, Irving, and Diana Vreeland. *Inventive Paris Clothes, 1909–1939*. New York: Viking Press, 1977.

Picken, Mary Brooks, and Dora Loues Miller. *Dressmakers of France*. New York: Harper & Brothers, Publishers, 1956.

Steele, Valerie. *Paris Fashion: A Cultural History*. New York: Oxford University Press, 1988.

——. *Women of Fashion: Twentieth Century Designers*. New York: Rizzoli International Publications, 1991.

Steele, Valerie, Patricia Mears, and Clare Sauro. *Ralph Rucci: The Art of Weightlessness*. New York: Yale University Press, 2007.

White, Palmer. *The Master Touch of Lesage*. Rungis, France: Chene, 1987.

Wilcox, Claire, and Valerie Mendes. *Modern Fashion in Detail*. London: Victoria & Albert Museum, 1991.

Yohannan, Kohle. *Valentina: American Couture and the Cult of Celebrity*. New York: Rizzoli, 2009.

*Yves Saint Laurent*. New York: Metropolitan Museum of Art, 1983.

## FITTING

Amaden-Crawford, Connie. *The Art of Fashion Draping*. New York: Fairchild Publications, 1989.

Bray, Natalie. *Dress Fitting*. London: Granada, 1978. (Distributed by Sheridan House, 145 Palisade St., Dobbs Ferry, NY 10522.)

Hilhouse, Marion S., and Evelyn A. Mansfield. *Dress Design: Draping and Flat Pattern Making*. Boston: Houghton Mifflin, 1948.

Joseph-Armstrong, Helen. *Draping for Apparel Design*. New York: Fairchild Publications, 2000.

King, Judith E. *The Custom Dress Form*. Dayton, Ohio: Designing Lady Studio (325 Maysfield Rd.), 1989.

Kopp, Ernestine, et al. *How to Draft Basic Patterns*. New York: Fairchild Publications, 1991.

Liechty, Elizabeth L., et al. *Fitting & Pattern Alteration: A Multi-Method Approach*. New York: Fairchild Publications, 1986.

Stern, Suzanne Pierrette. "Padding a Dress Form." *Threads* 44 (December 1992): 35–37.

## SEWING AND PRESSING TECHNIQUES

Cabrera, Roberto, and Patricia Flaherty Meyers. *Classic Tailoring Techniques: A Construction Guide for Women's Wear*. New York: Fairchild Publications, 1984.

Coffin, David. "Irons, Boards and Presses." *Threads* 10 (April 1987): 40–43.

di Bello, Angelina. *Haute Couture Techniques*. Montreal: Angelina di Bello, 1990.

Hopkins, J. C. *Edwardian Ladies' Tailoring: The Twentieth-Century System of Ladies' Garment Cutting*. 4th ed. Reprint, edited by R. L. Shep. Mendocino, Calif.: R. L. Shep, 1990. (Available from Lacis—see Sources of Supply.)

Kennett, Frances. *Secrets of the Couturiers*. London: Orbis, 1982.

Liberty, J. E. *Practical Tailoring*. New York: Pitman Publishing Corporation, 1955.

Mansfield, Evelyn A. *Clothing Construction*. Boston: Houghton Mifflin Co., 1953.

Mauck, Frances F. *Modern Tailoring for Women*. New York: Macmillan Company, 1947.

Picken, Mary Brooks. *The Language of Fashion*. New York: Funk & Wagnalls Company, 1939.

Poulin, Clarence. *Tailoring Suits the Professional Way*. Peoria, Ill.: Chas. A. Bennett Co., 1953.

*Reader's Digest Complete Guide to Sewing*. Pleasantville, N.Y.: The Reader's Digest Association, 1976.

Rhodes, Elizabeth A. "Charles Kleibacker." Unpublished manuscript.

Shaeffer, Claire B. *Claire Shaeffer's Custom Couture Patterns*. New York: Vogue Patterns, a division the McCall Pattern Co.

———. *Claire Shaeffer's Fabric Sewing Guide*. 2nd ed. Cincinnatti, OH: Krause Publications, 2008.

———. *The Complete Book of Sewing Short Cuts*. New York: Sterling Publishing Co., 1981.

———. *Couture Techniques Workshop: Basics with Claire Shaeffer* (DVD). Newtown, CT: The Taunton Press, Inc., 2010.

———. *Sew Any Patch Pocket*. Radnor, Pa.: Chilton Book Co., 1989.

———. *Sew Any Set-In Pocket*. Radnor, Pa.: Chilton Book Co., 1989.

*Threads Magazine Archive 1985–2009* (DVD). Newtown, CT: The Taunton Press, Inc., 2009.

*Vogue Sewing*. New York: Harper & Row, Publishers, 1980.

Wilson, J. King. *The Art of Cutting and Fitting*. London: Crosby Lockwood & Son, Ltd., 1950.

Yanagi, Amy, ed. *Fit and Fabric*. Newtown, CT: The Taunton Press, Inc., 1991.

———. *Great Sewn Clothes*. Newtown, CT: The Taunton Press, Inc., 1991.

———. *Jackets, Coats and Suits*. Newtown, CT: The Taunton Press, Inc., 1993.

# Resources

**TAILORING SUPPLIES, INTERFACINGS, INDUSTRIAL IRONS & PRESSING TOOLS, DRESS FORMS, THREADS**

Atlanta Thread
& Supply Co.
695 Red Oak Rd.
Stockbridge, GA 30281
(800) 847-1001
www.atlantathread.com

Banasch's
3380 Red Bank Rd.
Cincinnati, OH 45227
(800) 543-0355
www.banaschs.com

B. Black & Sons
548 S. Los Angeles St.
Los Angeles, CA 90013
(800) 433-1546
www.bblackandsons.com
All supplies except dress forms.

Greenberg & Hammer
535 8th Ave., Rm 6N
New York, NY 10018
(800) 955-5135
www.gianuzzi.com
Boning, weights and chain,
horsehair braid and
tracing paper.

Wawak
P.O. Box 8589
Endwell, NY 13762
(800) 654-2235
www.wawak.com

**United Kingdom**
MacCulloch & Wallis
25–26 Dering St.
London W1S 1AT
England
(44) 20-7629 0311
www.macculloch-wallis.co.uk

**FABRICS AND MISCELLANEOUS SUPPLIES**

Apple Annie
Designer Fabrics
566 Wilbur Ave.
Swansea, MA 02777
(866) 675-9844
www.appleanniefabrics.com

Britex
146 Geary St.
San Francisco, CA 94108
(415) 392-2910
www.britexfabrics.com
Cotton tulle, interfacings,
lambswool, cotton batting.

G Street Fabrics
5520 Randolph Rd.
Rockville, MD 20852
(301) 231-8998
www.gstreetfabrics.com

Lacis
2982 Adeline St.
Berkeley, CA 94703
(510) 843-7178
Lacismuseum.org
Books, needles, tambour hooks,
threads, cotton tulle.

Michael's Fabrics
www.michaelsfabrics.com

Sawyer Brook
Distinctive Fabrics
P.O. Box 700
Clinton, MA 01510
(800) 290-2739
www.sawyerbrook.com

Things Japanese
9805 NE 116th St.
Kirkland, WA 98034
(425) 821-2287
www.silkthings.com
Silk threads.

# Index